SPORTSINSURE
BRITISH
SPEEDWAY
EUROSPORT
BIKERIGHT
MANCHESTER
RACING
THORNEYCROFT
ATPI
Recover8

NO BREAKS

NO BREAKS

A LOST SEASON IN BRITISH SPEEDWAY

RODDY McDOUGALL

pitch

First published by Pitch Publishing, 2021

Pitch Publishing
A2 Yeoman Gate
Yeoman Way
Worthing
Sussex
BN13 3QZ
www.pitchpublishing.co.uk
info@pitchpublishing.co.uk

A CIP catalogue record is available for this book from the British Library.

ISBN 978 1 78531 772 9

Typesetting and origination by Pitch Publishing

Printed and bound in India by Replika Press Pvt. Ltd.

Contents

Acknowledgements 9
Introduction. 11
1. September 2019 – Same sport, different worlds 16
2. October 2019 – A damp squib 33
3. November 2019 – If the points fit 52
4. December 2019 – Workington woman 70
5. January 2020 – Speedway's conundrum. 89
6. February 2020 – Sunlight through dark clouds 108
7. March 2020 – Lockdown 126
8. April 2020 – Fear and frustration 144
9. May 2020 – The speedway bubble 163
10. June 2020 – Closed doors 181
11. July 2020 – An elite sport 200
12. August 2020 – Some kind of normal 222
13. September 2020 – Best-laid plans 241
14. October 2020 – The unluckiest break. 261
Postscript 287
Select bibliography 288

Back cover:
Top: 'Speedway meetings attracted capacity crowds following the end of the Second World War with Wembley Lions one of the main attractions'
Bottom: 'Action from the first round of the British Youth Championship at Scunthorpe in August 2020, the first meeting after March's lockdown'

Front end paper:
'Rory Schlein (winner), Richard Lawson (second) and Jason Crump (third) on the podium at the end of the 2020 British Final at Belle Vue'
Back end paper:
'The first professional meeting after the lockdown was run behind closed doors at Belle Vue in September 2019 between the Aces and the ATPI All Stars'

Dedication

For Liz

The author's royalties from this book will go to the Speedway Riders Benevolent Fund, the only charity dedicated to looking after injured speedway riders.

Roddy McDougall worked as a journalist for several national news broadcasters. A producer and reporter for BBC News and BBC TV Sport, he moved on to senior roles in news editing with TV-am, GMTV and ITN, where he was Head of Home News. He has co-authored a walking book in his home city of Edinburgh, which is due for publication in 2021. He lives and works in London and tries to watch speedway when he can.

Acknowledgements

THIS BOOK would not have been possible without the help of the people listed below. From responding to emails or giving up their time on several occasions to answer my seemingly endless questions, they were always helpful and courteous. Given that 2020 was a difficult year for many, their time and generosity is hugely appreciated:

Paul Ackroyd, Oliver Allen, Josh Auty, Tom Bacon, Barry Bishop, Peter Bradbury, Hayley Bromley, Simon Downing, Jitendra Duffill, Georgina Faulkner, Scott Frame, Rob Godfrey, Graham Gordon, Katie Gordon, Ryan Guest, Alex Harkess, Bert Harkins, David Harris, Rachel Hellowell, Rory Hopkins, Mike Hunter, Nikki Jameison , Ian Jordan, Lee Kilby, Nicolai Klindt, Robert Mackenzie, Harry Maidment, Brian Mead, Amy Monkman, Laura Morgan, Graham Muncie, Peter Oakes, Rob Painter, Rob Peasley, Jodie Pledge, Pete Sampson, Peter Schroeck, John Short, Andrew Skeels, Ian Sinderson, Dave Tattum, Arthur Thomson and Sadie Wrigglesworth.

A select bibliography of books consulted appears at the back of this book, but I'd like to draw special attention to the one remaining weekly speedway publication, *Speedway Star*. It's been a real treasure trove of information and, frankly, this book would have looked considerably different without its coverage to read and follow up. Like most print magazines, it was already facing a tough time, which has been exacerbated by COVID-19. If you're a speedway fan, I'd urge you to consider a subscription to a magazine that remains vital for the sport.

Thanks to the Pitch Publishing team – Duncan Olner, Graham Hales, Andrea Dunn and Jon Hurst – and especially to Paul and Jane Camillin for both agreeing to publish the book andcontinuing to back it despite the upheavals of 2020.

Personal thanks to Ellen and Douglas for coming along with me to meetings in the past at the likes of Poole and Arena Essex. Above all, thanks to Liz for visiting more sports venues – speedway included – than she probably cares to remember, along with her encouragement and support over many years.

Introduction

I DON'T really like motorsports. Formula 1, MotoGP, stock car racing. I've nothing against any of them, they've just never really 'done it' for me. But I love speedway. You know, speedway? Motorbikes? Four riders, racing four laps around an oval circuit with no brakes? It's great.

Speedway was, not so very long ago, huge. It was reckoned to be Britain's second-favourite spectator sport. This surprises those who don't know anything about it. For those who do, it's a fact that hangs heavily, a sad reminder of better times. Immediately after the war, meetings were held in front of 90,000 spectators at Wembley. The Duke of Edinburgh and the Prime Minister's wife were among those invited to present the trophies. It's difficult to imagine the Duchess of Cambridge popping along to Swindon's Abbey Stadium to do the same today. Even into the 1970s, BBC radio would carry league results in its nightly sports bulletins, as would the following morning's national newspapers. Towns like Long Eaton, Weymouth, Eastbourne and Workington enjoyed a fleeting moment in the national spotlight. Speedway, with a couple of exceptions, is largely ignored, forgotten – it is Britain's left-behind sport.

Back in 1966, the year England won the World Cup, speedway rider Barry Briggs finished runner-up to Bobby Moore in the BBC's Sports Personality of the Year awards, the second time he'd done so. In 2018, Tai Woffinden, the one current British rider that those outside the speedway world might recognise, won the World Championship for a third time. He wasn't nominated for the BBC's main award and his achievement didn't even rate a brief mention on the programme. Sky Sports News, the UK's 24-hour sports channel, doesn't bother with speedway at all.

The last two main news reports on the sport that I could find when I started writing this book in September 2019 were from *The Guardian* and *BBC News Online*, the first headlined 'Out of time and on the skids: speedway's struggle for survival'; the second 'Does speedway have a future in the UK?'

When I do manage to get to a speedway meeting in Britain – not as often as I used to, not as much as I'd like to – and someone asks what I've been up to and I tell them I've been to speedway, I tend to get the same reactions.

The first – a particular favourite of most people under 40 – is a look of blank bemusement. Speedway? What's that? They've never heard of it, don't really know what it is. Whatever.

The second – more common than you might imagine – is a nod of recognition followed by something along the lines of: 'Speedway? Gosh is that still around? I used to go when I was a kid.' They'll tell you how they went to somewhere like Coventry or Wimbledon or Reading, most likely a venue that no longer stages speedway.

And that, unfortunately, sums up one of the main reasons why speedway has pretty much disappeared from general view. Much of its fan base is of an age that doesn't spend the majority of its waking hours on Instagram or Twitter.

Speedway's had a couple of golden periods, the first immediately after the Second World War and then again during the 1970s. Weekly crowds attending speedway were only surpassed, admittedly by some distance, by those going to football matches. That legacy of speedway as the second most popular sport lingers to this day. Thomas Jørgensen, a Danish rider who rides in Great Britain, still thought it very much a selling point to potential sponsors. This is what he said on his website during 2019:

'Speedway is an intense, explosive and very entertaining sport. It is very popular, particularly to attend live, and not too long ago it used to be the second largest spectator sport after football.'

Whether sponsors were, in fact, attracted by that historic claim to fame is probably open to debate. Speedway sponsors, vital for any sport in the 21st century, tend to be small, local and very often supporters themselves. With a few notable exceptions, you'll not find nationally known brand names associating themselves with speedway. Marketing executives take a quick look and decide it just doesn't fit their chosen 'demographic'.

You can see why the sport's in a bit of a crisis. And that was before the impact of the global coronavirus pandemic in March 2020.

Speedway is a sport of contrasts. Good and bad. And it was summed up perfectly in two short videos available online in the autumn of 2019. On its day, speedway can provide some of the most exciting moments of pure, sporting drama out there. Take, for example, a truly thrilling race that was the pinned video tweet on the Official British Speedway Twitter account for most of 2019. It was headlined: 'This is why we love speedway'.

It was heat 13 of a league meeting in Manchester between Belle Vue and Somerset. While riders do compete in individual competitions, most speedway meetings – unusually for motorsport – are team events, with clubs representing towns or cities rather than engine manufacturers. Over the course of four laps – one minute of action – the result of this race is in doubt right up to the last corner. If it's not quite reminiscent of those horse racing arcade games from seaside piers, where each coloured horse has a chance of winning until the very end, it's certainly not far off. But this is not a predetermined contest. And these are not manufactured metal figures racing for our entertainment. These are four human beings, travelling at speeds of up to 70 miles an hour, using their skill, strength and bravery to negotiate tight bends without the benefit of brakes, each trying his hardest to finish ahead of the others. The race was shown live on BT Sport, at that time the main broadcaster for British speedway, and the excitement in the commentators' voices as the race nears its end is palpable. 'What a speedway race we've got here!' 'We can't believe what we're seeing!' And then, in the final few seconds, as Belle Vue's Max Fricke gains speed on the very final corner to sweep from last to first and the home fans rise to their feet, they cannot contain themselves: 'Oh my goodness, gracious me – where did we get that from?' It's a genuine reaction to what they've just seen, speedway's equivalent of those famous South American broadcasters celebrating a goal by some Brazilian superstar.

Maybe it's just me, but every time I watch the clip, it really does make the hairs on the back of my neck bristle. And I'm not a fan of either Belle Vue or Somerset. It's just one race out of many over the years that are watched and rewatched on YouTube. Every speedway fan will have their own favourite.

Representing the other side of the profit and loss account for speedway in the modern era is another short video. This one appeared on the UK speedway bulletin boards in October 2019. It's another version of that famous clip from Hitler's *Downfall* film, the one that's been adapted so many times, over so many years, that, frankly, it's become a bit of a tired cliché. But what makes this one worth it is that it's topical, bang up to date and sadly accurate in the points it makes about the state of the sport in Britain today. Whoever's put it together clearly knows their speedway – and the ways in which it is perfectly capable of shooting itself in the foot. It's based around the British Speedway Promoters' Association's (BSPA) annual general meeting. The BSPA organises the domestic speedway leagues in the UK and makes most of the decisions that determine the direction of the sport. In the video, the Führer is portrayed as the head of the BSPA, with fellow promoters listing what's wrong with the sport in 2019. To pick out just a few: no one's coming to watch anymore; they can barely charge a tenner admission; the stadiums are all being demolished; and, when a finger jabs on the map around Berlin, the caption tells us that 'Cradley are track-sharing near Berlin' ... Cradley Heath, from Dudley in the West Midlands, and probably the most successful

British team of the 1980s, have been nomadically sharing tracks for the last nine years since their old track was built over for housing. The comment may prompt a rueful smile, but it also underlines an issue that too many speedway tracks are facing themselves.

As I'll discover, speedway people are acutely aware of the problems facing their sport – but it doesn't mean they don't still love it.

Being involved in running speedway in the UK or trying to make a living – beyond the very top level that a world champion like Tai Woffinden operates at – is not an easy job. And yet the spirit and generosity of what's known within the sport as the 'speedway community' continue to shine brightly. There may not be much money to go around, but when it's needed most, they'll go out of their way to make sure no one's left to struggle.

What follows in these pages is a look at the sport over one year from September 2019 to October 2020, as it heads towards its centenary. British speedway – in some form – will celebrate the 100th anniversary of the very first race in this country at High Beech in Essex in 2028. That track, unsurprisingly, has since been reclaimed by woodland.

Speedway is a sport out of time in many ways. Modern sport in the 21st century tends to be talked about in terms of big numbers, of millions and hundreds of thousands, whether that's crowds or viewing figures or salaries. Spend any time in the world of British speedway at club level and you'll quickly discover it's a sport of thousands and hundreds.

It tends to be referred to in the past tense: speedway used to be or it once was. It's rarely talked about in terms of what might happen. But there are people who continue to believe in its future, who put money towards that goal and spend more time than is probably good for them on trying to achieve it.

And you know what? Despite the odds seemingly stacked against them, they might yet succeed.

What follows are – some of – their stories.

September 2019 – Same sport, different worlds

LOOMER ROAD Stadium – or, to give it its original title, the Chesterton Greyhound and Speedway Stadium – wouldn't be many people's first choice for a great Saturday night out. It's hidden away, out of sight of the road, in the hinterlands of Newcastle-under-Lyme in Staffordshire, at the end of a featureless industrial estate boasting the likes of Burma Bacon Supplies and Dynamic Pump Services.

'Stadium' is a bit of a stretch, too, if we're being honest. There's a small brick and corrugated metal grandstand along one side of the track, rust-red steelwork holding up a sloping roof, which has 'STOKE SPEEDWAY' in black capitals across the front. It's functional rather than flamboyant. Glass windows offer good views from the bar area above a shallow concreted standing area, and there are red, metal barriers on either side of the grandstand for spectators to lean on as they fill in their scorecards. The other three sides are effectively grass banks where cars can drive up and park – American drive-in cinema style – to overlook the track in the middle. To the uninitiated this looks like a muddy and puddled construction site after a period of heavy rain rather than something that's going to be the centre of paid-for entertainment.

Yet, tonight, a sunlit evening in mid-September that can't decide if it's late summer or early autumn, there are hundreds of people heading towards this unlikely sporting mecca. A long line of cars and vans is queuing patiently to get through the stadium's narrow entrance from the east. From the west, there's a queue of pedestrians, their entrance money – £13 for adults, £11 for senior citizens, £2 for children aged 5–15 – ready to be handed over at the small brick turnstile block. They've all come out to watch their local speedway team, the Stoke Potters, race against the Leicester Lion Cubs. So many have turned up, in fact, that tonight's advertised start time will have to be pushed back by half an hour to half past seven.

Many are regulars, visitors to Loomer Road for many years. Some have probably made a special trip this evening, having not been for quite a while. Others – including me – are here because tonight is the last time that this stadium will host speedway. A sport that was first staged in Stoke in 1929 – and which has continued, off and on, in the area ever since – will come to an end. Loomer Road Stadium is to be demolished. It may be replaced with more warehouses or housing, no one seems quite sure yet. These good people of Stoke and the surrounding area will have to find something else to do with their summer Saturday nights.

* * *

It's easy to spot Dave Tattum, the promoter of speedway at Stoke. For a start, he's walking around in a red 'Stoke Potters Speedway' fleece jacket with his name neatly printed on the right-hand side. Spend any time amongst real speedway people – the managers who organise the riders on the night, the promoters who are responsible for just about everything else and, of course, the truly committed fans – and you'll soon discover there's real pride in wearing their clubs' branded jackets. But Dave's hard to miss anyway as he seems to be everywhere, chatting to people as they arrive and then moving between the riders in the pits, the volunteer track staff in the centre green and the supporters and former riders in the bar who've turned up to pay a last farewell to the old stadium. He also makes sure to look after the night's guests, including the sponsors of the club's £100 draw – Activity Mobility of Weymouth.

Over the years, the team has attracted a range of sponsors – from Signal Radio, the local independent radio station, to a long association with Easy Rider, a Stafford-based motorcycle and scooter dealer. Since 2016, they've been sponsored by A.R. Richards Ltd of Market Drayton who, amongst other services, specialise in concrete sleepers, farm waste disposal and wheelie bins.

Promoters are the people who run speedway clubs and hire riders to race, although the work involved covers a much wider range of jobs than the title might at first suggest. Dave had arrived at the stadium around 9.30, as he's done on just about every other race day. He unlocks the gates and the sheds to get various vehicles out of storage that will be needed later: two tractors, JCBs and the parade truck on which the winning riders will be driven around after the meeting to wave to fans. Dave makes sure they're all full of diesel and prepared, along with the generator. Then he keeps an eye on what's happening with the weather and whether he needs to put water on the track during the morning or a little more shale around the turns or at the start. Getting the track right is vital for both the riders and the spectators. Shale, a fine-grained sedimentary rock mainly composed of mud, allows the riders to skid around the corners at speed and, hopefully, encourages safe and exciting overtaking. If the track isn't well prepared it's dangerous for the riders. If there's not enough shale, and the track's too slick, racing can be processional and dull for the spectators.

There's always something to do for a speedway promoter and most of it is far from glamorous. Dave has a loyal band of helpers – Ron, Gaynor and Caroline – who help out too, all of them volunteers, looking after, among other things, the bars and the catering while Dave's off doing his many other jobs.

I catch him by the stadium entrance at six o'clock, his fleece collar up despite the warm evening sun. Dave's a friendly soul and, even if tonight's difficult for him, he's doing his best to keep everything together. He says that he was choked on air earlier in the week when he was doing interviews on local radio. 'I felt like a fool because I couldn't talk. It was very emotional.' But he's pulling himself together tonight: 'You can't let the fans see that. You have to go out as if you're the happiest man in the stadium.'

I tell him I'm an Edinburgh Monarchs' fan and he says he's spoken that morning to Alex Harkess, the co-promoter at Edinburgh who's been involved in speedway even longer than Dave has. It turns out that Alex was one of the volunteers who helped build Loomer Road Stadium when he was living in nearby Newcastle-under-Lyme.

'He wanted to phone and wish me all the best. He'd heard what had happened obviously. You know what? We both ended up in tears.'

Dave's been promoting speedway at Stoke for a quarter of a century. He'd only found out earlier in the week that the stadium owners had decided to sell up and that tonight's meeting, the last of the 2019 season, would be the final one. Full stop.

He's keen to make clear that it's all coming to an end because the owners have simply decided to sell the stadium. 'There's no hidden agenda here or anything with that sort of stuff you read on the internet. We've always paid our rent. We've had some good racing here and we've had some good crowds this year.'

The owners of the stadium have come to a logical decision. With no greyhound racing at the stadium anymore – the last meeting was back in 2003 – and increasingly fewer speedway meetings (tonight's is the 13th of the season when, back in the 1980s, there'd be at least double that number), the only other activity is stock car racing. It's not really enough to justify the maintenance and upkeep of a stadium and its large car parking area. Dave can understand completely. 'I feel certain the buyers have done their homework. It will be developed. I really think it will be under construction come January. They have invested a lot of money and they have to recoup that money somewhere. They don't want to sit on this empty.'

Since speedway first took place in Stoke in 1929, it's had a chequered history in the area. According to the club's website, the Sun Street Stadium at Hanley in Stoke hosted speedway before the Second World War until 1953 when the track closed. The entertainment tax

– a 48 per cent levy on the revenues of many sport and entertainment venues – hit many clubs that had sprung up in the post-war speedway boom. It reopened in 1960 but closed after just three years and only began again ten years later at its new venue here in Loomer Road. Apart from a single-season break in 1993 and a year as the curiously named Cradley Heathens/Stoke in 1996, the Potters have raced at Loomer Road – at different levels of league racing – ever since.

But Dave Tattum isn't banking on this being just a short hiatus before speedway starts up once again. He sees little prospect of a return. 'We're noisy and dusty. No one wants to be near a motorsport stadium. Unfortunately, it will be inevitable the club will end.'

And while there's been some talk of Stoke possibly carrying on by racing next year, 25 miles away, at Buxton in Derbyshire, that's not something Dave thinks likely. He doesn't see how you could move Stoke Speedway to Buxton and call it Stoke. He says it was tried with Cradley in 1996, when it was called Cradley Stoke, and it didn't work. 'The Cradley fans came and the Stoke fans didn't.'

I tell him it's a sad night, we shake hands and he moves on to his next task for the evening.

* * *

The meeting – a National League fixture – is run briskly and without any serious crashes. The National League is the most junior of the three levels of league speedway in Great Britain – although, as we'll see, there's a certain fluidity to riders taking part in different leagues. The Leicester Lion Cubs win 50-40, although no one's really bothered about the result, Leicester having already qualified for the end-of-season play-offs and Stoke out of the running.

Despite the fact that speedway is a competitive team sport, there's none of the latent hostility towards opposing supporters that football has suffered from over the years. During the meeting, I spot several Leicester jackets along with a couple from Wolverhampton, Coventry and Wimbledon, the last two tracks suffering their own closures in the 21st century.

Go into the bar during a race and you'll find a busy and friendly space. The tables by the windows have been carefully covered in tartan and gingham plastic tablecloths and are all occupied. Somebody's set up a trestle table to sell speedway memorabilia – old programmes, photos of riders past and present and club badges. There are glass cases on the wall highlighting Stoke teams from the past, one of which, titled 'Times to remember', seems particularly poignant tonight.

Strangers politely stop to let you pass, semi-apologetic smiles acknowledging the shared but unspoken fact that we won't be here again. When the racing starts, plenty of heads turn to follow the riders around their four laps. One of the great things about speedway – compared to other motorsports – is that you get to see the whole race, not just vehicles flashing by and then disappearing for a while until they come around again on the next lap. But you'll also see some couples or groups of people chatting over a drink, the speedway apparently incidental to their Saturday night out. For them, going to the speedway is much more than just the racing. It's the smell – the sweet aroma of methanol mixed with racing oil which, although less pungent these days, entices speedway aficionados, like the smell of freshly cut grass. It's the raw sound – the angry, impatient revving of the engines just yards away from the spectators. And it's the comfort of familiarity, with many spectators – either in the bar, by their favourite first-corner barrier or on the grass banks surrounding the oval track – in the same place, sharing a few words with the same people next to them, week in, week out. Going to speedway appeals to many of our most basic human needs, familiarity amongst them, and it's all the better for it.

Lots of people are, unsurprisingly, filming the final races on their phones or taking selfies against the backdrop of the grandstand or starting tapes. But not everyone is using the latest technology. I pass two men panning around the track with old-style video cameras, which must have been state-of-the-art back when they were bought in the late 1990s.

I don't actually see anyone in tears as I'm walking around, but the Stoke Potters' Twitter feed – 2,605 followers on the day of the last meeting – later makes clear that quite a few people most certainly were. After the final race of the evening, Dave invites anyone who wants to come down to the track to walk around it, a symbolic and moving experience for those for whom the Stoke Potters is much more than a slightly oddly named team competing in a largely forgotten sport; it is a real part of both their own lives and the wider community.

Later, in the one remaining weekly speedway magazine, *Speedway Star*, I'll read about Jess Sant, who has been coming here since she was a baby, nearly 24 years ago. She's devastated at the closure and says she's made many friends and memories at the stadium. There's Vickie Ellis, who has been following Stoke since 1973. For her, it's heartbreaking that they won't be there anymore. Her only consolation is that they've had this last meeting to say goodbye properly. She is well aware that other clubs weren't so lucky because they just closed and that was that.

Scan the most recent messages on the club's Twitter feed, those offering sympathy and condolences for what's happened, and you'll soon see a common theme emerging. 'I used to go there for birthdays at primary school', 'Rarely missed a meeting from '81 to '92' and 'My dad used to take me' are typical examples.

And that, along with the kind of sponsors the sport gets and the average age of those attending and those capturing their final memories on 20-year-old DVCAM video cameras, underlines one of the main issues facing British speedway in 2019. The audience for it, the people who know about it and want to watch it and care about it, is growing old. It's not being replaced by anything like the same number of young people.

Despite the long queues and the need for a delayed start, the final attendance is around 1,100. 'If we had crowds like this coming all the time, we could probably do something in future,' says Dave. 'But if we were running the week after, it would have been less than a third. When we were here in the late 90s, we had crowds of 1,200 to 1,500, right up until the mid-2000s. It's a shame. People have lost heart with speedway. It has gone and it's a great shame. It's a fabulous sport with fabulous people in it.'

But perhaps the saddest thing for us dwindling few who enjoy our speedway is that Stoke's closure will likely not be the only one. A week earlier, Peterborough responded to speculation about redevelopment at their East of England Showground track by saying they were safe in the short term. The Panthers, as they are known, race in the top league, the Premiership, but didn't have a home meeting at all between July 15th and September 5th – effectively prime summertime season for speedway as it covers the school holidays – because, like most speedway clubs, they don't own their own track and don't have first option on its use.

The year before, 2018, four tracks – Workington in Cumbria, Buxton, Lakeside in Essex and Rye House in Hertfordshire – closed too. Just 23 tracks opened for the start of the 2019 season. A 24th, the homeless Cradley Heath – whose track closed back in 1995 but who were revived by supporters in 2010 – race at Wolverhampton's Monmore Green track.

As ever, at the end of the speedway season, which runs from the end of March through to October, there are rumours that other tracks are in financial trouble and are considering their options for the following year. Whatever the truth, it seems highly unlikely that Stoke's closure tonight will be the only one.

Dave Tattum is the last person out of Loomer Road Stadium at around quarter past eleven, his trusty colleague, Ron Parry, still with him. He knows Loomer Road isn't the prettiest of sporting venues. His benchmark is Wolverhampton, one of the better-appointed speedway stadiums due to it being home to one of the country's remaining greyhound tracks. 'Loomer Road was coming on 50 years old, but we did keep it tidy. We spent a lot of money on it in the last ten years – me and the stock car man.' But now, as he locks the gate behind him, it's the end, an unheralded moment that brings another chapter of the British speedway world to a close. Belle Vue in Manchester is now the only surviving speedway club in the north-west of England.

* * *

Around 170 miles or so away, Jitendra Duffill is doing his best to keep speedway going in another part of the country. The town of Redcar sits just outside Middlesbrough town centre on the north-east coast of England. Redcar has a curious, split-personality history – once a popular seaside resort but also a centre for steel and chemical production. It has, like much of the United Kingdom where heavy manufacturing was the basis for employment, seen better days. Its steelworks closed in 2015, with unemployment increasing as a result. The area was featured in the BBC's 2018 series, *The Mighty Redcar,* which followed the real-life experiences of several young people trying to find jobs.

Jitendra – or Ben, as he's known outside the speedway world – isn't your typical speedway promoter. He's just 38 for starters, younger than most. He has an Indian mother and an English father. And he works part-time as an optometrist in the town. I'm guessing he's the only speedway promoter to be profiled in *Optician Online.* He first became interested in speedway when the Redcar Bears raced along the road at Cleveland Stadium in Middlesbrough before that closed in 1996. He rode for a couple of years – 'I wasn't very successful. If I'm really honest, the commitment wasn't there from me' – for Newcastle, Edinburgh and Glasgow and then moved to Redcar's third-tier league team, the Cleveland Bays, when speedway started up again on Teesside in 2006. In 2009, he became team manager. Then, in September 2017, he stepped up to become promoter. Except, as he says in his programme notes for this month's meeting against Eastbourne, 'promoter' isn't an accurate description of his role.

'The one thing I get to spend the least time on is promoting our club. That's not great, I know, but it's a fact. A more accurate job title would be general manager. I spend a minimum of 40 hours per week running our club, which includes staging events, press releases, cashing up, banking and resetting floats, invoicing, accounting, preparing the programme, dealing with all kinds of administration, from sponsorship to correspondence with staff, the Promoters' Association and riders. The list goes on and on and it eats up all my time, which is all given on a completely voluntary basis.'

Later, he'll tell me he does this because he loves Redcar speedway. 'I was brought up around speedway and my dad and my grandad both used to attend. It can be tough because us promoters get a hard time as the sport's not in a great position; crowds are not what they were years ago and we tend to get the blame. To be frank, we're just giving our own time and, a lot of us, our own money, just to keep the sport going. Whether we're doing things right or wrong, we can only use what's at our disposal. Finances and budgets are pretty tight. I think a lot of promoters deserve a lot more credit for what they do than they get.'

Ask him about the reaction of his patients when he mentions speedway and the answer is sadly familiar. 'It always surprises me because a lot of them don't actually know speedway is there. There are a lot who say they used to go years ago, when there was speedway in Middlesbrough.' He says the local press is very supportive – both radio and TV – and that they're very active on social media, but there are still too many people who don't know they exist. And there's another problem.

'When you ask people if they'll come and watch, it's tough to get them along once they are out of the habit. It's a shame because it's such a fantastic sport. We made admission for under-16s free and that brought quite a few new people in. Once they're there, they tend to be hooked. They absolutely love it. I'm not going to pretend to have all the answers. I'm not a marketing expert; I was brought in to run the speedway club with no experience in that field whatsoever. I have experience in business, but I'm not going to pretend I'm something I'm not. I'm not the answer to speedway's revival. If there was a big marketing push, we'd need experts to be able to do that. I still think we have something there to sell, 100 per cent. I think speedway is one of the most amazing sports in existence. It's just knowing how to get people in and selling that to them because once they're there, most people come back.'

Had he written his list of 'non-promoter' tasks a week later, a time when his Bears' team should have been focusing on the end-of-season play-offs, Jitendra would have had to include hospital visits and statements to the police. Three of his seven riders end up in casualty after on-track crashes. And their stadium – the Media Prime Arena – is broken into and vandalised. The cost of the damage and losses is over £1,000. Loose change to your average Premier League footballer, but real and vital funds for a speedway club that has no spare money.

'We're pretty vulnerable because, although we're only a five-minute drive from Middlesbrough town centre, we are on an industrial estate and there's nobody there on an evening or through the night. It leaves us vulnerable to theft and it's something that happens on a yearly basis, certainly since I can remember. Every time it does, it's a bit of a gut punch because you work so hard to build up what we have through blood, sweat and tears. Our directors and supporters make generous donations, so for somebody to come and take that away from us and cause the damage they do ...' He tails off. 'It's pretty devastating, every time it happens.'

Nevertheless, Jitendra is keen to make progress in his role – despite the time constraints and injuries and break-ins – and along with Bears' supporter John Gallon, he put together a survey of fans earlier in the summer. It's not the biggest survey ever – just 157 participants – but its results, revealed in the match programme, illustrate some of the problems facing speedway in general.

The main – and worrying – finding backs up what I've seen first-hand at Stoke. Namely that more than half of those answering the survey have been supporters for at least 41 years. That suggests they're at least in their 50s. As *Speedway Star* says after reprinting the survey in full: 'No sport is going to be able to flourish and grow when half its audience is in its collective 50s, 60s or even older.'

However hard it's going to be to attract the time-poor, short-attention-spanned, mobile phone-fixated younger generation, it's clear that speedway is going to have to try. The alternative is a continuation of the seemingly downward spiral the sport is in at the moment.

* * *

As ever with speedway, though, there's another side to the sport, a more positive and, dare one say it, glamorous side. And it can be glimpsed – however briefly – in the middle of September.

The current speedway world champion is British. He's spoken of how he is often recognised when he does his supermarket shopping at his local ASDA in Long Eaton in Derbyshire. But he'd probably manage Harrods Food Hall in London's Knightsbridge without being spotted. Relatively unknown or not, Tai Woffinden is not just the country's best rider but, in publicity terms, he's the sport's biggest asset too. At 29, he's been world champion three times. He's a man who clearly doesn't suffer fools gladly and hasn't been afraid to ruffle feathers in the past. Peter Oakes, co-author of Tai's new autobiography, *Raw Speed*, says Woffinden is a workaholic, willing to bend his back to be successful in anything that he does.

Raw Speed has just been published and Woffinden is promoting it with book signings and media appearances. The book is selling well. It enters *The Times* list of best-selling hardback non-fiction books at number ten, alongside new titles by the likes of Jamie Oliver and former Prime Minister David Cameron. It's apparently speedway's fastest-selling book ever. This morning, he's live on BBC TV in Salford.

It's fair to say, given that BBC Breakfast's staple guests are politicians and business leaders, that Tai Woffinden stands out when he's sitting on the sofa. He's a man famous for his tattoos and several are on show, on both his T-shirted arms and up his neck. His trademark, lobe-stretching, gaping-gauge circular earrings are equally prominent.

Normally, when he's interviewed at a meeting in the pits, Woffinden is covered in sponsorship – on his leathers and on his cap. BBC guidelines – and no doubt attentive production staff – have made sure that he's as neutrally dressed as possible. But there's an unmistakable Monster energy drink logo – three lightning-like green lines on the side of his backwards-slung cap – which has squeezed through the pre-broadcast branding check.

The interview is introduced with a quick explanation of speedway to those watching (likely the vast majority) who aren't familiar with it:

no gears, no brakes, acceleration faster than a Formula 1 car – the last claim often made but technically open to debate. Woffinden speaks well and is remarkably down-to-earth about the daily risks of being a speedway rider. It's something that never seems to phase the people who actually do it, the riders, unlike those who are hearing about it for the first time. Woffinden has spoken about how it feels to be on a speedway bike when it slides into the corner and the front wheel tucks in and it pulls his arms up, about how close it is to being out of control but still in control. For him, that's the best feeling.

The BBC producers – to give them credit – have done their research and there are questions about Tai's relationship with his father, Rob, his main influence before he died from cancer in 2010. Tai also confirms that he wouldn't want either of his children – one daughter and another child on the way – to be a speedway rider.

It's not the first time he's been on the BBC Breakfast sofa. As *Raw Speed* details, he was invited on after winning the World Championship for the first time back in 2013. But the discussion then strayed on to the size of the stud in his ear and his tattoos, leaving him to reflect that he'd rather the BBC Breakfast team had been briefed about speedway rather than having them talk to him about body art and ear stretchers.

History repeats itself today, 18 September 2019. One of the two main presenters, Louise Minchin, is obviously unaware of what Woffinden has said about that previous appearance on the programme.

'Your tattoos are mesmerising, by the way,' she says. 'Have you got a favourite?'

'One on my back, which is a portrait of my dad and the letter he wrote me before he passed away,' says Woffinden. 'That's the one that means the most to me.' There are a couple of empathetic 'awws' off camera at this although, knowing the everyday cynicism that is hard-wired into most journalists, you do wonder how genuine they are.

But overall, it is good, and very rare, mainstream, national publicity for speedway. It comes in the week when Woffinden – and the other top speedway riders in the world – will take part in the biggest event of the year in Britain.

* * *

Once a year the centre of Cardiff is taken over by speedway fans from all over Europe. The reason? The British staging of the Speedway Grand Prix series. Once upon a time, the contest to decide speedway's individual world champion was held over a single meeting. But since 1995, it's been expanded into a series of Grand Prix – ten of them – which are, this year, held in Poland (three), Sweden (two) and one each in Great Britain, Slovenia, the Czech Republic, Germany and Denmark. The division pretty much reflects the current strength of speedway in each country.

The Grand Prix in Cardiff is the one moment each year that British speedway gets to feel like it is part of the same world as its much richer motorsport relative, Formula 1. For anyone who has never been, it is genuinely one of the best feel-good days out in the British sporting calendar, and Cardiff – the city and its residents – do their bit to make it a real event, even though the city itself hasn't had a speedway team since 1953.

Speedway fans in their thousands take over the city centre. Walk around on the Saturday morning before the event and, to the casual observer, speedway appears to be thriving. There's a sponsored fans' area outside Cardiff Castle and a giant inflatable speedway helmet by the castle walls. Pop-up stalls sell all manner of speedway memorabilia and T-shirts in the city-centre streets. Bars and restaurants are filled with good-natured and well-behaved speedway fans. And they *are* well behaved. While some might shudder at the thought of motorbike enthusiasts descending on their city, worried that they represent a rebellious and noisy collective, all too ready to cock a snoot at more civilised society, that's not the case here.

Councils, as we'll see, have not been the biggest fans of speedway over the years, but Cardiff Council Cabinet Member for Culture and Leisure, Peter Bradbury, is very happy to have it in the city. For him, it has become a well-established part of Cardiff's annual events calendar, with the city looking forward to offering fans from across the world a warm Welsh welcome. Figures from South Wales Police indicate that looking after speedway crowds is most likely one of their easiest jobs of the year. Over the 13 years since 2007 (since official figures have been available), there were just six arrests at the Cardiff Principality Stadium on the day of the Grand Prix. They were all for minor offences like being drunk and disorderly or using threatening words or behaviour. Speedway fans are most certainly not long-haired hooligans intent on causing trouble.

The Cardiff Principality Stadium is normally the venue for the Welsh rugby union team or big concert events for the likes of the Rolling Stones, Coldplay and Ed Sheeran. Every year, several days are spent installing a custom-built speedway track under the watchful eye of 1970s world speedway champion, Ole Olsen. It helps that there's a roof, which means – whether it rains or not – that the meeting will definitely go ahead. There are fireworks, champagne, glamorous Monster Energy models holding up rider numbers, and 40,000 expectant fans making lots of noise and – whether you like them or not – sounding air-horns as if their lives depended on it. Certain sections of the ground are, deliberately, kept air-horn free.

And yet, this is not what British speedway – everyday British speedway – is all about. It's light years away. It's the once-a-year birthday trip to the big city when the rest of the year is full of mundanities, of six o'clock in the morning starts and waiting for the bus to travel to work.

Many of the fans are bedecked in the red and white of Poland, there to cheer on the current Grand Prix leader, Bartosz Zmarzlik, and his four other Polish compatriots. As speedway declines in countries around the world – Britain is far from being alone – Poland stands out as its most vibrant venue.

Top league matches – all of them televised live – regularly attract capacity crowds in five figures, far in excess of the best that British speedway can offer. It means that riders can be paid much more and so, unsurprisingly, Poland attracts the best in the world. It's telling that, of the 15 permanent Grand Prix riders for the 2019 season, only one – Australia's Jason Doyle – began the season racing for a club in Great Britain. For the other 14, the focus is on Poland, with Sweden – where crowds are also higher – a close second. Woffinden himself hasn't raced in the British leagues since turning out for Wolverhampton in 2016. He has been vocal in saying that if he is to be the best speedway rider, he needs to ride against the best, week in, week out. 'Unfortunately, they're not racing in England. If all the best riders in the world were racing in England, then that would be the place to be racing. But the fact is that they're not.'

The riders riding tonight are on a different level of pay and sponsorship from those taking part solely in the British league system. Their support staff, the mechanics and back-up teams are much larger too.

The stadium is a mass of flags – many of them red and white from Poland, but plenty too from Denmark, Sweden, Australia and Russia, the other main countries on the international speedway scene in 2019. During the national anthem – which follows 'Land of My Fathers' – there's a cascade of union flags, a working-class Britons' version of the previous week's *Last Night of the Proms* at the Royal Albert Hall. I'm assuming there aren't that many – if any – who've attended both events. But, as the poet T.S. Eliot once said, for a nation to be truly complete, it must have both high and low culture, 'from the opera to a night at the dogs'. While some fans would say that speedway, at its very best, is a true art, most people would place it closer to the latter.

Of the first six heats, five are won by the rider in red, on the inside lane. None of the three British riders – Tai Woffinden, Robert Lambert or Charles Wright – makes it through to the semi-finals. For the many British fans, the only real moment to celebrate is when Lambert holds off Denmark's Leon Madsen to win heat nine. Charles Wright, this year's British champion (Woffinden hasn't competed in it since 2015), gets two battling second places. Woffinden has a disappointing night in his bid to win his first-ever British Grand Prix title. It's perhaps not surprising. He's just back from two months out of the sport after being involved in a crash in a Polish league meeting, which resulted in a compression fracture to his spine along with a broken shoulder blade and a bruised lung. In terms of injuries, Woffinden has, during his career, broken just about every bone that it's possible to break. But, like so many speedway riders, he keeps coming back.

He's excluded in his first race ('unfairly' according to BT Sport's co-commentator and former rider, Kelvin Tatum) when he clips Freddie Lindgren's back wheel after the Swedish rider has effectively left him with no space to ride. He ends up in the safety fence but has insult added to – thankfully – non-existent injury when he's excluded from the rerun, judged by the referee to be the 'primary cause of the stoppage'. He ends up with just five points, disappointing for him and for all the British supporters in the crowd.

At the end of the meeting – not a classic British Grand Prix, by any means – BT's main commentator, Nigel Pearson, and Tatum are watching the night's top riders – the winner, Denmark's Leon Madsen, second-placed Emil Sayfutdinov from Russia, and Poland's Bartosz Zmarzlik – spraying each other with the customary champagne. Pearson reveals that members of his family have attended the meeting, some of them for the first time.

'And I've just had a text saying they've loved every minute of it. How good is that?'

Tatum agrees it's good, but warns that Pearson will have a lot to live up to the next time he takes them to speedway. It will have to be even better than this. 'I'll take them to Cradley!' says Pearson, whose genuine commitment to speedway goes beyond media duties, as he helps to run Cradley Heath, the third-division National League track.

'Okay. Good luck with that,' is Tatum's verdict.

Tatum's not being unfair to his colleague. Or to Cradley Heath. He probably has some idea of what's going to be announced later in the year.

October 2019 – A damp squib

SPEEDWAY, LIKE cricket and baseball, is a summer sport. It's best played – or, in this case, ridden – on warm, dry afternoons and evenings, shirt-sleeved crowds enjoying the sun on their faces instead of worrying that they've forgotten their umbrella. If a speedway track, covered with mud-based shale to start with, becomes waterlogged or deeply rutted because of rain, then it's too dangerous for racing to take place. There's also the small matter of riders, already lacking any brakes, needing to see where they're going – even harder in wet conditions. As a result, the British speedway season starts, some would say optimistically, in the middle of March and carries on until the end of October.

Three main leagues make up British speedway in 2019. The third division, the most junior, is the National League, where Stoke and Cradley Heath race. It has eight teams. The middle tier, the Championship, is very much a northern league, with only two of its teams – Eastbourne and Somerset – south of Birmingham. The top league, the Premiership, has seven teams – Belle Vue in Manchester, Wolverhampton, Swindon, Poole on the south coast and three teams in East Anglia – King's Lynn, Peterborough and Ipswich. London, once a hotbed for British speedway, boasting some of the most famous team names – Wembley, Wimbledon, Hackney, New Cross and West Ham – doesn't have a single club. The closest to the capital is at Sittingbourne in Kent, nearly 50 miles away.

At one time, the league champions were the team that finished at the top after the regular home and away meetings had been completed.

That was simple. And then someone noticed end-of-season play-offs. They'd been used in the United States for baseball, American football, ice hockey and basketball for many years to decide the champions. Closer to home, the Football League introduced them for a promotion place in 1987, and rugby league went further in 1998, using them to determine the overall Super League champions. Extra fixtures, at the 'business end' of a six-month-long season, mean more revenue and guarantee a tense league climax rather than a runaway, if deserved, winner. Sky Sports, by then holding the live TV rights to British league speedway, were keen too. As a result, speedway promoters introduced play-offs to the top league in 2002 and have become fixated with making it into them ever since. Read an interview with a rider or a promoter during the season and you'll find that it's all about 'making it into those play-offs'. And it's in October, with the leaves turning and the nights quickly drawing in, that the finale to the season takes place.

But getting to see a speedway meeting in Britain in October is very much a case of crossing your fingers and checking the weather forecast, particularly if you live some distance from the track. Of course, it's not just October. Britain's recent weather patterns mean you're just as likely to find a meeting rained off in the middle of July. But there's no doubt the capricious British climate gets worse the further north you go. Glasgow and Edinburgh, the most northerly tracks, know full well that they're battling to keep the dust down one week while the next they're trying to stop the track turning into a swamp.

This particular autumn seems particularly bad. At the start of the month, prime time for play-off meetings, the solidly torrential rain sweeping much of the country dominates the news, along with the seemingly never-ending wrangles over Brexit and President Trump's increasingly bizarre conversations with other world leaders.

You have to feel for those organising speedway in this country – and, of course, the riders trying to earn a decent living from it – as the rain plays havoc with the schedule. Postponements are inconvenient and frustrating enough for supporters, but much worse for those with a financial stake in the sport. For riders, every cancellation means lost wages and, particularly if it's within a couple of hours of the start of a meeting, long and often tedious motorway journeys for no purpose. In some ways, it's worse for promoters who still face costs like programme production, stadium rent, BSPA fees, riders' travel costs and, if it's not called off by lunchtime, the referee's travel costs too. One promoter tells me that every postponement last season cost him £2,500, more in the Premiership – real money in the world of British league speedway.

There's no real solution, short of staging speedway under cover, as happens at Cardiff for the British Grand Prix. But that's a one-off, the costs justified by the 40,000 crowd. Track covers have been tried at some tracks – most notably at Berwick in the Championship – with mixed results. If rain is forecast and there are enough volunteers to help both lay and then remove the covers, it can mean a meeting that would have been cancelled going ahead. But there's nothing that can be done when the heavens open half an hour ahead of a 7.30 start. And covers are neither mandatory nor widely used.

Out of 29 meetings scheduled between 22 September and 7 October, 16 are postponed. British Speedway vice-chairman Rob Godfrey – also the Scunthorpe promoter – says the weather has been a nightmare. And he's not wrong. With the speedway season due to end before November rolls round, the pressure to complete the season is on.

Every league's showpiece meetings are affected. The individual championship for National League riders is rained out at its original venue at Leicester. It's then moved to Scunthorpe before being postponed and pushed back to the penultimate Sunday in October. It's eventually abandoned after 14 heats because of torrential rain, and is not restaged.

Redcar – having their most successful season on the track despite injuries and burglaries – end up having to schedule three of their most important meetings on consecutive days: at home to Newcastle in the first leg of the KO Cup Final on the Friday, away at Leicester in the second leg of their Championship Final on the Saturday, followed by the second leg of the final at Newcastle on the Sunday. The first two go ahead, but the meeting at Newcastle is rained off. Rescheduled for the following Sunday, that also falls victim to the weather before finally going ahead on the final Sunday in October. BBC's regional news programme, *Look North*, does its bit for speedway by mentioning the Tyneside-Teesside derby each time it's due to be staged. But it soon becomes a matter of reporting that it has, once again, been postponed. Newcastle promoter George English bemoans the impact of the weather in spoiling what should have been a fitting climax for speedway in the north-east of England.

Glasgow and Somerset suffer two postponements for their Championship semi-final play-off. The first leg of the National League semi-final play-off between Belle Vue Colts and Kent is rained off twice before going ahead; the second leg takes place in persistent rain, the tail end of Storm Lorenzo. Belle Vue boss Graham Goodwin says there is no way it should have gone ahead, but because of the time of the season they just had to get on with it.

I'm determined to make it to some of the Premiership play-offs, to experience end-of-season speedway for myself, but when you're based in London and still working, that's easier said than done. Three times I make tentative plans, shuffling meetings to fit around the play-off schedule; three times I'm thwarted by the rain. With each postponement, the finale of the British speedway season is effectively shunted further and further back into the autumn.

Some people would say that scheduling play-offs for a league that only has seven teams to begin with is a bit odd. But that is what's happening in the Premiership this year. Out of the seven teams, just three haven't made it through. The unlucky ones this year are Peterborough, King's Lynn and Belle Vue.

Poole, who finished top of the league, are meant to race against Ipswich in the first leg of the play-off semi-final on Monday, 23 September. But that falls victim to the weather. So the second leg, scheduled for the Thursday at Ipswich, is replaced by the first leg at Poole. The Ipswich meeting goes ahead two nights later and, despite both taking place on very wet tracks, they're completed, with

Ipswich causing something of an upset to reach the final. For a team new into the Premiership this season – they had moved up from the Championship – they had not been expected to make the Grand Final.

The other play-off semi-final between Swindon and Wolverhampton is not so fortunate. The first leg at Swindon is cancelled because of the weather. The second leg at Wolverhampton suffers the same fate. The rescheduled first leg at Swindon is also postponed. The BT Sport schedule struggles to keep up with the changes. Finally, after three postponements, the first leg takes place at Wolverhampton on Wednesday, 9 October. But it quickly becomes clear that it's going ahead under far from ideal conditions. The start time is delayed for half an hour because of more rain. In the early stages, on a wet track, any riders at the back are quickly covered in shale and struggle to see where they're going. Not surprisingly, several riders fall as a result of the conditions, including former world champion Jason Doyle, who comes off on the first bend with no one near him. He describes track conditions as 'atrocious'.

I'm sat at home, in the dry, watching on TV. It's a hard job for the BT Sport commentators to find the right balance between objectively calling it as it is and not demeaning the quality of the racing to the extent that anyone watching will simply switch off.

'Unfortunately, at this time of year, they're just going to have to make the best of it,' says Kelvin Tatum, himself a former world finalist.

'I would say it's just great that we've got any speedway whatsoever here,' adds Nigel Pearson. 'Another five, ten minutes of rain and I think we'd have been going home.'

With times much slower than normal, Wolverhampton's Rory Schlein agrees, telling viewers in between races that it's nothing like normal riding conditions. He'll go on to point out that Wolves haven't ridden a match for three weeks and haven't been at home since 2 September, five weeks earlier; hardly ideal preparation for any team, in any sport, facing a crucial semi-final.

'Look at the race suits,' says Pearson a little later, observing the mud-spattered riders on display. 'It's not a good night for team sponsors to have their branding advertised on television.' Then, realising what he's just said, he does some elegant backpedalling. 'I'm sure they understand, the respective team sponsors. They do a great job for speedway clubs up and down the country. Well done to them. Without sponsorship, of course, the sport becomes unviable. It is an important part of modern-day speedway.'

At the end of the evening, Swindon have a ten-point lead to take into the second leg at home, which is now taking place the following night. Unless something unexpected happens, Swindon will face Ipswich in the final.

'It's not the best speedway meeting they're ever going to witness,' says Tatum with admirable honesty as the home crowd head off into the wet streets of Wolverhampton. 'Ordinarily I don't think this meeting would be on. I think it would be run at a different time. But at this time of the year it's never easy.' *Speedway Star* describes the meeting as a damp squib.

Twenty-four hours later, Natalie Quirk opens up BT Sport's coverage in a coat and scarf. The Swindon manager, Alan Rossiter, is interviewed and looks like he's about to head off for a hill walk in the Lake District rather than spending the next two hours trying to guide his team into the showpiece final of an allegedly summer sport.

We learn that 14,000 gallons of water were removed from the Swindon track the previous day and, with more rain forecast, the aim is to get through the meeting before it arrives. Overall, there's a real feeling of 'grin and bear it' to tonight. The end result – getting this semi-final finished and out of the way – justifies the means, which, in turn, results in less than thrilling racing for those spectators who've turned up. It's a slick track with little grip for the riders to use to overtake and therefore little of the exciting passing that really makes speedway a true spectacle.

After six races, Swindon lead 26-10 and there's no doubt they're heading to the final. The riders realise it too. They come straight back to the start for heat seven after Swindon's Troy Batchelor is warned for moving at the tapes. Normally there would be a frustrating two-minute gap involving trips back to the pits, but not tonight. The riders want this over as quickly as possible too.

There's still time for some chirpy comments from the BT commentary team. Kelvin Tatum, wearing a Biggles-style jacket (which he generously says has been borrowed from Paul in the pits), spots the former Swindon rider, Frenchman David Bellego, watching the action. 'I think I might prefer the South of France at this time of year.'

Nigel Pearson is more worried about what's still to come. 'I wonder if this scaffold tower is going to remain here for us for next week? I must remember a scarf and gloves.'

Five days later, on 15 October, it's the – delayed – first leg of the climax to the British speedway season, the Premiership Grand Final between Ipswich and Swindon. The BT Sport production teams have juggled outside broadcast units and schedules to make sure they're able to cover it live.

Although this is the final, there's been no attempt by either club to increase ticket prices. Given all the postponements, and the added costs those have undoubtedly brought for both promotions, that's admirable and very much in keeping with speedway's value-for-money reputation.

That's not the only positive news. There's a good crowd inside Ipswich's Foxhall Stadium. 'The management here must be delighted with the turnout,' says Kelvin Tatum. 'One of the better crowds I've seen here in a long, long time.' Promoters don't release official attendances, but it's estimated at between 2,500 and 4,500.

Sadly, for the home side, that's where the good news ends as they go down to a 41-49 defeat, which makes Swindon virtual certainties for the title. There's been – no surprises – heavy rain in the Ipswich area and while the track staff have done an excellent job to prepare a rideable surface, it's still far from ideal. Jason Doyle talks later about how it turned really icy after heat 11. Doyle is made of strong stuff. He has two falls in his first two rides, and has his ankle ridden over by team-mate Adam Ellis into the bargain, but keeps going.

The racing, bluntly, isn't great. There's little passing and, as can happen at speedway meetings, the winner of the heat is, more often than not, the rider that 'gates first' – the one that's first away from the starting tapes – and leads going into the first corner. These are criticisms often levelled at speedway, that it's sometimes processional, dull and predictable. Sadly, tonight wouldn't convert many new supporters. Then again, given the number of adverts for over-50s insurance in the commercial breaks, it doesn't look like many are expected anyway.

Heats 13 and 15 are notable for the rare sight in Britain these days of two Grand Prix riders, Jason Doyle and Niels-Kristian Iversen, riding against each other. It's also apparent, after a quick look at Ipswich's fixtures, that of their last 11 matches – all the way back to Thursday, 8 August – all but one has been against either Swindon or Peterborough. Not exactly a variety of opponents to put before an audience, whether committed or new.

Two days later, it's the second leg at Swindon's Abbey Stadium and, again, there's a good crowd inside. Estimates put it at between 3,000 and 3,500, which is excellent for British speedway in 2019. If tracks could regularly attract that every week they'd be delighted. Earlier in the month, *Speedway Star* tantalisingly reminded readers of the 1967 season when 12,000 turned up for Swindon's match against West Ham, with mile-long traffic jams queuing to get in.

But, nevertheless, tonight's crowd is so big that the often grumpy *British Speedway Forum* – where speedway fans post messages that often arrow in on the negatives – will be positively ecstatic about it later. 'A great night. The place was rammed.' 'The crowd ... was huge, I've not seen a crowd like that for years.' 'The atmosphere was terrific. Chanting at speedway? Never have I heard that before.'

The result is never in doubt. Swindon have a 20-point aggregate lead on the night after just six heats and the title is officially sealed after heat ten, Jason Doyle and Adam Ellis celebrating in front of the home fans with wheelies – lifting their front tyre up off the ground and riding just on the back one – down the home straight. The Swindon fans undoubtedly enjoy it, the Ipswich fans in attendance much less so as their team doesn't really compete, which means it's a less than enthralling night for the neutrals.

Once victory is secured, the night turns into a retro-disco celebration from the 70s interspersed with a few speedway races. 'We are the Champions', 'That's the Way I Like It', 'Hi Ho Silver Lining' and 'Celebrate' all echo across the stadium. The fact that it's cold and starting to rain doesn't seem to bother anyone.

Swindon's trophy is presented to them after the meeting by Eddie Kidd, the former motorcycle stunt rider who was a household name in the 1970s and 1980s before an accident left him paralysed with brain damage in 1996. It's a sobering reminder of the dangers of riding any kind of motorbike for a living.

When it's time for Swindon's winning team photos, with fireworks going off behind them, five of the riders are nattily attired in bobble hats, possibly for sponsorship reasons but more likely because it's getting on for ten o'clock and it's now even colder.

* * *

The morning after Swindon win the Premiership Grand Final is a good moment to check how much coverage British speedway's showpiece gets. Both BBC regional TV stations – *Look East* from Norwich and *Points West* in Bristol – included the result in their late-night bulletins, which is a good start. Regional TV broadcasters, traditionally closer and more responsive to their audiences, have tended to stick by their local speedway teams in a way that national news organisations simply haven't.

I start by looking at *BBC Swindon News* online. The lead story is a stabbing by a gang of youths followed by news of a hidden St Christopher statue discovered in Lydiard church, along with the 'last imported great bustard chicks released in Wiltshire'. Scroll down and there's news that Swindon's Morrisons store is to shut and that a council tenant 'can see daylight through cracks in their house'. The last of these stories is four days old. Even if cutbacks have meant *BBC*

Swindon News doesn't get going until later in the day, there's still no mention of speedway when I check back in the evening.

Sky Sports isn't covering it either. Their Speedway Twitter feed hasn't been updated for more than a year. A cynic might suggest that Sky's interest has waned somewhat since it no longer covers it live on its own channels. Sky Sports will tell me later that speedway is a sport that doesn't have a media backing and sports that don't have this will struggle for coverage as a result.

At eight o'clock in the morning on the *BBC Sport* national website, there are 14 stories on the main page, most of them football-related, but there's also room for the Rugby World Cup, Andy Murray and an injury to the Kansas City Chiefs' star quarterback in the NFL. British interest in American sport has grown over the last 30 years but, still, isn't the BBC a British news organisation, first and foremost?

It's something that annoys speedway fans. The previous year, the *Speedway Star* columnist Peter Oakes named the BBC *Sports Personality of the Year* programme as one of his 'losers of 2018', for not only failing to mention Tai Woffinden's third world championship win, but also for ignoring the deaths of former world champions – and household names at the time – Ivan Mauger and Ronnie Moore. Oakes, a considered and thoughtful columnist, calls it 'scandalous'.

Many speedway fans thought so, too, and complained to the BBC. In reply, they received a standard response, aimed as a catch-all for any sports that felt they had not been represented properly in the programme: it had been an incredible year of sport, there hadn't been enough time to mention all of them but, rest assured, the comments had been passed on to the production team.

To be fair to the BBC, it hasn't always been so sniffy – at a national level – towards speedway.

Browse the excellent Genome website – which lists BBC programming in every edition of the *Radio Times* from 1923 up to 2009 – and you'll see that speedway has had its share of coverage. The 1930s saw live commentary of big meetings from the likes of Wembley,

Belle Vue and Southampton. After the war, world championships and major international test matches were regularly covered, along with top-division matches from New Cross and West Ham. In the mid to early sixties, speedway coverage of the Internationale meeting at Wimbledon often kicked off the BBC's Saturday afternoon sports programme, *Grandstand*, with Alan Weeks the regular commentator. Speedway found a regular home on ITV – its natural home, some would say – when *World of Sport*, the commercial alternative to *Grandstand*, began in 1965. Speedway was a regular feature, with Dave Lanning's distinctive and enthusiastic commentary helping to attract top ratings of eight million. But *World of Sport* came to an end in 1985, with channel controllers looking more to live action rather than pre-recorded highlights. As a result, there was little speedway on British TV over the next decade. In 1994, *Sunday Grandstand* covered the World Individual Final from Denmark, and the last time the BBC appears to have shown any real speedway coverage was the British Grand Prix in August 1998.

Speedway world champions – Hans Nielsen, Sam Ermolenko, Greg Hancock, Mark Loram and Jason Crump – were invited onto *A Question of Sport* in the late 1990s and early to mid 2000s. But since then – with the contract for live coverage in Britain going to first Sky Sports and then BT Sport – the BBC, nationally, has pretty much ignored speedway. *Flog It!* in April 2007 did come from Poole in Dorset 'where Paul Martin found out about local sporting team, the Poole Pirates speedway'. But Speedway, the short-lived Scottish rock band, had more live appearances on the BBC in the 21st century than the sport from which they took their name.

But it's not just the BBC. A quick look through any speedway history book will show that newspapers were regular sponsors of speedway competitions and trophies – from the *Daily Mirror* and *Sunday Mirror*, the *Daily Express* and the *Daily Mail* to long-gone names like the *Evening Dispatch*, the *Daily Sketch* and the *London Evening News*. Now? They rarely, if ever, cover the results.

Alex Harkess, the long-time Edinburgh co-promoter, is as frustrated as anyone. He was chairman of the British Speedway

Promoters' Association for six years from 2009 to 2015. He says they had an All-Party Parliamentary Group for motorcycle speedway – now dormant – which had one function every year at Parliament in November, at the end of the season. Promoters and top riders were invited along with 50 to 60 MPs. 'Every major newspaper was invited to it and every year not one of them turned up. That used to annoy me greatly. I thought what else have we got to do? It's a freebie, it's in London, they've all got journalists in London. Okay, speedway's maybe not their sport, but for the sake of two or three hours? I always blamed speedway a bit as well, because we're obviously not promoting ourselves well enough to get them to come. But if a speedway rider does something outside speedway – gets caught taking drugs or whatever – you can guarantee it'll be in the paper, a full-page spread. There's nothing about what he does on a bike.'

Whatever the reason, British speedway's biggest team prize has, once again, passed by with virtually no national coverage. More Britons, it seems, are interested in the health of an NFL quarterback in Kansas.

* * *

Since mid-August, there's been speculation that BT Sport is giving up live coverage of British speedway. It's not clear, if that's the case, who'll replace them. Sky Sports broadcast domestic speedway for 20 years from 1997 and was an enthusiastic partner, covering not just world individual events and top league action but also meetings from the second tier. Between 2007 and 2009, anything from 100,000 to 145,000 viewers were watching meetings. However, Sky turned down the final two years of its contract for 2017 and 2018. There were suggestions that declining viewing figures and frustration with frequent rain-offs and meetings overrunning were behind the decision. Sky asserts that everyone involved in covering speedway really enjoyed it, that there was no one reason for them giving it up and that it was down to the ebb and flow of contracts in sport.

In some ways, speedway should be an ideal sport to cover live on television. Races are short – around a minute – so should appeal to the younger, smartphone-addicted generation. There's no problem building in commercial breaks and, as the action takes place on an enclosed track, the riders are in view the whole time. But, despite laudable innovations like helmet cameras, production hasn't really moved on much since Sky Sports' day.

Opinion – as ever – is divided amongst the speedway world on BT Sport's coverage. On the positive side, they stepped in to keep live British speedway on TV screens and regularly promoted their coverage around bigger audience sports. Critics say they cover too few meetings, with no Championship coverage, and that they only begin broadcasting once the football season has ended, when the domestic speedway season is already underway. There have also been grumbles about how much the contract is worth financially to the sport, with BT Sport effectively being the only bidder at the time Sky Sports pulled out.

Not in doubt are the viewing figures for British speedway that are publicly available on the BARB (Broadcast Audience Research Board) website. While a fraction of what a Premier League or Champions League match attracts, they are sometimes the most-watched live sport events on BT Sport in a week when there's no football.

The average for the season just finished is just below 34,000, with the highest being the 43,500 for Swindon's second-round Premiership Grand Final at home to Ipswich, and the lowest 19,700 for King's Lynn's July league win over Poole. While that doesn't look great compared with Sky's figures ten years earlier, it's not a fair comparison because of the rise of streaming over that period and the fact that Sky Sports has more subscribers than their rivals.

For comparison with BT's non-football sports, live Premiership Rugby is watched by around 140,000, and Premiership football by anywhere from 600,000 to 1.2 million. MotoGP consistently gets bigger audiences than speedway, as you might expect, but league speedway does get better audiences than Hyundai A-League football from Japan and live Bundesliga 2 soccer matches.

BT is said to be happy with the contract and likely to bid again. One wag on the *British Speedway Forum* suggests the *Comedy Channel* would be the best home for it. But, on 21 October, it's announced that Eurosport has agreed a five-year contract for British speedway. It's heralded as 'a major boost for the sport', especially as Eurosport is promising to cover more domestic meetings than BT Sport did – and provide a highlights package, too.

It's fair to say that Eurosport has historically been seen as the poor relation of the sports broadcasting elite, with fewer 'big-ticket' sports to offer viewers. But, since being fully taken over by the American media company, Discovery, in 2015, Eurosport has been – quietly but steadily – building up its portfolio. It has exclusive coverage of the Tour de France, holds the rights to broadcast the Olympic Games for most of Europe and, from 2022, for the UK and France. It already covers a considerable number of motorsports, including the British Superbike Championship and, in speedway, the European Championship and the Under-21 World Championship.

No agreement satisfies everyone, but the general reaction is positive. Meetings will not just be broadcast on Eurosport, but highlights will also be shown later on Discovery's 'free-to-air' channels, Quest and DMAX, and will also be available to stream on the Eurosport Player app. For the much-criticised BSPA, hiring an external company to handle the bidding process seems to have worked well. A five-year commitment – with the money that guarantees for the sport – is a genuine plus.

* * *

It's 23 October, the very last week of the 2019 speedway season, and – better late than never – the first international test match of the season involving the Great Britain team is taking place this evening at the Saddlebow Road home of the King's Lynn Stars. I've checked the weather forecast daily since the hastily arranged meeting was announced last week and have decided to take my chances and drive up from London, even though there's no guarantee it's going to stay dry.

The fixture is the first for the new Great Britain management team of Olly Allen and Simon Stead, who were only appointed last month. Despite the absence of Britain's top two riders – Tai Woffinden, back in Australia for the birth of his second child, and Robert Lambert, who is resting an injured back after an incredibly busy season – it's going ahead to give younger and less experienced riders a taste of test-match action. Denmark aren't at full strength either, but that doesn't detract from the fact that it's an international and a good idea that deserves support.

Test matches used to be regular fixtures on the speedway calendar, with Great Britain or England (the titles have varied over the years) taking on the likes of Sweden, Denmark and the United States regularly during the 1970s and 1980s. Some people believe the emergence of the Danes during the 1980s – regularly beating a British side that had dominated world speedway over the previous decade – is one of the main reasons why mainstream national press interest started to decline. The ITV speedway commentator of the time, Dave Lanning, was in no doubt, telling speedway's *Backtrack* magazine in 2014 that Fleet Street was 'notoriously xenophobic'.

At noon on the day, the chances of the meeting going ahead seem to be diminishing. The BBC weather app tells me that there's now a 72 per cent likelihood of rain by seven o'clock – half an hour before the start time.

I wonder if they'll bring the start time forward to six thirty, so I set off north up the M11. As I head past the Harlow turn-off there's a burst of late-afternoon sunshine. I sense it will prove just as illusory as the overhead motorway signs outlining the need for new documents for driving to the EU from 1 November, given that it's patently clear that Brexit is not going to happen – as planned – at midnight on 31 October.

The trees on either side of the M11 are turning a muddy brown and golden yellow. The sun goes down and the skies darken just after four o'clock as I reach Cambridgeshire. I've had unsuccessful motorway trips in search of speedway outside London before. Despite a new tweet from King's Lynn speedway promising 'perfect conditions!', I'm more convinced by the weather app telling me there's a 74 per cent chance of rain at eight o'clock. In fact, after I've crawled past the trucks and tractors on the A10 into King's Lynn, there are, as predicted, specks of rain on the windscreen as I arrive at Saddlebow Road.

Despite that, there's a reasonable crowd inside – I'm guessing 2,000 or so by the time the racing gets underway. Most, I suspect, are from the local area. The British riders sign autographs for the fans after their track walk. They're all kitted out in GB leathers – or kevlars, to give them their modern name. The *Daily Star*, national team sponsors and one of the only daily newspapers still reporting on speedway, has its logo emblazoned on their backsides. Another national brand, Smyths Toys, are on the fork covers of the British riders' bikes – proof that the new management team of Rob Painter and Vicky Blackwell, who'd taken over the running of Great Britain Speedway 18 months earlier, is managing to attract new and nationwide sponsors.

Speak to Rob and, within seconds, you're struck by his genuine belief that there really are commercial and sponsorship opportunities out there. 'We think that speedway's a fantastic sport and, at the highest level, which is where Great Britain compete, we have a lot to offer. We have a lot of TV time.' He has his own view on why it's been difficult for national media to embrace speedway. 'It's very regionalised. There's not a speedway club in every town, whereas Great Britain is still important to everyone. It doesn't matter where you're from, this is your national team.'

Like many people I'll speak to, Rob's interest in speedway came from riding, but it wasn't something that lasted. 'I learned pretty quickly that my skillset wasn't in steering a speedway bike.' But he began to work as a mechanic for Jason Crump when he won the world championship and that led to Rob working with other riders, too. He then decided to do something 'a little bit different'. Taking a leaf out of other motorsports' books, like MotoGP, he created a standalone race team to have their own bikes and their own coaches to go racing and formed Revolution Speedway. He and his partner, Vicky Blackwell, researched the Great Britain speedway team. They realised they were 'underachieving, which pushed us into working out what could be done and here we are now.'

Rob and Vicky's immediate aim was to professionalise the Great Britain team, taking their inspiration from the British Olympic Association and Team GB. 'We liked the way that all the athletes pulled together to represent their country and that's really something that we felt we should strive towards. We try to do the best job we can with the relevant budgets that we have.'

Introducing a fitness regime, a new concept for many British speedway riders, was an early innovation. Performance specialist Chris Neville, who has been involved with England football at four major tournaments, and psychologist Jeremy Holt are involved in this side. 'We're fully aware that speedway isn't football, but what we need to do is find out what it takes to physically make an elite speedway athlete and then we'll have the foundations that we can replicate. We're very lucky that we've got the most successful British rider of all time right now so we can do a lot of work with Tai Woffinden. Hopefully in the years to come we'll be able to produce more riders who can reach the elite level.'

Professionalising the Great Britain team set-up certainly struck a chord with Woffinden. In *Raw Speed* he details his frustration at previous national set-ups and how he'd campaigned for better training, fitness tests and advice on nutrition. Failing to get anywhere, he announced he would not ride for the Great Britain team at the World Cup in 2017. When Rob and Vicky took over, one of their first jobs was to bring the country's best rider back into the fold.

They nearly – literally – struck gold within a few months when only a perverse scoring system, since amended, meant that Great Britain finished second to Russia in speedway's World Cup, the Speedway of Nations, despite scoring the most points over the two days of competition. This year's tournament was much less successful: Woffinden was missing because of his back injury, and Robert Lambert and Craig Cook collided in their first race. Lambert had to pull out after the first day. Cook rode on but was later discovered to have broken his wrist. Unsurprisingly, they finished last of the seven nations competing in the final. Tonight's international is the first outing for Great Britain since then.

I'm up in the stand, open to the elements, and spot Charles Wright, the current British champion and one of tonight's team, watching the opening race with the rest of the crowd on the first bend. It's another reminder of how – reassuringly – speedway, despite its problems, really does remain a community sport, with riders mixing with the people who pay their wages. It harkens back to the days of footballers getting the bus home at the end of a game with their team's supporters. Not something that's likely to happen nowadays.

The first race has to be rerun three times because riders fall off around the first and second bends. The new Great Britain co-manager, Olly Allen, is interviewed as we wait and he admits that it's greasy out there. Riders from both sides gather on the track for what looks like a conference and I wonder if the whole thing's going to be called off. But they carry on and, while the rain continues for the rest of the night, it remains light. There are no more fallers until heat 14 and, by then, the British team have guaranteed themselves victory. There's been some decent racing, too.

In the end Great Britain win 53-37, with the highlights being the performances of young riders Anders Rowe and Drew Kemp. Interviewed after the meeting, Kemp talks of how his confidence had dipped during the season. Just a couple of weeks after becoming British Under-19 champion, he'd been axed by his Championship club Sheffield to make way for a rider who was returning from a broken collarbone injury. It was still mathematically possible for Sheffield to make the play-offs (they didn't) and despite clearly having a big future ahead of him, Kemp had been struggling and was the rider who was cut. Ironically, Sheffield's manager is the same Simon Stead who is now co-manager of the Great Britain team.

But that's put to one side tonight. It's been a good opportunity for young riders and an encouraging example of planning for the future.

The *British Speedway Forum*'s correspondents are positive. Comments like 'a good advert for speedway', 'excellent', 'good to see commitment from riders on both sides' and 'some good racing on a miserable damp night' sum it up well.

* * *

Dave Tattum, the Stoke promoter, isn't a drinker. He's not one for black-tie events either. In fact, you sense he'd rather be pottering about in a shed than having a posh night out. But a few people have encouraged him to attend this month's 'Potteries' Heroes Awards' at Crewe Town Hall. These aren't just for sport but for the whole community, recognising bravery and courage, like, for example, a police dog and his handler who were shot in the line of duty. Dave has been invited to the awards a few times in the past and hasn't always gone, but he's been persuaded to attend tonight and is seated at a table along with his wife, Bente, his son, Lloyd, and daughter-in-law, Suzanne.

In Dave's own words, he and his family are treated like kings. When it comes to the winner of this year's Sporting Hero award, Dave is staggered to find they're calling his name out. It's been given to recognise his efforts in going 'above and beyond' for Stoke Speedway over the years.

'I was totally in shock. I was really humbled because I couldn't imagine anything like this happening to me or the club.'

But if the award is a shock to Dave, then it's nothing compared to the surprise that many of those in Stoke and the surrounding area, Potters fans amongst them, will have for the country in general later in the year.

November 2019 – If the points fit

ALTHOUGH IT has teams up and down the country taking part in competitive leagues, British speedway isn't overseen by an independent body in the way that, say, the Rugby Football Union, the Lawn Tennis Association or the Premier League run their sports. The British Speedway Promoters' Association manage British speedway. They make the important decisions and come up with the rules. A separate body, the Speedway Control Bureau, oversees the rules, adjudicates disagreements and discipline, and appoints and manages referees. Everything else is down to the BSPA.

Because, as the name would suggest, it's made up of the promoters who actually run the clubs, the people with 'skin in the game', this has led to criticism over the years that it is an organisation geared towards looking after promoters' interests rather than the sport as a whole. Take a quick look at the *British Speedway Forum* message boards and you'll soon get a feel for how the BSPA is viewed by many supporters. Tin hats aren't, as far as I know, supplied when promoters take up positions on the committee – but they would probably come in handy.

This month, while there's not a speedway wheel turned in anger, is in some ways the most important month in the British season. Because this is when the main decisions for the following year are made.

In the past, British speedway promoters have taken themselves away from the rain and dark winter nights of a British November and headed for the sunnier climes of Tenerife for their annual meeting.

This year's three-day conference is being held in Coventry. I'm told that conferences are – generally – good-natured with promoters enjoying the chance to catch up with each other in a positive environment to make decisions for the good of the sport. Critics say too much time is devoted to trivial matters – like whether to make a change to helmet colours – rather than focusing on marketing the sport and trying to get new people to the tracks.

This year there isn't the same feeling of crisis that there has been in previous years. A year earlier, *Speedway Star* devoted a whole issue to the future of speedway with a series of probing articles. It outlined what a variety of interested parties – promoters, riders, supporters amongst them – felt should be done to rescue a sport that was seemingly only heading in one direction – continued decline. This year there's no repeat. The clamour for fundamental change seems muted.

Which isn't to say there's nothing to talk about.

* * *

Unless Nigel Pearson managed to take his family to one of Cradley Heathens' final two National League matches at the start of October, he'll have failed Kelvin Tatum's challenge at the end of BT Sport's coverage of the British Grand Prix in September. And not just for this season but very possibly forever. Because, after much speculation, Cradley Heathens have decided to close. While it's not entirely unexpected, it's still a sad day.

Cradley Heath is a suburb of Birmingham and, from 1947 until they were evicted from their Dudley Wood Stadium in 1995, the Heathens were one of the top sides in British speedway, particularly during the 1980s. Seven world champions won their titles while racing for Cradley Heath. But their stadium was bought by new landlords to be knocked down and turned into housing, a wearily familiar story for speedway fans over the years. The club – backed by a strong hard core of fans – was revived at the third level of British speedway in 2010 without a home track. During those ten seasons, meetings have been run mainly at Wolverhampton's Monmore Green, but also at Birmingham's Perry Barr Stadium.

Now, the consortium running Cradley – which includes Pearson – is admitting defeat. Just as at Stoke, it's stressed that it is not as a result of poor crowds; attendances have been encouraging for National League level. Rather, there's been no progress on getting planning permission for their own track near Cradley. Their statement is very carefully worded: 'The search for a new piece of land, which started back in 1995, has been unsuccessful with little or no encouragement going forward.' Their supporters can read between the lines, with some pointing the finger at Dudley Council, where Cradley Heath were based, for failing to make any of the many disused industrial brownfield sites in the borough available for a speedway track. Former Dudley Council leader, Les Jones, had told local radio earlier in the year that there was 'no chance' of the club returning to the borough given all the environmental issues around trying to build a new speedway track. Whatever the true community spirit the sport can engender, its image – and the noise and dirt that comes with it – is clearly a big obstacle for its future.

The final meeting was Cradley's Golden Hammer individual meeting at the end of October – an annual fixture that once attracted the best riders in the world. Now Cradley Heath have joined other famous names like Wembley, Reading and Hackney on speedway's scrapheap, lovingly remembered by a loyal group of fans but with no prospect of racing again soon.

That means that the third tier of British speedway, the National League, is now down to just six teams. There's speculation that both Kent and Plymouth are keen to move up a level into the Championship, which would leave just four teams: Belle Vue's junior team, the Colts; Leicester's junior team, the Lion Cubs; Mildenhall in Suffolk; and the Isle of Wight.

But this isn't the main issue facing the British Speedway Promoters' Association at this month's annual meeting. In fact, it's unlikely to feature heavily because the BSPA gathering is for owners and promoters of clubs in the top two divisions. National League clubs can send a representative but have their own separate meeting later. Instead, the BSPA meeting will be sorting out a much bigger issue: the decision of the Poole Pirates to voluntarily drop down from the Premiership to the Championship for financial reasons.

The reason why this news has had such a seismic impact on British speedway is that Poole have been, over the previous ten years, the most successful club in the country. They're often referred to as the 'Manchester United' of speedway. Since owner Matt Ford bought the club in 2009, they have won eight top-flight league titles and five Knockout Cups, along with 12 other national shields, pairs titles and league cups. They'd just finished top of the Premiership league table before losing to Ipswich Witches in the play-off semi-finals.

Matt Ford says that, financially, it's been the worst season Poole have ever had since he bought them and that something has to change. In the local paper, the *Daily Echo*, Matt points to a 22 per cent drop in attendances since having to switch from Poole's traditional Wednesday race night to Thursday – one of the two days on the European speedway calendar set aside for meetings in Britain's top division. With the best riders regularly racing in Poland and Sweden, the international body overseeing world speedway – Fédération Internationale de Motocyclisme (FIM) – consults with national associations to allocate set days for each country to allow riders to compete in all three. Monday and Thursday are set aside for Britain, whether they've been traditional race nights for clubs or not.

The Poole owner says that moving down to the Championship will allow the club to return to their preferred Wednesday night as lower-league clubs can choose their own day of the week to run. It'll save them 75 per cent of their current costs, with lower wages and reduced travelling bills. He adds that they've had lower crowds when their meetings are televised on BT Sport and they've also been hit by the liquidation of their main team sponsor, No. 1 Carpet Cleaning. Losing Sky Sports a few years earlier also had an impact. According to Ford, the current TV agreement with BT Sport only provides a fraction, 15 per cent, of what they were getting two or three years earlier. He'd felt the writing was on the wall and had put the club up for sale in October 2018 – without any buyers coming forward. He says that although the Eurosport TV deal is better, the 2019 season has put the club in real financial jeopardy. He's canvassed fans to get their views on moving down a league and says they're very positive about it.

While that means speedway will, at least, continue at Poole, it will leave just six teams in the top division; hardly a healthy number to kick off a five-year TV contract aimed at building a new audience. There's a real need for the number of teams in the top division to remain, at the very least, at seven, but ideally more.

There's speculation – as there always is at this time – that teams might decide to move up. Championship Berwick are rumoured to be considering it, but they end up staying put. Kent, currently in the National League, but with one of speedway's better-equipped stadiums at Sittingbourne, a wily promoter in the shape of the veteran Len Silver and the advantage of being the closest track to London, are another. And then there's Sheffield. After some discussion, Kent decide to make the move up to the middle tier of the Championship, rather than risking a two-division jump at once.

That just leaves Sheffield who, to the relief of British speedway, announce ahead of the AGM that they will be making the move to the Premiership. The BSPA is expected to approve this at their meeting. The 2020 season will have, in its top division, a new team – Sheffield Tigers – who finished sixth out of 11 in the Championship. They're replacing the club – Poole Pirates – who finished at the top of the Premiership but who have chosen to drop down a league into the Championship.

Such are the vagaries of British speedway.

It's something that, after the initial shock, speedway fans take in their stride. But, to an outsider, it looks strange and, frankly, a bit amateur. This rearrangement of teams based on considerations independent of sporting merit has happened several times before. In his book, *The Golden Age of Speedway*, Philip Dalling records how, in 1950, a sceptical national media took a poor view of the sport's refusal to promote 1950 Division Two champions Norwich. At the same time, Plymouth were demoted to the third tier, allegedly because promoters and riders, mainly in the north and Scotland, didn't relish the travelling and the cost of trips to the far south-west of England. 'It means that it all gave valuable ammunition to journalists who, for many reasons, refused to take the sport seriously.'

Of course, football and rugby teams have been demoted for reasons other than their on-field performances, suffering penalties for financial irregularities or going into administration. But in almost every sporting league structure in the world – outside the closed memberships in the United States, where the possibility of relegation would be unthinkable for financial and commercial reasons – there is some form of relegation and promotion. The bottom teams in a league at the end of a season are either demoted or go into play-offs and their places are taken by the best team or teams from the division below.

Speedway isn't like this. At all.

At various times in its existence, British speedway has attempted the traditional form of promotion and relegation with play-offs between the team at the bottom of the top league and the one at the top of the second league. Invariably this has resulted in a fairly substantial win for the team in the top league. There has never been much appetite amongst some teams, happily operating in the middle tier of British speedway with what they feel is an appropriate level of costs, to push on to the top level where budgets need to be bigger. Either they feel their crowd levels won't support top-level speedway or they're geographically situated where they'll struggle to attract the top riders they need to compete. A perfect example of this was Berwick, who surprised the speedway world by taking the plunge in 1991 to move from the second tier up to the top league. An enthusiastic – but inexperienced – promoter soon found out about the economics of speedway and Berwick dropped back a year later, having nearly gone out of business.

So while speedway is often set alongside football – after all, its claim to once be the second most popular sport in the country has invited that comparison – it's often not helpful or appropriate or, indeed, fair. Clearly, today, football is light years ahead in global appeal, TV coverage and the amount of money its top performers are paid. Promotion and relegation are decided on where teams finish in the league table. Speedway has shied away from that model and, in some ways, there are good reasons why that's the case.

To understand why speedway in Britain has been seemingly cavalier in its approach to merit-based promotion and relegation – or why promoters sometimes move clubs, franchise-style, from one city or town to another – it's important to remember that it's always been, to quote a famous business expression, a 'top-down' sport rather than a 'bottom-up' one. Most football clubs grew from a grassroots base. A group of young men would get together and decide they wanted to form a football club. They'd find a patch of land and rent or buy it and their progress from then on would be based on the many local connections and networks that then developed. Whilst speedway is, at its best, a true community sport, it is – and always has been – operated largely at the whim of owners or promoters who risk their own money in running speedway. If they're not making money or losing too much, they can decide to drop down a division to cut costs, move to somewhere where they believe they'll attract bigger crowds or close altogether.

Take Wembley, perhaps the biggest club name in British speedway until their demise in the 1950s. Wembley Stadium was originally built for the British Empire Exhibition of 1924–25. Completed early, it hosted the famous 'White Horse' FA Cup Final in 1923, in front of a crowd estimated at anywhere between 126,000 and 300,000.

Once the exhibition ended, Wembley was very much a white elephant, a large site that was only going to be used sporadically – for the FA Cup Final and the occasional England football international. Step forward entrepreneur Arthur Elvin, who bought the stadium and looked for ways to host different events and maximise its use. He introduced greyhound racing in 1927 and, when speedway began in Britain in 1928, he built a speedway track the following year. In many ways, speedway isn't just a sport but an entertainment in the widest sense of the word. The original Belle Vue stadium at Hyde Road was just one of the attractions at the Belle Vue Zoological Gardens. Edinburgh's first speedway track, at Marine Gardens, was part of an entertainment complex in the city's seaside resort of Portobello. When there was speedway in Southampton, their Banister Court track also hosted greyhound racing and boxing and was next to an ice rink. The great majority of football teams the world over have developed from the grassroots. Speedway clubs, much like choosing where to put an amusement park or a cinema complex, have been set up at the whim of owners.

So it might be fairer to acknowledge that the main driver for promotions and relegations – or indeed closures – has always come down to finances. If it's cheaper to run a team in a lower division – paying lower wages to riders, but keeping speedway alive – then that's what promoters and owners will do. It's what Poole Pirates have done this year.

* * *

Rob Godfrey loves his speedway.

'There's just something about speedway. That 60 seconds of one race can just make you happy for days on end.'

Rob also loves his garage at Yaddlethorpe in Scunthorpe, which he has run for 30 years. He's been the promoter at the local Eddie Wright Raceway for 14 years. I've been told that if it wasn't for him, there wouldn't be any speedway in Scunthorpe. And he's not in it for the money.

'There's a great saying, which Neil Machin, the former promoter at Sheffield and Leicester, said to me when I first came into speedway: "If you want to make a small fortune out of speedway, you'd better start with a large one." And that's how speedway is. It's not a sport where you open the doors and you're going to be a millionaire, because you're not. It is down to a group of individuals who put their lives and their businesses and everything else on the line so that we can all enjoy it. We're not doing it out of pity for the spectators, we do it because we love it.'

He's been on the board of the BSPA as vice-chairman for four years. But it's now time for a change. Rob has become chairman, replacing King's Lynn promoter Keith 'Buster' Chapman, who's been in the job since 2015.

Chapman has been one of the most powerful figures in British speedway. In addition to his BSPA chairmanship and ownership of King's Lynn, he bought Ipswich and Peterborough in November 2018, making the investments, he said, to do what was right for the sport. He certainly, in the short term, saved the Premiership. By buying both clubs, then in the Championship, and immediately moving them up to the top league, he made sure the number of Premiership teams remained at seven. Without his intervention, it would have been reduced to just five and struggled to continue. Both Leicester – to move to a more convenient race night – and Somerset – for financial reasons – had decided to drop down a division. At the time, Keith said he'd invested a lot of time and money because a three-league structure had to be maintained. 'One big league would never work. We explored that possibility but reached the conclusion we have to have three leagues. I've done what I feel is right and I really don't see how anyone can knock me for that. I'm driven by a desire to see British speedway progress, which I believe it will.'

It's not the first time Keith has intervened to help save clubs. In 2016, he stepped in to save Leicester and was also instrumental in introducing new owners at Belle Vue. But for some critics, Chapman owning three of the league's clubs – and so having three out of seven Premiership votes at the BSPA AGM – is yet another reason for having an independent body running British speedway.

Rob Godfrey rejects the criticism that the BSPA shouldn't be running the sport. 'I can speak for every single promoter in this country and say every person that runs the clubs does it because they believe and love the sport. When we do come together, at the AGMs, we get on really well, because we're all in the same boat. We all hope that, one day, it will become profitable. It'll never emulate football, but I believe it will become an attractive sport again.'

As well as Rob's appointment, the headlines from the AGM revolve around rubber-stamping the already well-publicised league moves. Sheffield, who are owned by the same family – the Bates – that own Leicester, have their request to move up to the Premiership accepted, so seven clubs will again take part in the top league. Poole will move down to the Championship. As expected, Kent will be in the Championship, meaning there will be 12 clubs taking part in that league. But Plymouth's request to move up from the National League has been rejected. The club say later that they were told at the AGM about new and previously unforeseen conditions of entry, which would have meant increased financial commitments and bonds having to be paid immediately. They withdrew to safeguard the future of the club. They'll remain – for now – in the third tier of British speedway, which is set to run with just five clubs.

But there's a late fly in the ointment. Newcastle, who have just celebrated the 90th anniversary of speedway in the city, may not be the 12th team riding in the Championship. The current promoters say they need new investment and fresh ideas after a 'testing' 2019 season. They're in talks with potential investors and have been given extra time to sort things out.

Newcastle have been one of the mainstays of the Championship, the second level of British speedway. Losing them – and their loyal support – would be a major blow to the sport.

* * *

While supporters often look to the AGM as some sort of magic wand for the sport, that tends not to happen. There are many moving pieces to speedway in Britain, as we've seen, and shifting one can upset others in ways no one could have anticipated. In addition, Rob Godfrey says one message that came out very strongly from supporters ahead of the AGM was that they didn't want things tinkered with. It is felt there's been enough of that in the past and it has been taken on board this time.

In particular, it has meant keeping the same points limit for each league for the forthcoming season. Speedway fans are well aware of what this involves, but for those who don't, it's worth explaining because it determines a huge part of which riders can race for which team.

Imagine you're building a fantasy football team. There's a set limit – either points-based or financial – and each player is given a value. While it would be nice to fill a team with David de Gea, Harry Kane, Kevin De Bruyne and Virgil van Dijk, that's not going to be possible. It's the same for a speedway team of seven riders. You can't just get the best seven that you want.

There will be three top riders called heat leaders, two middle-order riders and two reserves, normally younger riders. Every time a rider takes part in a race, he gains points – three for a win, two for second and one for third. These are totalled and count towards the team total. For the rider, they go to what's called a CMA – calculated match average – which gives an accurate figure for the number of points that rider would be expected to get over four races in a single meeting. The maximum would be 12 if a rider was exceptionally talented and won every single race he competed in. No one ever has. Normally, heat leaders will average between eight and ten (Jason Doyle had the highest average in the Premiership in 2019 with 9.89), the two middle-order riders will likely be on anywhere from five to seven, and the reserves below five. In putting a team together, promoters have to assemble a squad based on a rider's CMA average and then make sure that it's under the total permitted. I'm told that promoters invariably work out what the best points limit will be for their own team and lobby for that. The loudest voice or the best political player is the one who wins.

For the coming season, the maximum for the Premiership will be 42.5 and for the Championship 41. Sometimes, team places are decided on tenths or even hundredths of points. What it also means is that teams that have had a successful season – like Swindon who won the Premiership Grand Final – will invariably have to break up their side, because their riders' averages, as a result of their success, will be higher than the permitted team total.

It emerges that Swindon have been pushing – hard – for the points limit to be raised to allow them to bring back the same seven riders. It was clear – both on that chilly night when the Grand Final was clinched and before – that Swindon fans liked their team the way it was and wanted all their riders back. Swindon promoter Lee Kilby, who's been at the club for three years in a working capacity, and has 42 years as a supporter, had wanted continuity. Instead he'll only be able to keep five of his seven riders.

'I'd be lying if I said we were happy. We knew it was a tall order. We wanted to keep the same team to sell to the supporters. The promoters didn't feel they were in a position to try and run it next season. But they listened and there was will in the room for it to be tabled next season.'

What having the points limit in place does mean, however, is that promoters now know what points they have to play with so they can go about team building and contracting riders for 2020 in earnest.

* * *

Of the 2014 graduates from Leicester University's Business Management course, most are, as you might expect, now employed in predominantly business-type careers. Some work in accountancy, others at insurance companies, several in marketing departments. But one graduate, one of the real stars who walked out with a first-class degree, decided to do something completely different. Which is why, today, Thursday, 21 November, he is at Cambridge's Addenbrooke's Hospital for an operation to have a large piece of metalwork removed from his back.

Tom Bacon is a speedway rider.

'Yeah, I know,' he'll cheerfully tell you. 'I went into what you'd call a normal job straight from university, but I just missed riding so I went back to it.'

Because Tom's father, Mike, is a former speedway rider who rode for Coventry Bees in the late 1980s, you might think that Tom was encouraged from an early age to sit on a bike. 'Far from it,' he says.

'My dad tried to stop me getting involved in speedway. He'd seen what could happen and he didn't want that happening to me.'

Tom says that in his last year at university, he was going to classes during the day and then, as soon as he was finished, he'd drive to somewhere like Sheffield to go and race after the league meeting, and it started from there. 'My dad got back into it and now he's even keener than me!'

After university, Tom got onto a graduate sales scheme at a very large technology company, Telent, where he worked for two years in Warwick. But when he signed for Peterborough in the Championship, as well as riding for Birmingham in the National League, he realised he would have about 80 meetings and would need about 55 to 60 days' holiday. That was never going to work, so that's when he gave up his job to focus fully on speedway.

Tom is now 26 and has suffered his fair share of injuries over the years. Breaking his back stands out. Not once, but twice. And, as I'm quickly getting used to when hearing speedway riders talk about what most of us would consider serious injuries, he talks about them in a low-key, 'nothing much to see here' kind of a way.

Just over a year earlier, in 2018, he was riding for the Birmingham Brummies in the National League and Peterborough in the Championship. He was having a good year and was at the top of the National League averages. But a crash towards the end of the season caused a fractured vertebra – the L2 for those, like Tom, who now know their back structure a lot better than most of us. Doctors operated on it and wired it together with metalwork across the adjoining bones – the L1 and L3 – in his lower back.

That allowed Tom to start the 2019 season with Redcar Bears in the Championship. The season began well. In the opening meetings of the season he was beating the best home riders – Scott Nicholls at Leicester, Stevie Worrall at Newcastle and Rory Schlein at Somerset – on their own tracks.

Then, riding for the Bears at Peterborough, he was involved in a big crash.

'I just thought I'd aggravated the previous injury where they'd put the metalwork in. Since the operation last year, I'd been in pain nearly every day so I thought it was that. I didn't realise that I'd broken my back again. I missed one meeting and spent all week just resting it, putting ice on it. I felt okay and rode five days later when Redcar met Edinburgh. I did a practice start, realised something wasn't right, but decided to carry on anyway so I didn't let the side down. I actually won heat 8 and then slid off in my next race when I couldn't even stand up. The pain was unbelievable. I went to the hospital the next day in Coventry and spent ten hours in A&E. They said I'd broken a different vertebra and I was going to need to be in a back brace for three months. That was a bit of a shock. It was probably because I had the metalwork in my back from the year before that caused the injury.'

This time Tom had fractured the L4 bone – the fourth lumber spine vertebra, to give it its medical name. It meant he was out for the rest of the season; hugely frustrating for a rider who had made progress every year he'd ridden and who was set to ride in his first British Final.

Initially, Tom was told he wouldn't be able to get back on a bike until early 2020, but a later consultation concluded that the injury was healing better than expected. As a result, he's here at Addenbrooke's today to have the metalwork taken out by the same surgeon who operated on him last September.

When you ask him if breaking his back – not just once, but twice – isn't a sign that it's time to put that first-class business degree to a more appropriate and perhaps safer use, he'll tell you that riding speedway is like a drug. 'You just want to do it. It's a combination of nerves, excitement and adrenaline. You are sat on the start line on top of a very powerful machine, fully concentrating, knowing that in a few seconds you'll be racing at high speed, and on top of that you only have 60 seconds to get it right. There is nowhere to hide. There is nothing else that quite compares to that.'

But he will concede that breaking his back twice in nine months is 'unlucky, to say the least'.

Two days later, the metalwork safely removed, Tom gets the call he's been hoping for: a team place for the 2020 season. He'll be riding down at Sittingbourne with the Kent Kings, who are moving up from the National League into the Championship.

* * *

Just before the end of the month there's encouraging news – on two fronts – for British speedway. To the relief of their loyal fans, the Newcastle Diamonds will run in 2020 under new ownership. Former rider Rob Grant, now a butcher in the north-east of England, has stepped in as the new promoter. He says he's done his sums and he's not just here for the short term but wants to make Newcastle speedway secure for the long term too. A familiar face will be joining Rob on the management team: former Stoke promoter Dave Tattum, who clearly couldn't stay away from speedway for very long.

But, with the greatest respect to Dave, the second announcement at the end of November is probably more significant. Sheffield Tigers, returning to the top league for the first time since 1996, have announced three-time world champion Nicki Pedersen as their marquee signing. No matter that the last of those world championships was in 2008, that he is no longer a Grand Prix rider or that he's now 42. Pedersen remains one of the biggest names in world speedway – apart from the age, think Gareth Bale returning to the Premier League after his ups and downs in Madrid for a comparison. Pedersen's return to the British leagues – for the first time since 2011 – is a real coup for Sheffield. He has a reputation as a hard rider – he's no shrinking violet – as he acknowledges in the official press release announcing his signing: 'I know there are people who don't like me.' But he adds that it's good that people want to come and see him race and he hopes British speedway can benefit from that too.

* * *

Someone else who's managed to confirm a team place relatively early in the off-season is Scunthorpe's Josh Auty. It's not that surprising as he's been with Scunthorpe for eight years – unusual in this era when riders rarely spend more than a couple of seasons at the same club – and has been one of the most consistent performers at Championship level.

While a top rider like Tai Woffinden is able to head off to the sun and his second home near Perth in Western Australia, Auty is typical of most riders looking for work to see them through the British winter until the new speedway season starts again in March. Speedway riders are self-employed. They may have a contract to ride for a club – and some may get a signing-on fee – but they only get paid when they ride. Unlike football, speedway riders aren't paid automatically. They may have agreements for travel expenses or, if they're lucky, a guaranteed minimum wage, however well they do, but they are the ultimate 'performance' artists, paid at the end of the evening according to how many points they've won for their team. The number of races isn't set either. Normally it's four or five but can be as many as seven or as few as three, injuries permitting.

Auty says he works 'on and off'. The previous winter, he was at a scrapyard for a few months from November, but trying to fit in a full-time job with speedway during the summer is impossible.

'Employers aren't interested in, "Oh, can I have a day off work?" The bottom line with racing is you cannot commit to anything during the season. All companies want is someone who's going to turn up nine to five, do the job and that's it. Next season I could have Poole on a Wednesday night, that's a full day. Or I've got to go to Edinburgh, that's a full day on a Friday. You could travel to a meeting, you get there and it's rained off and you've booked a day off work, so you'll need another one for the rearranged fixture. It's really difficult for everyone.'

Speedway has pretty much been Auty's life since he left school in West Yorkshire. He first rode competitive speedway in 2005, when he was 15, and went full-time a year later. He rode in the same third-tier Scunthorpe Conference team as Tai Woffinden for two years. Both began riding in the Elite League (then the top league) at the end of the 2007 season – Woffinden with Poole and Auty with Coventry – but their careers have diverged since then. Auty's had several seasons in the top league but has never quite cracked it. But he's always been near the top of the second-tier rider averages. He's totted up more than 300 appearances for Scunthorpe since 2012, more than anyone else.

He's very honest about why he's never quite made the very top. Sometimes, he says, he can make 'really good gates' and reach that all-important first corner ahead of the other three riders. 'I've sat there and analysed it afterwards and thought, "I don't know what I did to make that start." Speedway's getting more and more about gating and that's an Achilles heel for me.'

He says he's tried everything – different clutch plates, different engine set-ups and so on – but he's put it down to technique as to why he's never progressed further in the sport. 'The higher up the ladder you get, you can't give good riders split-second advantages because it's impossible to pull it back within a 60-second race.

'I'm an honest guy, I've always done my best throughout my career. We all have aspirations to be world champion and things like that, but sometimes those dreams don't materialise and you just have to accept it. The past two seasons I've looked at it and thought, "You know what, I probably haven't got the operation that some of the other guys have got." The top riders have people working for them full-time, nine to five – probably even longer than that – making sure the bikes are right and their equipment is in order. They pick them up from airports and take them to events.

'Last season, I did a lot of the away meetings on my own and I did all the driving myself, which was just a killer. As a result, I didn't perform as well as I should have done. I was still top of the Scunthorpe averages but I didn't feel that I rode to the standard I should. But it wasn't easy because I was knackered from all the driving. I'm travelling back and not getting in until sometimes two or three in the morning, and then there's work to do on the bike. A full bike wash is a day in terms of getting everything absolutely bang on, all your kit washed, everything, then loading it back into the van to go to your next meeting. There is a lot of work involved in prepping a bike, which a lot of supporters don't realise.

'I just go out, give my best and that's all anybody can ask of you. For the past couple of years, that's the attitude that I've gone with. Sometimes I've ridden quite well and sometimes I've not ridden very well. Sometimes I've scored good points, sometimes I haven't. You've just got to accept it and move on.

'Maybe I should have done things differently in my career, but it comes down to cost as well. I do wish on my long-haul meetings I could have stopped in a hotel, virtually next to the track the night before. It wears you down after a bit when you have five or six hours' travelling time and then you've got to jump on a bike.'

It probably explains why he's staying at Scunthorpe. It's his favourite track, somewhere he's always been happy and where he's just been awarded a testimonial meeting.

It's going to be at the very start of the 2020 season, on Sunday, 22 March. As long as the weather holds, it promises to be a good and well-deserved celebration for one of British speedway's unsung mainstays of the last 15 years.

December 2019 – Workington woman

DECEMBER IS one of the quietest months in British speedway. The annual general meetings have been held. The first rush of riders signed up for the following summer is complete, leaving just a few team-slots for those still looking. *Speedway Star* is filling its 48 pages with 'off-season' content – track reviews from the year just gone, year-by-year reports of individual riders' championships and nostalgic features on teams from the past: 'Where are they now? Crewe Kings 1972'.

Instead, it's politics – in various forms – that shines a light on the current state of British speedway this month.

* * *

'It's the Sun Wot Won It' was the characteristically bold claim by *The Sun* newspaper following the Conservative Party's victory in the April 1992 General Election. Nobody, to the best of my knowledge, has so far described this month's contest as the 'speedway election'. It's doubtful, frankly, if anyone ever will. There are just too few speedway supporters to be able to make that claim. But, once all the votes have been counted and the scale of the Conservative victory is firmly established, it becomes clear that quite a few key Tory gains, those seats that had been staunchly Labour for decades – part of their so-called 'red wall' – have an existing or past connection with speedway.

Scan down the names of those seats that changed hands in the north of England and the Midlands and the pattern soon emerges:

- Redcar (speedway still running)
- Barrow and Furness (track closed 1974)
- Workington (speedway ended 2018)
- Scunthorpe (speedway still running)
- Stoke – three seats: Newcastle-under-Lyme, Stoke North, Stoke Central (speedway ended 2019)
- Crewe and Nantwich (speedway closed 1975)
- Wolverhampton – two seats: Wolverhampton South-West, Wolverhampton North-West (speedway still running)

Even below the northern 'red wall', where fewer seats, just six, changed hands from Labour to Conservative, it's striking to note that half of them – Peterborough, Ipswich and Eastbourne – are areas where speedway still takes place.

In many ways, it's not surprising. Speedway has been, from the start, an unashamed, blue-collar, working-class sport. Go back to that epic race from Belle Vue that featured on the Official British Speedway Twitter account during 2019 and, in the comments underneath – the great majority rightly positive on a thrilling minute of sporting drama – you'll find one that, scathingly, dismisses it as a 'council house sport'.

I've heard it myself. When I wrote earlier about telling people I've been to a speedway meeting, I didn't mention every reaction I get. I'm also sometimes met with a slight narrowing of the eyes and a look of some confusion, which seems to suggest disbelief that someone – middle class and living in north London – could possibly like something as noisy, dirty and, frankly, common as speedway. Round here, if you say the word 'Tai', you're most likely talking about a meal from south-east Asia.

There's a good reason speedway has never found a home in the likes of Cambridge or Harrogate or Bath. Its natural home was near steelworks or car plants, large industrial complexes where workers would look forward to a few hours of exciting and escapist entertainment. Speedway clubs often share venues with working-class sports like greyhound racing and stock car racing. All three have, for different reasons, struggled to find their place in 21st-century Britain. The demise of greyhound racing is even more startling than speedway's. From attracting millions of spectators to several hundred licensed and unlicensed tracks at its peak, there are now just over 20 greyhound tracks today. Both are sports that have their loyal fans, but for a lot of people – some of them from Auberon Waugh's delightfully coined 'chattering classes' – they are considered slightly beyond the pale. They are aware the sports exist and that some people enjoy them, but they're just not for them. The new Prime Minister, Boris Johnson, did make a lunchtime visit to the Somerset Rebels' Oaktree Arena – not on a raceday – in June 2019 as part of his Conservative party leadership campaign. Somerset promoter Debbie Hancock described him later as a 'top man' but said he'd admitted never having been to speedway.

The phrase 'left-behind Britain' was coined for those towns, mainly in the Midlands and the north of England, that have struggled after the closure of whichever industry had been the basis of their existence in the first place. While some British towns and cities have benefited over the last 20 years from Government-backed expansion of universities or new investment from tech companies or retailers, that's not happened to the likes of Scunthorpe or Redcar. Both were reliant on British Steel which, in 1971, employed 320,000 people across its many sites in the United Kingdom. In 2016, that number had dropped to 24,000 and it's likely to be even lower today. Forgotten about, ignored and fed up with Westminster indifference, many used the Brexit referendum of 2016 and this month's General Election to remind the country that their voices could still be heard. Stoke's voice was one of the loudest: with 69.4 per cent voting to leave the EU, it became known as Britain's 'Brexit capital'.

'Workington man' was – to the bemusement and amusement of locals – identified by Conservative pollsters ahead of the General Election as representative of a typical type of voter whose disenchantment with Labour would help decide the result. They said he was over 45, white, without a degree, a Leave voter in the 2016 referendum, worried about crime and preferred security over freedom. Some of those characteristics may well have applied to people in the town. But, for speedway fans, the mention of Workington reminds them of something else. Because the town is synonymous with one of the sport's sadder stories which, in many ways, sums up the dilemmas and issues facing team speedway in Britain as it enters its tenth decade.

* * *

Sit high up in the main stand at Workington's Derwent Stadium, with your back to the Irish Sea, and you can see – on the horizon, on a good day – the soft mounds of the lower, northern fells of the Lake District. But that's the closest that Workington gets to the genteel tea rooms and Beatrix Potter world of day-tripping coach tours. It's an industrial town, the banks of wind turbines dotted all along the same horizon a much truer indication of its purpose.

Like many northern towns, it grew up around heavy industries – shipbuilding, coal and steel. But they've all gone and the main employers are now the Sellafield nuclear plant 20 miles down the coast and a Swedish-owned paper factory. According to a report in *The Guardian* the previous month, it is Britain's least diverse constituency with a population age at twice the national average.

Aside from its short-lived fame during the 2019 General Election campaign, Workington – a town of around 25,000 inhabitants – doesn't attract much national attention, certainly not when it comes to sport. Its football club were members of the Football League for more than 25 years but were voted out in 1977. Since then, they've slowly slipped down the non-league pyramid and are currently three divisions below the Football League in the Northern Premier League. The rugby league club, Workington Town, play in the second tier, their all-too-brief heyday way back in the early 1950s. Now, with gates of 500, it's a case of struggling to keep afloat.

Workington Comets – the town's speedway team – had similar issues. Founded in 1970, they disappeared after the 1981 season when they finished second bottom of the league and lost money due to poor crowds. The club didn't reappear until 1999. A few highlights followed, notably when Comets' Carl Stonehewer became the first rider from the second tier of British racing to qualify for the Grand Prix series. But the same problems that had forced their closure – lack of success and poor crowds – threatened their future again and, by 2012, the then promoter pulled out. Which is when Laura Morgan stepped in.

Laura was far from the traditional image of a speedway promoter. A senior teaching assistant at a school in Maryport, just up the coast, she'd been a speedway fan since her father took her to meetings as a six-year-old in the 1970s.

In December 2007, her life changed in an unimaginable way.

She was travelling with her then boyfriend, her sister and another friend in Denmark. Their car was hit from behind by a van, the force of which forced them off the road and into a field. Laura says she knew before she was cut out of the car that she would be paralysed. She'd broken her back and, with no feeling in her arms and legs, spent 12 months in a Danish hospital undergoing endless operations and rehabilitation.

She received more than £1 million in compensation for the accident and, in her own words, 'put a pot aside, which I referred to as fun money'. While most people facing up to the rest of their life in a wheelchair might not choose to spend 'fun money' on keeping speedway going in a remote outpost on the north-west coast of England, that's what Laura did.

Laura was realistic – she said at the time there wasn't a bottomless pot – and, while she knew she wouldn't make money from keeping speedway going, she hoped she and co-promoter Tony Jackson could break even. But it wasn't just about money.

'Speedway is more than a sport, it's a community. It's a country-wide community as well as each track having its own little community. You develop friendships. When a speedway club closes, people lose friends that they've sat beside for years because we all like to sit in the same place each week. It's almost like a family break-up.'

But Workington kept losing money. While speedway may be a community, it's a small world too. Riders mix with and talk to spectators in a way that would be unthinkable in other sports. Rumours and stories of Workington's financial problems became an open secret.

Laura and Tony sat down at the end of 2017 and, if their heads had ruled their hearts, they'd have called it a day then. Instead, they decided to keep going but try and put together a cheaper team to safeguard speedway in the town and bring their costs down. 'We didn't want to win the league. We wanted to stay middle of the road, just to keep it ticking over and hopefully bring more sponsors in.'

If that sounds odd – the owner of a sports club saying they didn't want their team to finish top of the league – then remember the reality of economics in speedway. Each speedway meeting has 15 heats. In each heat, the winner gets three points, second two points and third one point. With 90 points up for grabs, a winning team generally – excluding races where there are fewer than three finishers – needs 46 points. But, if a team wins with a blow-out score, say 66-24, then the promoter faces paying out nearly 50 per cent more. That's not all. In addition, there are things called bonus points, which can confuse those new to the sport. Bonus points don't count towards a team's score, but they do for a rider's pay at the end of the night. To explain, say two riders from the same team secure a 5-1 – finishing first and second. They score five points for their team but the rider finishing second will be 'paid' for three points, the same as his winning team-mate, his reward for not being beaten by an opponent.

Despite planning for a middle-of-the-table finish, Laura and Tony found themselves paying out on quite a few 5-1s in the early part of the 2018 season. That led to another problem. Speedway promoters only make money from their home matches – but they are responsible for paying their own riders when they race away from home.

'We used to have this joke, when we knew we'd won a meeting, the other team couldn't catch us up, and there was another 5-1, we were like: "Oh God, slow down! Just somebody go and tell the riders they don't need to push so hard now because we've won!" It was only ever a joke but, by God, it was true.'

There was a seven-week period when the Comets had just one home match and eight away matches. From the start of May until the end of August, the prime summer period for speedway, Workington only managed seven home meetings as a team. It wasn't just bad weather causing postponements. There was a row with the BSPA over their preferred race night. Cash-flow problems inevitably followed. For those more used to hearing about the millions lavished on top-class, international footballers, the figures might seem quaintly inconsequential. But in the world of British team speedway today, a few thousand pounds here and there really does make a huge difference.

One weekend, they had a wage bill of £11,000 after two big away wins, without a home meeting to provide any income. Riders weren't getting paid. It reached a point where the BSPA were on the verge of closing them down. But they managed to borrow and scrape money from various places to eventually pay the riders and escaped closure by an hour.

Whatever financial problems Workington had, the riders continued to do well on the track. They finished third in the Championship to reach the league play-offs. They made the final of the Knockout Cup. And, for good measure, they reached the National Shield Final, the third main team trophy for Championship sides.

The problem was that all those finals were concertinaed into the final days – not even weeks – of October, not the best time of year to attract decent crowds. The Comets found themselves racing three finals at home in just five days – Scunthorpe in the cup final on Thursday night and then Lakeside from Essex in both of the other two finals on the Sunday and Monday immediately after. It left them no time to advertise the meetings properly. It was hard on the fans too, asking them to pay out for three matches one after the other. Admission prices were reduced but, even then, crowds were down. They had 992 spectators for the play-off final but, if it had been held a month earlier in warmer weather, Laura thinks they'd have had another 500 attending – and possibly an extra £7,500 as well.

Those fans who did manage to get along to Derwent Park were glad they had. On the Thursday night, Workington lifted the Knockout Cup, overcoming a huge 18-point deficit at home to Scunthorpe. On the Sunday – a day after travelling to Lakeside in Essex for the first leg of the Championship Grand Final – they won 61-29 to secure that too. On the Monday, they beat Lakeside again to take the Shield Final. There were huge celebrations with the riders and the fans on the track and in the bar afterwards. Ironically, for a town said to be the least diverse, the seven-rider team had three Danish, two Australian and two British riders. Equally ironic, for a town with an ageing population – and speedway a sport attracting an older demographic – not enough of them came along.

'It was definitely the year that we didn't mean to win. And we went and won,' was Laura's verdict.

Because of their success on the track, and the extra 12 matches – semi-finals and play-off finals – she reckons they lost an additional £35,000. That wasn't all. No prize money comes with winning trophies in speedway. The club even had to buy medals for their own winning riders.

Once again, Laura and Tony sat down and worked out how much they'd need to defend their three national titles in 2019. They'd later reveal the costs in a detailed interview with the local Workington paper, the *News & Star*. Estimated costs for the forthcoming season were around £220,000. Money from spectators paying at the gate – the only real income source for the Comets other than sponsorships – was estimated at £145,000 with a further £6,000 coming from food and drink. Laura says the rugby league club got all the takings from the bar, even on speedway nights. They would need crowds of 700-plus every week to make sure all the overheads were paid. During 2018 they had averaged 500. Without those 200 supporters paying £15 or so every week, they'd be looking at an overall loss of around £75,000.

'We thought that winning the treble would bring more sponsors in. We didn't rest on our laurels. We went out to find them. Most of the sponsors that we had were supporters as well, doing their bit to keep the sport in the town. We didn't have any big business from Carlisle, for example, throwing tens of thousands of pounds at us. But sponsors who'd promised us money fell by the wayside. The money just wasn't there.'

And so, after originally committing to run again in 2019, Laura and her team made the difficult decision to close Workington speedway.

At the end of January 2019, she and Tony spoke with each of the riders they'd already contacted for the coming season and told them the bad news. Laura describes it as 'probably the most traumatic thing I've ever had to do' – which, given all she's been through, speaks volumes. They rang riders in Australia, New Zealand and Europe to tell them they didn't have a job. 'It's not as if they could nip down to the job centre and look for something else. Most of the other teams had already signed all their riders up.'

Imagine a professional sports club that has never won a major trophy in its history. Nearly 50 years after its formation, it finally wins the national knockout cup competition. Three days later, it secures the national league championship. Then just 24 hours later it wins a third, the national shield competition – a historic treble of the major honours available.

And then imagine that the club – just over three months later – goes out of existence.

That is the story of the Workington Comets speedway team. Winning the treble bankrupted them. Success is not always beautiful.

* * *

Of course, when businesses close unexpectedly, there are those who lose out. Laura was still sorting out money owed months after the season finished and, while speedway riders chasing their wage isn't uncommon, it's never a good look for any sport. Of the seven riders already contracted to ride for Workington in 2019 before they announced their closure, six did manage to find other teams. But one, Australian Mason Compton, hasn't ridden in Britain since. The club were criticised for saying at the November AGM that they would run, only to pull out two months later. Some will say that Workington's financial problems were too deep-seated to sort. That there were never enough fans to make it viable. It's not even the first time that winning the league one season and then folding the next has happened in British speedway: White City in London didn't appear after winning in 1977; the Bradford Dukes closed after their 1997 title win. And those were both top-league championships.

But, speak to people in speedway about Workington now and there's genuine sadness that they're no longer running. Nicolai Klindt, one of the Danish riders in the treble-winning team, says riding for Workington was one of the most enjoyable seasons he's ever had. Alex Harkess, the long-time Edinburgh promoter and former chairman of the BSPA, is sympathetic too.

'To win matches, you prepare for 50 points. That's probably as much as you can afford. If you start to win matches away from home and score 60 points, you've got a serious financial problem. I know, because we've had one or two very successful teams that won every single away match or only lost two or three in the whole season.

'Speedway clubs have a hard core and that's what they live on. People believe if they get a wee bit of success, the crowd will go up. Well, it does a bit, but you've just got to appreciate what you've got and make the most of it. We know we're going to struggle at Edinburgh to break even so we set our stall out to raise enough money so that the pressure's not on.

'Laura's lovely, she put heart and soul into it. But she didn't have the backing she deserved. We survive on volunteers. We pay the doctor, we pay the paramedics, we pay the referee. Once you get past that we don't really pay anybody. Whereas because they were in a stadium, they had to take on the security and the turnstile operators and all these kinds of things. That all adds up.'

Speak to Laura Morgan and she says she'd do it all again. She does feel let down by sponsors and by businesses in the area who could have come and helped out. She misses speedway although she didn't go to a meeting in 2019. 'Some of the rules are so ridiculous. You can't explain to people how it runs. The actual racing, the sport, I do miss. I don't miss a lot of the work. Everything was becoming more expensive, we weren't always on brilliant terms with our landlords, all of that I don't miss.'

Overall, she thinks that running Workington speedway for six seasons cost her quite a large amount of that pot of 'fun money' – probably more than £750,000. She says now that if she'd known she wasn't going to secure the future of the sport in the town, then she would have thought seriously about the investment before she did it.

At the time of their closure, Laura said she was putting the Workington licence on ice so that they could, hopefully, open again in 2020. By not running in 2019, and suffering another hefty loss, she was safeguarding the club's future. But that now looks like an increasingly forlorn hope – not least because their track no longer exists.

There were plans for a revitalisation of Workington's sporting facilities to coincide with the town hosting games at the 2021 Rugby League World Cup. Derwent Park was to be demolished and redeveloped with a purpose-built stadium built on the edge of town. But just for the football and rugby league clubs. There was to be no new home for speedway. It wasn't a consideration for the council.

But those plans collapsed with a change of council leadership. Both the football team and rugby league team remain – for now – at their original grounds. In the second half of 2019, the council spent £174,000 on Derwent Park. Nearly half – £77,000 – was used to buy the rugby league club out of its lease with speculation that it could be used for 'alternative uses' in future; £4,000 was given to the rugby league club in June 2019 to pay for the removal of the speedway track used by the Comets.

'I let my heart rule my head because I desperately wanted to keep speedway there, not just for me but for the whole speedway community. But you've got to start looking around and thinking: "Good grief, I've got three grown-up daughters, I've got a growing number of grandchildren, I can't just keep throwing money at something that's not going anywhere." I feel that I more than did my bit. But I do still feel really sad and I do still miss it.'

* * *

On the face of it, Oxford is an unlikely place to have any association with speedway. It's much better known for its university colleges, elegantly spired buildings and punts down the River Cherwell. But outside the academic centre, in the south-east suburbs, is the district of Cowley where, for much of the 20th century, cars were produced for three totemic UK manufacturers – first for Morris Motors, then British Leyland and finally Rover. By the early 1970s, more than 20,000 people worked at the Cowley site – fertile ground for both speedway and greyhound racing.

But while car production has continued at Plant Oxford – now under BMW ownership with 4,500 workers producing the MINI – speedway at Sandy Lane, a brisk walk away, has ended. The club formed in 1949 and won the championship five times. Equally impressively, Oxford ran continuously for nearly 60 years until they closed in 2007. No agreement could be reached with the stadium's owners, the Greyhound Racing Association (GRA). Greyhound racing continued for another five years but, with talk of the stadium being sold for housing, it has remained empty since then. The council has blocked plans for development, saying they would prefer the site to be used for leisure purposes, and two groups – the Oxford Speedway Supporters Club (OSSC) and Save Oxford Speedway (SOS) – have campaigned for speedway to return. Which is why, today, Tuesday, 10 December, around 60 of them are crowded into Oxford's largest multi-purpose conference and event centre, the King's Centre, to put their case to the city's planning officials.

Rob Peasley is amongst them. Rob, as we'll discover, has done – and continues to do – just about everything in speedway other than ride a bike. He tried that once at a training school when he was 39 and says he was 'pretty hopeless'. He went to his first meetings in 1979 when he was six and, the following year, started to attend regularly, learning to 'fill in the programme and add it all up correctly'. When he started going, Oxford were a struggling second-division side but, with new investment in both the stadium and the team, they moved up to the top league, then called the British League. Rob's favourite season was 1985 when Oxford, with world champion Hans Nielsen in their team, won the British League, the Knockout Cup and the Midland Cup. His love of the sport grew from there.

'For ten years of Oxford speedway, from 1997 to 2007, I hardly missed a meeting at all – home or away. In 2007, when we were running teams in both the Elite [the new name for the top] League and Conference League, the only two meetings I missed that season were because the two teams were running on the same night. It wasn't actually possible to be in two places at the same time.'

Rob started editing a fanzine and, as someone who was at every meeting, he began covering the Conference League for the *Oxford Mail* as well as filling in for the paper's main speedway reporter when he was on holiday. But, halfway through 2007 – with crowds down to below 500 and the club losing money – the Elite League team was shut down. The Conference League team continued and there were plans to run a team in the middle league for 2008. Rob had taken over as the *Oxford Mail*'s speedway reporter, but the first story he had to write was that Oxford wouldn't be running after all. There was no agreement with the stadium landlords, the Greyhound Racing Association.

'It was horrible when Oxford closed. I still went to speedway in 2008. I remember going to Coventry on Good Friday and then it really hit me that Oxford weren't running. I felt like I should be at Oxford. I hated that meeting at Coventry. I was quite glad when it was over so I could go home.'

Since then, Rob and fellow campaigners have worked to bring their team home. There have been complicated and time-consuming legal directives to navigate through. Rob says their campaign goes in ebbs and flows. The main campaigner is a supporter called Ian Sawyer, who Rob says has done a brilliant job. 'It can be quite dispiriting. It takes so long for it to all happen. We almost went 18 months without anything and now we've got this planning inspectorate meeting and we had to tell everybody to get up here. What's fantastic is how much support there still is. This meeting couldn't have been at a less amenable time of the year – the run-up to Christmas, in the middle of the week and the middle of a working day – and yet we still got about 60 people. The planning inspectors could see the level of support in front of them.'

But every week and month that passes means further deterioration in a moribund stadium. The good news for those like Rob, who are hoping to see speedway bikes racing around Sandy Lane once again, is that Oxford City Council have placed both heritage and conservation status on the stadium. That has effectively tied the hands of the stadium owners who want the entire site for housing development – a frequent fate for former speedway venues.

Rob and the others on the committee have hired a legal representative to collect personal evidence from fans – underlining the benefits the stadium, in its various roles, has brought to the community. The best examples are to be selected and put to the council as part of their consultations for the Oxford Local Plan, which is to be discussed early in 2020 and will determine development in the city up until 2036.

Even more encouraging for Rob and the campaigners is that there's a businessman keen to reopen the stadium – with speedway as a central part of it. The £20–25 million facelift would aim to make use of the stadium seven days a week, with speedway and greyhounds making a return. There would be some housing on the site, too, but it's the return of speedway that excites the campaigners.

They're not getting carried away. The current stadium owners would need to agree to sell up. They'd need to get planning permissions through the council. Then there's work that would have to be done on the stadium to repair and upgrade it after so many years without any care and attention.

It's not unusual for speedway tracks that have closed to feature in the press every so often as being candidates to reopen. Fans of

Coventry, one of speedway's really big names, whose closure after the 2016 season was a real hammer blow, continue to campaign for a return to Brandon Stadium. There's also occasional talk of Bradford's Odsal Stadium, which hosted two World Finals and was home to the Bradford Dukes, possibly staging speedway again one day.

The next milestone for Rob and the Oxford campaigners is getting the planning inspectorate's verdict. That's likely to be May or even June.

'That's what people don't appreciate, how long it can actually take.'

Then again, if you've been campaigning for 12 years, another six months isn't that long. Hope springs eternal for the exiled speedway fan.

* * *

For those living near Alexandra Palace in north London, the period leading up to Christmas means one thing. Young, and not so young, men and women in a variety of costumes – superheroes, leprechauns, Ali G lookalikes, chickens, Teletubbies and Father Christmases – all of them heading to the grand Victorian building for the William Hill World Darts Championship. For two and a half weeks, the sport enjoys time in the national spotlight amidst a singularly British party atmosphere of fancy dress and communal karaoke all washed down with copious amounts of alcohol. It's been estimated that around three-quarters of a million pints are sold during the tournament. That works out at around 11 per spectator.

For many years, speedway fans have cast envious glances at darts and snooker, whose Dafabet Masters tournament takes place at Ally Pally in January. Both are traditional, working-class sports that have moved with the times and adapted to the new world of television – and thrived as a result. Why, many in speedway have often wondered, could someone like Barry Hearn not be given free rein to sprinkle some of his magic dust over their sport? Riders like Tai Woffinden have speculated on what kind of impact the entrepreneurial impresario could have.

Unfortunately for Hearn's advocates, that's not going to happen. As he tells the BBC's Jennie Gow in her podcast series, *Speedway*, he doesn't like motorsport and he doesn't do anything in his life that he doesn't like. He hasn't got the time.

But, still, he can't quite work out why speedway is in decline. 'It's in your face, it's very raw, it is exciting, it's very simple – just drive faster than the other bloke. Somewhere along the road they made a wrong move or didn't maximise or maybe got complacent that it was easy. I won't say it's in terminal decline because there will always be hard-core pockets of resistance, but would you want to be a speedway rider, put your life on the line for very little? It's really difficult to stop the decline. You either invest and work to take it forward or you give up. What you don't do is just sit there in a slowly declining market because it's boring.'

Barry Hearn doesn't do 'boring' and this month, in his role as chairman of the Professional Darts Corporation, he has even more reason to be excited.

A woman has beaten a man in the early rounds of the competition – the first time this has ever happened – and coverage and interest in the competition has gone off the scale.

Fallon Sherrock is 25 and from Milton Keynes. She has reached the final of the Women's World Championships and has won many women's titles across Europe – from Wales to Slovakia – without attracting that much media coverage. But now, newly nicknamed the 'Queen of the Palace', she's everywhere – from BBC Radio Four's *Today* programme to CNN International. TV ratings for her matches on Sky Sports attract the highest-ever ratings apart from finals. Even Barry couldn't have bought that kind of publicity.

Speedway can only look on with a touch of envy. It's not fair to say that speedway is a closed shop for women. One of the most respected post-war promoters was Alice Hart – or Miss A. S. Hart as she preferred to be called – at Belle Vue. There have been others, from Pat Bliss at Reading in the 1980s through to Debbie Hancock at Somerset who's just been appointed to the BSPA management committee, the first woman since 1992. Many women have always been enthusiastic supporters of speedway. It has helped to give the sport its family, community atmosphere and remove some of the worst aspects of tribalism.

But speedway, particularly in Britain, has never really managed to bring women riders through to the highest levels. Danish rider Sabrina Bogh not only rode – with the men – for the Danish under-21 team in 2001 but actually beat them to win the Danish under-21 Championship that year. Barry Bishop, now the co-promoter at the Isle of Wight, started the first 'ladies-only' speedway school at the Iwade training track in Kent in 2011. Barry, who is a firm believer that women should have the same opportunities as men, has three or four young girls riding regularly alongside boys at the Isle of Wight's First Skid training school. Every so often, a female rider emerges: Jessica Lamb rode at Wimbledon in 2004 and 2005; Montana Jowett at Scunthorpe a few years later. Even this year, three women rode in the Development League, one below the third-tier National League.

One of them is Rachel Hellowell. Her dad, Kevin, is 'motorbike mad' and got her interested in the sport. She began riding a bike competitively when she was 15 in 2009 and, for the last two years, has ridden for the Birmingham Bulls. She was their rider of the year in 2018. Rachel has found that being a woman in a male-dominated sport can help. 'Because I'm a girl, I get quite a bit of support from people giving me oil and fuel. Even £10 can buy me methanol for a meeting.'

But she doesn't want to be seen as any kind of trailblazer because of her sex. 'I'm not bothered about raising awareness to get women riding, because I'm quite happy just doing my thing. I don't want to be treated differently. I don't want to be pinpointed as a female rider and have a big song and dance made about it in *Speedway Star*. I just want to get on track and ride my bike and impress people.'

How do male riders react when – as has happened – Rachel has finished ahead of them? 'I have heard some comments, through the grapevine, that "so and so" is going to retire if you beat them and then

I have beaten them and I've had great satisfaction from that. But no one's ever passed any comment – good or bad – saying, "Oh I can't believe you just beat me." I'd love to know because in a way it might push me a bit more, knowing that someone doesn't want to get beaten by me so I can say, "Right, I've got to now!"'

Rachel has been lucky with injuries. She hasn't actually broken anything apart from a few mudguards, but does admit to having some impressive bruises over the years. Speak to her and you sense that she can be hard on herself. 'When I don't do as well as I'd like, I beat myself up quite a lot for it.' As a result, she's got no plans to go higher in the sport. 'I enjoy the level that I'm at and I'd never want to go professional, purely because I don't think I would cope with the pressure. I think it would take away the element of enjoyment a bit too much.'

While Rachel won't be the Fallon Sherrock of British speedway, she doesn't see why it couldn't happen. It could be another female rider, someone like Katie Gordon from Knutsford in Cheshire, who is determined to do for speedway exactly what Fallon has done for darts. She tells *Speedway Star* that she's totally focused on going as far as she can. She'd love to be the first woman to get into a Premiership or Championship side. Katie's young – just 15. 'I know I've got such a long way to go, but I've set my ambitions high. I want to be that woman. I want to be that trailblazer. It's being done in other sports so there's no reason it can't be in speedway.'

Others, though, wonder if it will ever happen. Peter Schroeck rode for a number of teams in Britain from 1983 to 1992 after coming over from Germany. Settled in Britain, he is team manager at King's Lynn as well as running a training school at Rye House in Hertfordshire. It would be hard to find a bigger supporter of young riders, but he's sceptical that women can make it to the very top. He says there have always been a few female riders around in his time but nobody's broken through yet. And he doesn't know what the answer is.

'A lot of the time, the dads are very enthusiastic and the girls are young and they have a go at speedway, and then their lives change as well – boyfriends, getting married. I don't want to be too disrespectful but I just can't see it. There's no role model at that top level. If there were ten or 15 girls racing at that level, you would have growth. I have full respect for anybody who puts their leg over a speedway bike. It doesn't matter to me whether you're a man or a woman. But for girls, it has been a lot more difficult over the years.'

Difficult or not, there are plenty of people – female and male – who'll be hoping that Katie or Rachel or someone else can do what no British woman has managed before. British speedway, on a number of levels, would undoubtedly benefit if they did.

January 2020 – Speedway's conundrum

THE OPENING days of the new year are dominated by news of the United States' assassination of Iranian commander Major General Qasem Soleimani. Amidst genuine concerns of a possible all-out war between the two countries, other news slips by without much notice. On 5 January, China notifies the World Health Organisation of an outbreak of 44 pneumonia-like cases in the city of Wuhan. It's thought the virus might be linked to SARS, severe acute respiratory syndrome, which killed more than 700 people worldwide in 2002–03. A WHO spokesman says they will monitor the situation closely.

* * *

Before we go on, it's worth reflecting on the term that is bandied around a lot – 'the golden age of speedway' – because it offers useful perspectives on the sport's health today. Speedway in Great Britain has had several periods when it's generally thought to have prospered. The one that most people would point to – because it boasted the sport's largest crowds – is immediately after the Second World War through to the mid-1950s. Like almost all forms of sport and entertainment, speedway benefited from the end of the war when a weary population was finally able to get back to some form of normality and enjoy itself.

A casual browse through the many books looking back on this period reveals facts that stand out, particularly given the benefit of knowing where speedway stands now. A *Daily Mail* survey on the popularity of sports in the UK in 1947 found that speedway rated fourth behind football, cricket and boxing, well ahead of racing, rugby union, tennis and golf. League gates for single domestic club meetings were as high as 80,000. In one season, 1946, Wembley attracted over one million spectators to their home meetings. That is, by some way, more than the combined attendances of all speedway tracks, at all levels, in Britain in 2019. Post-war crowds may well have been even higher than officially recorded. The Government's entertainment tax was set at a punitive 48 per cent and while some sports, like football and boxing, paid a reduced rate of 15 per cent, speedway was oddly classified as a 'non-live sport' and paid full whack. The then Chancellor of the Exchequer, Hugh Gaitskell, was questioned on it in 1951, and admitted that while there was skill in speedway racing, that wasn't 'a factor in determining liability to entertainments' duty'. As a result, some owners, promoters and managers across a range of leisure activities 'fudged' the size of their attendances to escape paying so much.

The Government even felt speedway was a threat to the recovering post-war economy. In 1947 they worried that weekday afternoon crowds for speedway were so large that factories would suffer reduced output as a result. They called promoters in for a meeting at the Home Office, warning them to cut the number of midweek meetings – or the Government would do it for them. Fortunately for speedway, the national press came to the rescue on this occasion, stressing the strong community element to the sport and its benefits in keeping post-war morale up.

Speedway was considered important enough for the most high-profile public figures of the day to be associated with it. In 1948, the Duke of Edinburgh, Prince Philip, presented the Riders' Championship winner's trophy; Violet Atlee, the wife of then Prime Minister Clement, presented a £500 cheque to the winner of the 1948 World Speedway Championship in front of 93,000 at Wembley.

Back in the late 1940s, if you lived in London and liked speedway, you could watch it on five consecutive nights: Monday at Wimbledon,

Tuesday at West Ham, Wednesday at New Cross, Thursday at Wembley and Friday at Harringay. But it wasn't just London. Photos of the time show packed crowds at tracks in Bradford and Bristol and Liverpool, all large cities where, like London, speedway has long since ceased to take place.

Speedway riders were – it is generally thought – the highest-paid sportsmen in the country. This was, of course, at a time when footballers were subject to the minimum wage. In Philip Dalling's book, *The Golden Age of Speedway*, five-time Swedish world champion Ove Fundin remembers his days as a Norwich rider. In the late 1950s, he was out golfing with some Norwich City footballers. They were still on a fixed wage and Fundin, one of the very top riders of the day, could make as much in one night at speedway as the footballers earned in a week. He was riding virtually every day in England, Sweden or elsewhere. The footballers, he said, were 'quite envious of me'.

But, even during speedway's golden age, there were difficulties. It's important to remember them too. As with so many things, it wasn't simply a case of famine or feast but rather a woollier, greyer area with good and bad mixing at the same time. Tracks, often opened speculatively by promoters keen to make money from a new audience, sometimes closed down within months of a new season opening. The track at Hastings in Sussex had to close after one season at the end of 1949 because local residents complained about the noise.

The speedway bible of the times, *Stenner's Speedway Annual*, proclaimed that 1951 – in the era when we think speedway was at its zenith – was 'crisis year' for the sport in Britain. The big question, author Jim Stenner explained, was whether speedway would survive as it was, with a good geographical spread of tracks, or be reduced to just a handful as it had after the initial 1928–1930 boom. Some issues that he highlighted – another wet summer and the continued high rate of entertainment tax – were largely outside the speedway promoters' control. But there were three things, said Stenner, that the sport could do something about. Firstly, it could seriously consider automatic promotion and relegation between the three leagues. Money, rather than sporting excellence on the track, seemed to be the main driver for who would take part in which league. Secondly, it should stop revealing its plans for a new season at the last minute. Finally, Stenner argued, several clubs were guilty of sloppy presentation, which he felt offered spectators poor value for money. Speedway, too, never enjoyed the same attention – for better or worse – that betting brought to similar working-class sports like horse racing and greyhound racing.

It's also important to bear in mind that, by 1958, British speedway – buffeted by the rise in the number of television sets keeping people at home and, at many tracks, the competing attractions of the mid-decade introduction of stock car racing – was in a real slump. There were just 11 tracks operating as the so-called golden decade came to an end.

The sport reorganised itself – most notably creating a British League in 1965 for all clubs to compete in – and entered a second 'golden' age in the late 60s and 70s. Names like Ivan Mauger, Barry Briggs and Ole Olsen were known widely by sports fans, not just those interested in speedway. Briggs finished runner-up twice in three years for the BBC *Sports Personality of the Year*. There may well have been a concerted campaign amongst speedway fans to vote for him but, even so, it reflects the size of the audience at the time. There was regular coverage of the sport on ITV's *World of Sport*, and crowds for league meetings, while not reaching the same levels as the immediate post-war period, were still respectable. The White City Rebels filled 30 coaches for their league decider at Wolverhampton in 1977. The media generally gave speedway coverage too, helped, in part, by the fact that England or Great Britain dominated international speedway until the rise of Denmark in the 1980s. Many older fans say the last World Final held at Wembley Stadium in 1981 – watched by 92,500 and won by the charismatic American Bruce Penhall – was the second golden age's high point.

Since then, however, speedway – certainly in Great Britain – has increasingly fallen out of national consciousness.

* * *

While some speedway riders may have occasionally cursed Paul Ackroyd in his previous role, you'll struggle to find anyone in the sport who has a bad word to say about him these days. Paul was a former speedway referee, a job he did for 28 years and which his son, Craig, has taken on himself since 1999.

Paul Ackroyd is chairman and trustee of the Speedway Riders Benevolent Fund (SRBF), the only charity anywhere in the world set up to look after riders when they're injured or, in more serious cases, permanently disabled. It was set up in 1948 by Arthur Elvin, when he was the promoter at Wembley.

Paul got the job the day after he retired as a referee to take over from the then chairman who was having health problems. He reckons he spends up to 20 hours a week on the fund. He's helped by four other trustees – former riders Kenny McKinna and Tony Noel, current Edinburgh co-promoter Alex Harkess and Wolverhampton promoter Chris Van Straaten, along with secretary/treasurer Stephanie Babb. All do it voluntarily. There are no highly paid charity executives at the SRBF.

'We spend what we get in, every penny,' says Paul. 'We get £120,000 income per year and the expenditure is £120,000.' Currently, that's less than a third of the weekly salary paid to the highest earner in football's Premier League. The contrast isn't lost on Paul. 'I just can't believe what those guys earn. Our boys get knocked off their bike and a minute later they're ready for the rerun. I can't believe fans pay money to go and watch a football match to keep those guys in the luxury that they get.'

The SRBF's £120,000 is made up as follows: 40 per cent comes from a special, one-off meeting held every year, the Bonanza, with the Ben Fund getting money from ticket sales and special raffle and merchandise sales on the day; 25 per cent comes from collections held at every British track, once a year, with riders literally walking the terraces and stands with buckets, for people to donate what they can. Every year there's a competition to find the track that raises the most. In 2019 Ipswich raised £2,331.93. The remaining 35 per cent comes from donations and other events.

Anyone who has ever tried to get car insurance for a newly qualified, teenage driver knows how expensive it is. Imagine being a speedway rider, driving with no brakes and knowing that injuries like broken fingers, wrists and collarbones are common. Some riders complain that, even with insurance, companies will use loopholes to avoid paying up.

Paul outlines what is effectively a two-tier insurance world. 'The very top riders pay a lot in premiums but their pay-out will be very high. They'll probably have three or four policies. Moving down the scale, there'll be riders where they'll be scraping together to have decent insurance. The middle and lower league? They probably won't have private insurance, just the legal one that the BSPA insist they have for each meeting, although the pay-out for that isn't very high.' Paul says a lot of riders don't see insurance as a priority and feels the authorities should better educate young riders. 'Instead of buying a fancy mudguard, they'd be better investing some money in health protection.'

The Ben Fund generally helps 40 to 45 riders throughout the year who are injured and can't ride – or earn – and need short-term cash to supplement that small insurance pay-out to put food on their families' tables and pay the bills. They also help 13 permanently paraplegic riders and one rider with brain injuries.

Much of their work is done quietly, visible only to those being helped. 'Two days before Christmas, we helped one of our paraplegic riders. He's been in a wheelchair for 40 years and had to go back to hospital because of heart issues, which tends to happen with a lot of them. His carer is his 92-year-old mother and the hospital wouldn't let him go back home unless he had a specialist mattress to lie on. There was no way his mum was going to be able to do that. We heard about it and got them one. It was delivered at four o'clock on Christmas Eve and he was back home two hours later. It was a small thing, but it's something that does make a real difference to people.'

Paul is still struck, even after so many years in his role, by the generosity of speedway people – not generally the country's most affluent – when disaster or injury strikes. He mentions the case of Ricky Ashworth, one of the saddest and most salutary examples of the dangers of racing a speedway bike in recent years. Ricky was a British international rider who was left with serious brain injuries after an accident at Scunthorpe in August 2013. He spent 91 days in a coma. Paul says it was one of the darkest moments in his time as Benevolent Fund chairman. 'You can't begin to imagine how his family cope with that, not just financially, but mentally. It was astounding what people did. They raised enough money to allow Ricky to build a downstairs extension at his parents' house to cope with his new circumstances. The fund is a real lifeline for a lot of people.' It was speedway's own – and largely unheralded – version of BBC TV's *DIY SOS*.

He does wish that younger riders could see the value of the fund. 'If you're a 20-year-old rider, it's sometimes hard to understand what the benefits of helping us are. Speedway's exciting at that age and they don't see the potential downsides. If a well-known rider goes around the terraces with a bucket, he's going to get ten times the amount of money someone like me can collect. A few years ago, we had big-name riders like Jason Crump, Shane Parker and Jason Lyons who really understood what we were about and who helped drive the Ben Fund. But now they've retired we haven't really got the same level of well-known riders who buy into the fund.'

Former rider and promoter Graham Drury would go further. He thinks it should be in the contract of every rider in Britain that they ride in the Ben Fund meeting if asked. Without naming names, Paul will say that it's quite disappointing when there are riders who have been helped by the Ben Fund who are not prepared to give something back later.

January is a busy month for Paul because he's busy sorting out a date and a track for that much-needed annual Bonanza meeting. Paul was the driving force for it with the first one held at Sheffield in 2009. 'Two years ago, the Beast from the East – remember that? – wiped out the meeting we'd arranged at Peterborough. It was really difficult to rearrange so we didn't have any income until July of that year. But we were paying money out from April onwards.' Paul says they dealt with it through savings they'd held 'for a rainy day'.

New BSPA chairman and Scunthorpe promoter, Rob Godfrey, has already offered his home track for this year – Saturday, 14 March. For Paul, it's now a question of contacting riders to check if they'll volunteer their services and, of course, keeping his fingers crossed for dry weather.

* * *

Ask a British speedway fan to pick their favourite race from the 2019 season and there's a good chance it would be from the individual British Final at Belle Vue. But it didn't involve the rider who won the title, Charles Wright, or either of those who finished on the podium alongside him. The standout race of the night, and possibly the whole season, featured a rider mainly known for his exploits at the third level of British speedway, Danny Ayres.

Danny is no wide-eyed youngster. He's 32 and only began racing speedway at the age of 27. He's never had a regular place in the top league. But he's been one of the best riders in the National League and he rode for Scunthorpe in the Championship during 2019. He'd finished third in his semi-final to qualify for his first British Final.

No one would describe Danny as a fluent or stylish rider. He can be a bit out of control, but those who love their speedway know that he's an old-school rider. By that, they mean he's an entertainer, something they really appreciate. The kind of rider who, even if he misses the gate or isn't leading after the second corner, will spend the rest of the race trying to get past whoever's in front of him – whatever position he's in. Danny goes into heat 19 knowing he hasn't scored enough points to qualify for the night's final rounds but he's determined to do his best anyway. He starts on the outside gate, up against the veteran Chris Harris, a former Grand Prix rider who, even

New Cross and West Ham line up in front of a packed post-war crowd in April 1946 – London now has no speedway teams

Wembley stadium was regularly filled to capacity for speedway meetings – 93,000 were inside for the world championship in September 1949

When speedway really was a national sport. Of these tracks, 14 survive today – four at different locations to where they were in 1974

Stoke promoter Dave Tattum – in red fleece – greets visitors for the last night of speedway in Stoke

Stoke fans watching the final speedway meeting at Loomer Road

British fans waving Union flags after Robert Lambert wins heat nine at the British Grand Prix at Cardiff

The annual Grand Prix at Cardiff is by far the best-attended speedway meeting in Britain

October's international meeting against Denmark was the first for the new management team of Simon Stead and Ollie Allen

Danny Ayres' death at the start of February 2020 was a huge loss for the sport

Bert Harkins surrounded by a treasure trove of speedway memorabilia at the National Speedway Museum

The annual Celebration of Speedway event is an opportunity to enjoy the sounds and smells from the past

Tom Bacon on the Kent Kings' stand at the Celebration of Speedway event in February 2020

Riders waiting to get on the Rye House training track

At one point it looked like the only speedway meeting in the 2020 season would be the Ben Fund Bonanza at Scunthorpe in March

this summer, represented Great Britain. Ayres leads coming out of turn two but Harris comes up the inside to pass him as they head into the straight at the end of lap one. Into the first corner of lap two and Ayres retakes the lead, sweeping around the outside, making full use of Belle Vue's always raceable surface. It's thrilling stuff and the Manchester crowd respond, willing the underdog to keep his nerve and win a race, which would be his first in such exalted company.

All goes well until the third bend of the final lap, when Danny wobbles and drifts wide. It looks like he's going to slide off but he manages to right the bike, only to have it jerk up wildly as he tries to control it. He's like a rodeo rider trying to control a bucking bull. While he manages to stay on the bike, he loses vital speed and Harris slips past on the inside to take first place. Ayres, visibly frustrated, crosses the line second.

'That's entertainment, folks. That's what speedway's all about,' says commentator Nigel Pearson, as thrilled as anyone to have witnessed what he's just seen.

The crowd rise to Danny Ayres, some consolation for him finishing second. But, as he'll say later, he really wanted that first place for someone special – his mother, Anne, who died in 2018 and who, it's clear from interviews he's done since, he still misses terribly.

A week later, with the kind of cruel luck for which speedway is notorious, Ayres breaks his leg racing for Mildenhall, his National League team. His season is over. But his exploits at the British Final haven't been forgotten. This year, 2020, he'll be racing, for the first time, in the top league of British speedway for Ipswich Witches. Scunthorpe have retained him for the Championship. Danny can't wait.

In *Speedway Star* he tells Phil Lanning he's targeting a podium spot at the British Final for the coming season. He still misses his mum but he's got a great partner and two lovely daughters.

Chatting to Scott Frame and Graham Muncie on the *Talk Speedway* podcast, Danny says he's very proud of what he's achieved but that it's only the start.

'To come round and see everyone on their feet applauding me at the end of heat 19 in the British Final just blows my mind. I can't thank everyone enough. I finished 11th overall but it was almost like I won it. I'm just clucking for more of that. I want more and I want it all the time. I was fully in the zone. It was like poetry, I just felt part of the bike.' Danny goes on to say that he felt so relaxed as he went into the final bends, he clipped the fence. He thought he was 'going into the old Belle Vue stadium', which is next to the new one. 'My arms are back and forth and then she started to go on the bucking bronco, but if you actually watch, I never shut off, which I think is what actually saved me. Then I realised the race was over and that's when I started thinking of my mum and the tears came out. That race will never leave my mind. This is what I thrive on now, to get that feeling.'

'The people's champion of speedway – Danny Ayres!' says presenter Scott Frame, wrapping up the *Talk Speedway* interview. 'I don't think you'll hear a more enthusiastic speedway rider taking part in the show.'

It's no surprise when Danny is the first to volunteer for the Ben Fund Bonanza in March.

* * *

Imagine you work as part of a department in, say, sales or customer care with half a dozen others. You're not the most important person in the team, but you're doing a decent enough job, pretty much what was expected of you. One of your colleagues isn't pulling their weight. Maybe they're struggling to keep up with their workload or they're always late, or their attitude is poor, or they're not hitting their sales targets.

One day, you're all called to a meeting to be told that your underperforming colleague won't be coming back. Somebody new is being brought in to replace them. But, as well as this, they're making another change and it's not great news for you. They're terribly sorry, it's no reflection on your work at all, really, but there's the door and thanks for all you've done.

Welcome to the world of the British speedway rider.

Now, it's important not to get carried away and think that these kind of summary dismissals happen all the time. They don't. But in the increasingly pressurised mid-season, when teams are focused on reaching 'those play-offs', team changes are made that have unfairly affected some middle-order or reserve riders. The reason? Speedway's famous – or infamous – points limit.

Remember that each rider will have a match average based on their finishing positions in each race. This changes every month, with the release of 'green sheets' reflecting how well – or badly – a rider is performing. Green sheets alter the shape of the side, with the top five averaged riders in the team going into the main body of the team, and the two lowest dropping to reserve. That's what normally happens.

But let's say it's the middle of the season and the team – let's call them team A – aren't firing on all cylinders. Their team average is at the permitted level, but one of their heat leaders is underperforming. Instead of delivering an expected nine-point average, he's down around 6.5. Then, for whatever reason, a rider becomes available who would be a good heat leader for team A. But let's say his average is high, around 9.5. The promoter of team A can't just swap him for the struggling heat leader because that would put them over the permitted overall team points limit. But if the promoter looks at his team and sees he's got a middle-order rider on 5, then there's a chance he can do something. If he takes out the middle-order rider and the underperforming heat leader together, there are 11.5 points to play with. That would allow him to bring in that top heat leader on 9.5 points and then look around for a young reserve on 2 points. It's a gamble – the young reserve won't score as many points as the solid middle-order rider – but getting that top heat leader into the team is often worth the risk. And so the change is made. The heat leader may well be expecting it, but not the middle-order rider, who suddenly finds himself out of a job because his average unfortunately fitted the bill for the promoter to make the change he wanted.

In these days of zero-hours contracts and the gig economy, we shouldn't be too surprised that speedway's version of this happens.

After all, if a rider isn't performing and is trailing in third or fourth in every heat he races, it's not just the promoter who'll want a change. Some fans will too. But it does seem unfair to those riders – whose livelihoods, after all, depend on being paid to race – who are doing more or less what was expected of them when they were signed.

So this month's news that British speedway is going to introduce a transfer window – in the Premiership at least, if not the other leagues just yet – is a positive step. Supporters like watching the same riders from week to week and season to season. The window now restricts clubs' opportunities to jettison riders willy-nilly and seems to be generally well received.

Being speedway, however, it's clear it's not going to be simple. There's no cut-off date – like the football transfer window closing at the end of January. Signings can now only be made after 25 per cent of Premiership fixtures and before 75 per cent are complete. But Rob Godfrey, in his role as BSPA chairman, is clear that clubs will have to be particularly careful when making signings and can't just make changes for the sake of it.

Cynics within the speedway community seize on the one exception to all this – 'subject to proven injury' – which they feel could offer a convenient escape route for promoters. But, even so, it's definitely a move in the right direction.

* * *

It's always dangerous to oversimplify but – with apologies to sponsors who we'll come to later – there are three key groups of people in speedway. First, there are the riders who earn their livelihoods – and risk them too – through the sport. Then there are the promoters and owners who put their own money on the line, hoping to attract enough fans to meetings to pay the bills and, ideally, have a bit left over at the end of the day. And then there are the fans who go along to speedway wanting to be entertained and watch good, competitive and exciting racing.

Every so often, those three groups' interests come together and, instead of harmoniously blending together, they produce a set of circumstances that satisfies no one and leaves those who don't follow speedway scratching their heads.

A prime example is the number of teams that speedway riders in Britain can race for. Go back to that *Downfall* video that was circulating online in autumn 2019 and you'll hear the problem highlighted several times because it's a real bugbear for many fans: 'How many riders out there are doubling-up?' (riding for more than one team regularly during the season); 'God damn guest riders' (riders from other teams who are brought in for one meeting to replace someone who's injured to make sure each side has a full team); 'Riders having three different teams' (it happened in 2019).

Forget any ideas that – like football or cricket or rugby – a rider will appear for just one team over the course of a season unless they're transferred during it. This is speedway, it's different and there are good reasons for it.

Even so, it still sometimes leaves the sport tying itself up in knots in a truly circular conundrum.

Where to start? Let's start with the need for guest riders – filling in for another team on a one-off basis – during the season. Go back to speedway being slightly different from other sports in that, from its very beginnings, it should provide entertainment. If you're a speedway fan and you head along to watch your team one evening, you're hoping you win of course. But you don't want to sit through a meeting where your team wins every heat easily and every race is pretty much over after the first bend. That's dull and hardly likely to tempt spectators to return or encourage much-needed media coverage. Both teams have to be competitive, in as much as they can be, so that each race will feature relatively evenly matched riders.

That's the theory, except speedway, as everyone knows, is a dangerous sport. Riders get injured. British speedway clubs can't afford – because of the economics of the sport – to have a squad of riders. They can't have substitutes sitting around on the off chance they might get to ride. Anyway, if a heat leader is injured, replacing him with a reserve will make the meeting uncompetitive.

Let's say a team has a heat leader who's averaging ten points a meeting but gets injured. The easiest option for a manager is, ahead of their next meeting, to choose another team's heat leader, someone who's not already booked to race elsewhere that night. They need to make sure that his average isn't higher than their injured rider's – that's not allowed – and they can then put him in their team for the meeting as a 'guest' rider. Basically, they're looking to replace like with like to make sure there's an entertaining meeting for spectators.

To a speedway fan, this has become the norm. To those outside the sport, it looks distinctly odd. As Josh Auty knows very well.

Josh has ridden in all three leagues of British speedway since 2005. He tells the story of how one of his friends went to Belle Vue. The friend had his photo taken with one of the home riders, the same Max Fricke whose fence-scraping exploits were featured in the pinned video on the Official British Speedway Twitter timeline for most of 2019. But then, when he was watching a few months later on TV, Josh's friend saw Fricke riding for another team. 'I thought he rode for Belle Vue?' he asked. Josh explained he was guesting, because of injury to one of the team's top riders, to keep the meeting competitive. To which his friend replied: 'That's a bit of a joke, isn't it? It's like Manchester United bringing Agüero in when Rashford's not fit for a game against Chelsea.'

Perhaps the most extreme case of using guests happened in June 2019. Scunthorpe, in the Championship, used Eastbourne's Alfie Bowtell as a guest for their home match against Sheffield. In the Sheffield team was Broc Nicol. Just a day later, Scunthorpe were away at Eastbourne. This time Bowtell was back racing for Eastbourne, his home club. Guesting for Scunthorpe for the night was Broc Nicol.

This is a particularly extreme example, but while it may seem odd, the alternatives are even less appealing. There's an option – which teams do choose – called 'rider replacement', which sounds simple but, particularly to a newcomer to the sport, is actually quite complicated.

It means that a team will turn up with six riders only and, in heats where the injured rider was programmed to appear, give one of them an extra ride. Their match average – apart from the rider directly above – has to be below that of the missing rider and they can only take one extra ride. Still with us? All it takes is one of those six riders to be injured during the meeting and the team will be down to five, which means that some races will have only three riders. Many people have tried to think of another way to make it work for British speedway, but no one has come up with a solution. It continues to perplex and frustrate spectators, as well as contributing to the Speedway Control Board's annual rules and regulations running to a hefty 178 pages.

This leads on to the issue of 'doubling-up', whereby someone will ride for a team in not just one league, but two – and, very occasionally, all three.

Listen to BT Sport commentator Nigel Pearson, commentating during October's Premiership Grand Final between Swindon and Ipswich. One of Swindon's reserves during the season, Ellis Perks, was also a middle-order rider with Leicester Lions in the Championship and a heat leader with the Leicester Lion Cubs in the National League. Pearson pointed out that he could win all three leagues in British speedway this season. He did. 'I know it sounds strange.' It is.

It's a situation that annoys speedway fans. As we've seen, it's another aspect that makes the sport hard for 'outsiders' to take seriously. Jim Lynch, the former Great Britain manager, says the worst thing to happen to British speedway was riders doubling-up at the top two levels. He never saw sense in it and thinks it led to a loss of identity.

Armed with the team sheets for all the competitive meetings staged in Britain during the 2019 season across the three leagues – Premiership, Championship and National League – I open up a spreadsheet to find out just how widespread doubling-up really is.

I discover that 178 different riders raced in British league speedway in 2019. Of that total, pretty much two-thirds – 119 – rode for more than one team on at least one occasion. The remaining 59 were strictly 'one-club' riders.

In the top league, the Premiership, exactly half of the 80 riders – 40 – rode for just one club. That includes former world champion Jason Doyle, who helped Swindon Robins win the double. At the other extreme, Scott Nicholls rode for five of the top league's seven clubs at some point. He began the season at Wolverhampton, filling in for an injured rider. Then, at the end of May, he moved to Peterborough. He also made two guest appearances for Poole and one each for Ipswich and Belle Vue, meaning the only two teams in the Premiership that Nicholls didn't race for were Swindon and King's Lynn.

In addition, of those 80 riders who appeared in the Premiership, nearly three-quarters – 58 – rode in the Championship and/or National League as well. Speedway in Britain, as currently configured, just wouldn't function if they didn't.

Ben Barker is a former Great Britain international who rides at both Premiership and Championship level. He began the season with Peterborough in the Premiership and Redcar in the Championship. He left Redcar after a few weeks and joined Scunthorpe. While with Peterborough in the Premiership, he made a guest appearance for Poole. In the Championship, over the course of the 2019 season, he made guest appearances for Berwick, Edinburgh, Glasgow, Newcastle and Somerset. That means that of the 11 teams competing in the Championship, Ben Barker rode for seven of them during the season.

This is not to criticise the likes of Ben Barker – who's the only rider to have appeared at every Ben Fund Bonanza – or Scott Nicholls or any of the other riders who have invested money in equipment, have free time and help ensure that spectators can watch a night of competitive racing. Riders need to earn a living and speedway careers are often short. Every so often – as happened with Workington – some clubs are late with payments or fail to pay at all. Riders will say there just aren't enough meetings to earn a living riding for one team. Chris Harris has said, with some justification, that he risks his life every time he goes out on a bike and if doubling-up was banned it wouldn't be worth it for what he would get out of it. Graham Drury, who rode in the 1970s, reckons he was riding as many as 150 meetings during one season. Today, a Grand Prix rider like Niels-Kristian Iversen, competing in Britain, Poland, Sweden and Denmark, can expect 80–90 meetings a season. A team in the Premiership or Championship probably has 40 meetings at most, with even fewer in the National League. As a result doubling-up, especially for those who don't have continental opportunities – and then adding in guest bookings whenever possible – is what many riders need to justify their investment.

For the coming season, of the 49 riders named in the seven Premiership squads, more than half – 30 – are already doubling-up for Championship teams. There aren't enough meetings for riders. Riders say costs keep going up but their pay is falling. There aren't enough teams to make up bigger leagues to provide those extra meetings. There are too few riders to go around the teams that do operate. There are even one or two, like Jack Smith and Adam Roynon, who do want to ride but can't because of the vagaries of the team points limit. Fans don't like seeing riders turning out for one team on one night and another the next. Fans like getting to know their riders but they also want to be entertained with good, close racing.

It's a conundrum with which British speedway continues to wrestle, a multi-dimensional Rubik's cube except without a solution to satisfy everyone.

* * *

Whisper it but, overall, January is a good month for British speedway. As well as the sensible introduction of the transfer window, it's announced that Newcastle – at risk of not running in the Championship back in November – will also run a team at the third level. While the Newcastle Gems will only compete in the National Trophy and not the league, it's a positive move, another opportunity for young riders. With Edinburgh having said they'll run a junior team – the Armadale Devils – and Kent confirming they'll still track their National League team despite their move up to the Championship, it means seven teams in the third league, just one fewer than in 2019.

There's cautious optimism elsewhere too. *Speedway Star*'s US correspondent – and current US Team co-ordinator – Steve Evans says he's pleased by the additions of former Grand Prix riders Nicki Pedersen (Sheffield) and Peter Kildemand (Belle Vue) and hopes that the new TV deal might encourage other big names to ride in Britain.

But, being speedway, there is always the odd hiccup where people who love the sport are left wondering what on earth is going on. Just such an example is the KO Cup draw for Championship sides. When the pairings were announced back in December, Edinburgh were drawn to face Poole in the first round. But now, with the full set of 2020 fixtures announced, Poole have mysteriously been moved straight into the second round to face Eastbourne. Newcastle – who'd originally had a bye into the second round – will take Poole's place in the first round against Edinburgh. Poole issue a statement, saying they'd requested the change due to a lack of available dates in the club's 'busy start-of-the-season campaign'. They'd held talks with Newcastle and agreement was reached. It means a couple of attractive 'local' meetings – Newcastle v Edinburgh and Poole v Eastbourne – will replace the original fixtures which, sort of, makes sense. But it does make you wonder why the original draw was made in the first place. It's a moment where speedway's lack of wider media scrutiny is a positive advantage.

But then it's not like other, bigger, better-financed sports are without their problems either. One look at the sports headlines in the middle of January proves that.

In rugby union, Saracens, boasting an array of England international talent, are to be relegated from the Premiership for their continued failure to bring salaries under an agreed cap. Already heavily fined and penalised 35 points for transgressions the year before, they've been unable to sort it out this season and other clubs have forced the league management's hand.

In football, after some poor FA Cup attendances and top clubs fielding reserve teams, there's more discussion of doing away with fourth-round replays to ease fixture congestion. Derby County face a fine and points deduction for financial irregularities around the sale of their Pride Park ground. There's also continued speculation around the future of some lower-league clubs, like Macclesfield Town, and whether they'll manage to get through the full season.

In the United States, the world of baseball is facing one of its biggest crises for decades. The 2017 World Series champions, the Houston Astros, have been found guilty of using illegal technology to 'steal signs' from their opponents during their winning season. That effectively means they'd had a hidden camera focused on the opposing team's catcher as he indicated – through a variety of hand movements – what kind of delivery he wanted his pitcher to throw next. Houston's general manager and team manager have been suspended from the game for a year by Major League Baseball, but Houston have taken their own action and sacked them. That's not all. Both the high-profile Boston Red Sox and New York Mets are now managed by individuals who were part of the illegal procedure back in 2017. Both are sacked from their positions as well. Baseball is reeling.

Given all that, perhaps British speedway isn't doing so badly after all?

February 2020 – Sunlight through dark clouds

FEBRUARY IS barely 20 hours old when there's truly shocking news. It's revealed on the Facebook page of Danny Ayres Racing, above a photo of Danny – thoughtful, focused – in his Mildenhall body colours.

'DANNY AYRES R.I.P.
We have some awful news to bring you.
There is no easy way to report this.
Danny has passed away.
His passing is tragic, extremely sad and very untimely.
To say we are shocked and devastated is an understatement.
Our thoughts and condolences are with Danny's family.'

Tributes – genuine, heartfelt and shocked – are made on social media. Online fundraising begins. Paul Ackroyd from the Ben Fund offers help and support to Danny's partner, Jodie Pledge, and their two young daughters, Lilou and Anaiya. The speedway community, as it always seems to do, does its best to look after its own in times of need.

While there's inevitably speculation about how he died, it is Jodie herself who releases a statement on Facebook two days later, confirming that Danny had 'lost his battle to mental health'. It's hard, in some ways, to equate this with the enthusiastic and effervescent character who had lit up the *Talk Speedway* podcast just a week earlier.

In his tribute in the following week's *Speedway Star*, columnist Phil Lanning reminds us of a feature he'd done with Danny just over a year ago. It wasn't – even at the time – your normal speedway interview. It was open, honest and raw, painfully so, in places. Now, knowing what has happened, it's achingly poignant. Danny talks of how he's suffered deeply from the loss of his mum, Anne, and how, for him, it's a daily battle. He begins to cry, admitting that he's been in a dark place since her death.

'I seek comfort all the time. I've got my mum's ashes made into a chain round my neck. It's got her date of birth, the day she passed away and her ashes in the back. Honestly, this is no word of a lie, when I feel like really s*** I grab it with my fingers and then all that hurt goes away. It is a very, very strange thing. I'm not a spiritual person but it's made the difference. I take comfort in that so much.'

The two-page feature ended with perhaps the most telling words of all when Danny talked about how he feels when he's riding his bike.

'Being like that is like me being the great pretender. I am brave when I've got the gear on, the suit, helmet and boots. I'm a different person, I'm more confident in myself, I feel invincible. It's my suit of armour. When I take my suit off, that's perhaps when life scares me a bit.'

Now, just over a year later, Lanning's elegantly written tribute reveals their last conversation.

'I spoke to him just six days before his untimely death and he said: "Oh mate, I'm absolutely buzzin' for the season to start." Yet just like that race at the British Final, and so many others, just when Danny appeared to have it all under control, he lost it at the very end.'

Danny's death will, very quickly, result in the formation of the 'Fuel Your Mind' organisation, aimed at providing support and advice for all speedway riders suffering from mental health issues. He's not the first and, sadly, won't be the last speedway rider – or sports performer – who struggles away from the sporting arena. It's a welcome development.

For now, there's just huge sadness that one of speedway's great showmen has gone just as he was ready to appear before a bigger and even more appreciative audience.

* * *

The terrible news about Danny Ayres – rightly – overshadows a small but significant announcement a few days later. Two track curators have been appointed to visit every speedway club across the three leagues to try and offer help and support on track preparation. It's a joint initiative from the BSPA – now known as the British Speedway Promoters Limited (BSP Ltd) – and the Speedway Control Board, and one that's widely welcomed. Rob Godfrey has been pushing for it to happen for some time.

'Your track is your performance stage. If your stage isn't very good, you fall through it and you crash. If your stage is very good then you've at least got a chance because most of the riders are racers and they want a track to race on. Of course, the weather might play a part but if you get the basics right then we've got a chance of every meeting being as good as the ones we see at Belle Vue or Scunthorpe. We've got a new media partner in Eurosport and we want the tracks to be as good as they possibly can because that has opened up a massive audience throughout Europe that can see what British speedway's about. Track inspectors have to go hand in hand with that.'

It's something that will likely be welcomed by Tai Woffinden. He's previously been critical of tracks in England, saying they're not as good, as well prepared or as safe as those in Poland and Sweden. He says his risk of getting injured is a lot higher. In *Raw Speed* he said it was like the hillbillies had prepared tracks in the UK and the professionals had done it in Poland and Sweden.

Not all speedway tracks are the same. There's no uniform design or size and Britain is famous for having smaller, trickier and more technical tracks. Edinburgh and Eastbourne are well known – and often not appreciated by visiting riders – for being small. Manchester's National Speedway Stadium is reckoned to have the best surface for racing and for providing visiting riders, who ride there much less frequently, a better chance of winning. Knowing your home track – how it's been prepared or, occasionally, if there's a hole to be avoided on one of the corners – can be a real advantage.

The four corners on a track can be different – in width or camber – and that's before getting down to the tricky issue of track preparation. Tracks used to be cinder but it's now shale that provides the surface grip. Too slick and there's no racing. Too dry and the spectators get covered in dust. Trying to decide when and whether to water the track – given the vagaries of the British summer – is one of the most difficult weekly decisions for any speedway club's track staff. Also crucial is the quality of the shale, something which has been, by many accounts, hard to source over the last few years.

While the appointments themselves won't guarantee exciting, safe and entertaining racing every week on British speedway tracks, they are most definitely another step in the right direction.

* * *

It is early February and Storm Ciara is about to lash much of Britain with rain and high winds. But, on this Saturday morning, there's a window of opportunity, certainly here in the south of England, for the budding speedway riders of tomorrow.

For most parents, ferrying their children around at the weekend means driving to football training or swimming or piano lessons. For the various parents dotted around the Rye House speedway track in Hertfordshire it involves often long journeys from different parts of the country to one of the few tracks where they can practise at speeds of up to 60 miles an hour. While league racing ended here in 2018, it's still used as a training track.

There are around 30 riders of varying ages – from the youngest who looks about eight to someone probably six times his age. There's a real range of abilities too. The current British Under-19 champion, Drew Kemp, is here and his practice laps are required viewing for many of those keen to emulate him. Several up-and-coming British riders – National League regulars or Championship reserves – are readily identified from the names on the back of their kevlars. There's one female rider amongst this morning's group.

Before arriving, I'd worried that it might be a bit disorganised, but I'm completely wrong. Riders are only allowed on the track in carefully selected groups according to their age and experience. There's a whiteboard by the track entrance where a man in a hi-vis jacket enthusiastically ushers riders on for their allotted number of laps.

The youngest rider – his helmet so big it looks like it might overbalance him, so small is the body underneath – takes to the track by himself and completes his laps without mishap, his father watching on.

Some of the riders gingerly take bends, others throw their bikes into the corners as if the 2020 season is already underway and this is their first real meeting.

There's a lot of shaking of heads as bikes are wheeled to the entrance gate and then turned back for some last-minute adjustment in the pits. There's also a great deal of parental assistance, pushing riders off on their bikes, tightening their helmet straps or slapping their backs for good luck. And there are more cans of trade-size WD-40 than I've ever seen, which come in useful when bike chains need lubricating.

Most of those here are – noticeably – fathers rather than mothers, although I spot a few girlfriends watching from the small stand by the first corner, their eyes flicking from the track to their phones with practised ease. Over to the right, a few hundred yards away, is the Rye House Kart Raceway where Lewis Hamilton began his motorsport career. But that's not who these speedway youngsters are aiming to emulate.

In charge of it all is Peter Schroeck, a 53-year-old German who rode for Rye House in 1988 and 1989 and who now also manages King's Lynn in the Premiership. He's been running training schools for four years. 'Passionate' is a much overused word, but if anyone feels that way about developing young riders, it's Peter Schroeck.

He says a lot of youngsters who come to speedway realise that with the right nurturing, environment and direction they could, in the long run, make a living out of it, as well as enjoying what they're doing. 'There are lots of gains to being a speedway rider. But we need to build what's going to happen in England for the future. The Jason Doyles of this world won't be around for the next ten years.'

He thinks there's a real need to look after those young riders as and when they do break into league teams. 'I'm quite big on getting youngsters – not total rookies – coming through and getting experience as reserves in the top teams. I believe you are the people you mix with and it'll make you stronger. Not everybody's going to succeed, but you've got to give these kids the opportunities they deserve without any pressure otherwise we'll have no growth in the long run.'

Peter says too many promoters simply build their teams to 'win, win, win'. He points to a few youngsters last year who'd started off at reserve and done well. They then moved up to the number-two position in the team, where they faced tougher opponents and, because they weren't scoring the points they had before, they struggled and ended up being replaced. He says it can put them back another six months. Peter's careful not to mention any names but I'm thinking of Drew Kemp, who was dropped by Sheffield before making a successful debut for Great Britain at King's Lynn back in October.

He goes on to talk about two riders who'd come to him at Rye House specifically to get their confidence back. 'They don't know what they've done wrong. You don't turn into a bad rider overnight. Everybody needs different treatment; some need pushing, others you need to leave alone. It's a tough game. There's no other sport where, in 60 seconds, you have to make decisions so quickly. Riders don't turn up to have a bad night, they want to do well. When things don't go well, that's when you have to be strong as a team manager to make sure they're going to come through the meeting. Because otherwise it defeats them for the long run.'

Something that you hear frequently from some fans is that there are too many foreign riders in British speedway. Peter, a German, would agree. He says overseas riders are sometimes brought into teams for a year but then their average doesn't fit and they're not seen again.

'What is the point in building an asset base like that when you have kids over here who would love to have a go at it? Not everybody's going to make it as a speedway rider, but we want them to have the experience.'

That certainly seems to be the case this Saturday morning, with all the riders – whatever level they're at – looking ahead to the new season in just a few weeks.

* * *

Dave Tattum is packing up at Loomer Road. He and a couple of helpers are at the stadium every day, collecting their things and trying to get a bit of money in return. It's early February and work to knock the stadium down hasn't started yet. Surveys have been carried out for all sorts of things – bats, noise and pollution. But Dave assures me that it will be demolished. 'It's not going to lie empty.'

He says there's been a backlash over the decision to sell the stadium. 'There's a lot of stick, a lot of things being reported by people who don't really know the circumstances. The owners have put their money into it, they've kept the stadium alive and allowed me to do what I want for 20-odd years. It's theirs, they deserve to sell. It's privately owned by a family, who are all 60 or more. It's time for them to cash in their chips and go.'

Then he puts his finger on one of the biggest threats to British speedway's future, the fact that the great majority of promoters are dependent on other stadium owners. 'I've been paying rent for 30 years here, one way or another. I could perhaps have bought it. We knew, for the last ten years, that it was up for sale. There was never any secret made of it. If anyone was really interested in investing in the stadium, they should have come ten years ago. Maybe we should have looked at motorsports' stadiums and put some kind of protection on them. But, obviously, we didn't think that far ahead, did we?'

Although he says he can't see speedway in Stoke again, it's clear he's not given up entirely. 'One or two people have messaged me and made various suggestions. There's still plenty of ground up for sale surrounding the Britannia Stadium, Stoke City's ground. We sit on 16 acres here at Loomer Road so you'd really want a minimum of 12 acres. Someone rang me and told me to get hold of the people who've got the land. I spoke to the estate agent. They were very nice. One of them said he'd read about us and they did have spare land. But they wouldn't want a speedway stadium being built down here. I said please don't get the wrong idea about speedway people, we're not the leather-clad and what-have-you sorts. We're nice ordinary people. He said, no, they wouldn't want it because they've got some classy places there, a lot of car garages and main manufacturers. Anyway, I asked how much the ground would be. He said it would be anywhere between £250,000 and £350,000. That's per acre. One acre. We want a minimum of 12. That's three million pounds at least. And all you've got for that is a flat piece of land.'

He did genuinely think it was the end of his involvement in speedway when Stoke closed. But his wife, Bente, knew better. 'I thought that was it for Dave Tattum and speedway. It was goodnight, like. And my wife kept saying, "No, you won't be out of it, one or two of them will be wanting you." And I'll help where I can. When I saw Newcastle needed help back in November, I thought Rob Grant would be in without a shadow of a doubt. Granty rode for me at Stoke and we've always stayed in touch during his time out of speedway. So I rang him up and said, "Newcastle?" And he said, "I've already done it!" I said, "Brilliant!" And he said, "I want you to come with me." And I said, "Bloody hell, Rob, like!" I said I'd do what I can to help because he's going to do a brilliant job. I think he's awoken a sleeping giant up in Newcastle and I hope the supporters get behind him. There aren't many speedway clubs around now and we need to protect the Newcastles and get behind the Rob Grants, don't we, like?'

* * *

Paradise Wildlife Park in Hertfordshire is a popular animal and amusement park. It's also the location of the National Speedway Museum – not, admittedly, the most obvious place for a collection of motorsport memorabilia. Yet, it's perfectly fitting given the fact the whole complex is run by former speedway rider Pete Sampson.

If you ever meet Pete and ask him about his career as a speedway rider, he'll be sure to tell you that he wasn't that great – 'Joe average' is how he describes himself.

But if his six-year career – which took him from Rye House in 1959 to Swindon in 1965 via Rayleigh, Newcastle and Swindon – isn't, in his eyes, worth spending much time discussing, what he's helped bequeath to the speedway world since then certainly is.

Pete has had a successful and wide-ranging career, building up a coach hire business and then setting up Paradise Wildlife Park – the Zoological Society of Hertfordshire – near Broxbourne. In a purpose-built building, in the same 30-acre complex as Sumatran tigers, meerkats and three-banded armadillos, is a treasure trove of speedway memories.

Setting it up here sounds perfectly reasonable when Pete talks about it. He was born about 500 yards from Rye House – 'it's a tragedy there's no speedway there anymore' – which is less than five miles away from the wildlife park across the A10. It's also just 15 miles away from High Beech in Epping Forest, where speedway in the UK started back in 1928.

'I had this piece of ground and I got to know George and Linda Barclay. They kept on at me that they wanted to do a speedway museum but there was nowhere to put it. I offered to do something here.' George and Linda went around tracks raising money. 'I didn't think it would happen but I said, "If it does, I'll match-fund it in some shape or form." George and Linda worked their socks off and raised about £30,000 and we supplied labour and materials to get it built.' The museum opened at the end of April 2007.

There are three of us sitting in Pete's office on the first floor of the park's Discovery Centre. We're joined by Bert Harkins, a former speedway rider who enjoyed international success in the 1960s and rode in two World Individual Finals. Bert is chairman of the World Speedway Riders' Association, which oversees the museum.

Pete will be 81 this year but doesn't look it. With a full head of near shoulder-length hair, he's more the keyboard player of a still-touring prog rock band from the 1970s than someone who was born three weeks after Britain declared war on Germany in 1939. Bert, just hitting 80 this year, doesn't look his age either. I'm left wondering if speedway – assuming you survive it on the track – keeps you young.

There are few signs of speedway in Pete's office. Instead there are lots of photos of animals at the park, which is clearly his number-one passion. Bert points to a photo on one of the shelves of Pete holding a tiger cub. The Wildlife Park raises and sends animals back to the wild, which Pete describes as 'a lifeboat' for endangered species. Two lionesses have gone back to Uganda and they're involved in a programme to send leopards to the Russian far east.

Unsurprisingly, for two former riders who experienced a more buoyant period in the sport's history, both Pete and Bert have their own views on what's wrong with speedway today.

Pete is forthright and blunt. 'Speedway today? I wouldn't know where to start, if I'm honest. Unless someone sits down and changes it, it's going to disappear. Or it needs to go back to basics, amateurs, and start again. You've got to create a new, younger audience.

'Modern-day speedway is all about fast engines and wheel-spin. They've all got the same style, it's all a bit follow-the-leader. Even the top riders, even Tai Woffinden, if he's third it's hard for him to get past. Tracks have become very slick, racing has become, to a certain extent, boring. They took away the smells, too. They've got silencers on them now so some of the noise has gone. I think the social part has gone as well. In the old days, riders would have a drink afterwards. Now they're off at the end of the meeting.'

Bert agrees. 'I think with the second halves [extra heats after the main meeting] people could watch a local novice wobbling around and then they could see him improve. Each year they could follow their progress. Plus, you kept pretty much the same riders in the team each year. You only changed one or two.'

Pete's also not a fan of that guest system where teams borrow another team's rider for the night to ensure they track seven riders. 'You never get this in football. If Arsenal are a bit weak for whatever reason, they go and borrow two from Tottenham? How does that work? One minute they're in your team, the next they're in the other.'

Bert throws in the quality of riders in the British leagues. 'Nearly all the top riders ride abroad, they don't ride here anymore. It used to be you needed to ride in Britain to become good enough to be world champion.'

The lack of regular meetings also annoys Pete. 'You need consistency. Most football clubs play at home once a fortnight minimum. Sometimes twice if they've got a midweek game. Rye House, when they were in the Premier League, went five weeks without a meeting. Then they had to squeeze five meetings into two weeks. People can't afford that. So crowds go down and down.'

Bert thinks modern speedway bikes – laydowns – aren't necessarily better than the old upright designs he and Pete used to ride. 'We used to ride in the wet with the old upright bikes and they'd put sawdust down. The laydowns are easier to ride in many ways on tracks that are slick, but if you get a bit of dirt, they pick up and take off and the riders can't control them. With the laydowns, you've got all that extra exhaust and engine that can hit somebody compared with the old uprights.'

But it's not all doom and gloom. Bert's still keen to go and see speedway and is a frequent visitor to the Rye House training schools. He reckons we've got a lot of good, young riders coming through. 'They're starting to ride at ten, 11 years of age. Some of these little kids, they're so fast. They're coming down the straight, pitching it sideways, right into the corner, not wobbling around at all.'

They're hopeful that speedway might resume at Rye House. Pete says they're trying to convince the owner of the site to reopen and run a league side. 'They should call it London Speedway,' he says, given there's no one else likely to claim that name.

It confirms what the BSP Ltd chairman Rob Godfrey has said in *Speedway Star*, that new leaseholders at Rye House want to see speedway return there. A big investment is being made at the stadium to make it multi-purpose and Rob has been assured speedway will be returning at some point, hopefully this season. He's hopeful of granting Rye House an open licence to allow challenge matches later in the season with a view to a Championship team racing in 2021.

It sounds, on the face of it, like really positive news. If it's not quite returning the sport to London, it's the next best thing.

* * *

I'm sure Bert Harkins has shown a few people around the National Speedway Museum over the years, but his genuine enthusiasm for pointing out exhibits on display hasn't dimmed one bit. There's one full-time, paid member of the team and a couple of volunteers including Bert.

The museum is in a single-storey, steel building roughly 45 feet by 40 feet. While there are a few private speedway collections around – I've been told about another excellent one run by former rider Ian Paterson at Loanhead near Edinburgh called 'From Cinder to Shale' – they're not always open to the public. The National Speedway Museum is open Thursday to Sunday during the summer and on special speedway event days at the park.

As we head in we pass some mementoes from long-gone speedway tracks: part of the Exeter fence from the County Ground stadium, which – built of solid metal – was a fearsome hazard in itself; a turnstile from Wimbledon; the tractor from Wembley Stadium used to re-grade the track between races – recently named 'Arthur' after its legendary promoter, Sir Arthur Elvin.

Inside, there's a veritable cornucopia of speedway memorabilia, including Douglas and Rudge machines from the earliest British speedway meetings at High Beech in 1928; a workshop with a rider working on his bike; a Japanese speedway rider's goggles (I didn't know there had ever been a Japanese speedway rider) made of wire mesh instead of plastic; team bibs and body colours aplenty – Barrow, Norwich, Exeter – and helmets too. Then moving through to the modern era's world champions: Sam Ermolenko's leathers and bike; a Grand Prix body colour of Greg Hancock – a real star of the sport for the last 30 years who's just announced his retirement at the age of 50; Jason Doyle's pit board from the British Grand Prix in Cardiff last year.

It's not the biggest museum in the world but it doesn't need to be. 'We have a lot of stuff. We keep running out of space,' says Bert.

As we walk round, Bert tells me about how he got into speedway. 'I grew up in Govan fire station in Glasgow because my dad was a fireman. It was just down the road from White City speedway at Paisley Road West and on a Wednesday night you could hear all the bikes roaring – before they had silencers. That attracted me and my dad took me along. I got hooked on it after that.' He never rode for Glasgow – apart from a single guest appearance – because at the time he started riding only Edinburgh were operating in Scotland. When Glasgow did reopen, he says he wasn't asked. He was established in the Edinburgh team and decided to stick with them.

Close your eyes, and Bert's voice has the same story-telling lilt to it as Billy Connolly's. Which isn't surprising, as Connolly's birthplace of Anderston is just across the River Clyde from where Bert grew up.

When he shows me the older speedway bikes, he's in his element. 'When I first saw speedway, all the bikes were like this. All chrome – mudguards, handlebars and chrome wheels. Underneath the track lights at nighttime it would all sparkle and create a tremendous atmosphere. Now you've got fibreglass and it doesn't quite sparkle in the same way.'

Safety has – thankfully – improved since Bert was riding. He picks up an old back protector which, to me, looks decidedly flimsy. Bert tells me it's made of sponge and offered some protection. 'I broke my back at Wimbledon – several vertebrae got broken – and I had this on, which saved me, otherwise I think I'd have been in a wheelchair. Now the modern ones are so much better. They've got this as a base and then they've got a hard shell on the outside.'

We're about to head for the exit but I hear Bert's voice behind me. 'Don't forget the tartan guy up there!'

Bert was famous for wearing glasses and tartan leathers and he proudly points to his own display up above us featuring his last bike, those tartan leathers and a succession of tartan-tinted helmets along with a pit sign warning 'Beware low-flying haggis', 'Haggis' being one of Bert's nicknames when he was riding.

'I think I invented those "See You Jimmy" hats. I should have got the commission!'

We look at a display showing that Bert and his partner, Jim McMillan, got to the World Speedway Best Pairs Final riding for Scotland in 1970 and finished fourth. 'We beat England actually, which was quite nice,' he says proudly. I reflect that there was one Scottish-born rider in the whole of speedway last year. The Scottish international team, like so much around us, a thing of the past.

There are, undoubtedly, grander museums devoted to a single sport. The National Football Museum in Manchester or those 'halls of fame' in the United States devoted to baseball or American Football. They're bigger and grander and flashier because sponsors and corporations have contributed. But there is something far more genuine about the National Speedway Museum.

It may be tucked away behind Pirate Cove and Wolves in the Wood in a wildlife park in Hertfordshire. But there's genuine pride in the way it's been put together and looked after.

* * *

The media loves big, round anniversaries. The bigger and rounder the better. 100 years, a centenary, is excellent, as are quarter centuries – 25, 50 and 75. A tenth anniversary is good and 20's not too shoddy either.

Ninety-two? Not so much.

That probably explains why there aren't many reporters or TV crews thronging the 92nd anniversary of speedway on the last Sunday in February at Paradise Wildlife Park. In fact, other than various representatives from *Speedway Star*, I'm not sure there's any other press here.

The World Speedway Riders' Association (WSRA), the body hosting the annual event, has changed over the years. Originally, its strict rules allowed only ex-riders to join after they'd been retired for eight years. But that didn't work because most had drifted away from the sport by then. 'The hardest thing is getting current-day riders to join,' said Pete Sampson when I'd asked him about it. So they opened it up to anyone who is a speedway supporter to keep the organisation alive. Let me declare an interest; I am now a member, despite never having sat on – or indeed wanted to sit on – a speedway bike.

They say they usually get 1,500 to 2,000 at their celebration of speedway event, and they also host a spring and August lunch and then a gala dinner in Leicester in November with awards. It all helps to raise funds for the WSRA and allows them to buy bikes and other items for the museum.

I'd asked Pete if it was easy to get young people along. He'd shaken his head and told me that the average age of those attending the celebration of speedway event is 68.

Today the museum is packed. While not everyone is 68, there aren't too many who'd be able to tell you that The Weeknd and Billie Eilish have been scrapping it out for number one in this week's UK singles charts.

The day itself is grey and blustery. The overflow car park is in operation from early on and while not everyone has come for the speedway – it's the end of the schools' half-term week – there's a good crowd.

As well as the museum, there are stalls selling old programmes, books and speedway memorabilia in the marquee building. I spot a special pile – 'Last ever at Loomer Road'. That final-meeting programme at Stoke last September has already become part of speedway history.

Outside, there are a dozen or so stalls set up by clubs – Peterborough, the Isle of Wight, the Kent Kings and the long-lost Reading Racers – along with engine and equipment manufacturers. There's much talk during the day of the past, of old engines and old tracks. At the top of every hour, a group of men of a certain age crowd around to see a parade of old bikes – Javas, GMs and the like – cranked up once more for our benefit. There's noise and smoke and, best of all, an unmistakable smell of methanol. I join them for the two o'clock session when Martin Yeates, a rider from the 1980s, fires up one of his bikes for the first time in 20 years, according to the master of ceremonies. We all enjoy a few minutes of standing very close to real bikes and, most importantly of all, savouring the smell as keenly as if it's freshly baked bread. Like many others, I suspect, I'm taken back to my first days of attending speedway.

But it's not just about the past. There's discussion – positive chat too – about the new season. Another big name has been tempted to return to British speedway. Jason Crump is a three-time world champion. He retired in 2012 and is now 44 years old, so his prime years are definitely behind him. Think of it as David Beckham returning to the Premier League. But he's a name that resonates beyond the speedway world if my wife, who's not that interested in speedway, is anything to go by. Crump had turned out for the Australian team over the winter at short notice and has clearly rediscovered the riding bug. He'll be at Ipswich this season.

When I drive off in the afternoon, I listen to the radio news. There's an update on the 30 Britons now in quarantine on the Wirral after being flown back from a coronavirus-infected cruise ship in Japan. But I'm not thinking about that. Instead, I'm enjoying the sunshine breaking through the February clouds, hoping this might just be a metaphor in some way for the coming speedway season.

* * *

When I catch up with Tom Bacon he's in Mâcon, a city in the east-central part of France. Every year, Tom arranges to hire a track for six or seven riders to head down for two days of pre-season practice. This year the group includes two of his new team-mates at the Kent Kings – Scott Nicholls and Rob Ledwith – who are taking advantage of the slightly more favourable weather further south.

Tom's recovered well from having the metalwork in his back removed and he's been able to ride six times this year already. 'To be feeling healthy in February, for me, is a good start to the year.'

He's lucky in that he has another job outside speedway – working four days a week – which is flexible and can fit in with his riding career. When he broke his back in 2018, he needed some work over the winter and found a job at a local company, which he's carried on since. Because he's only racing for one team, he'll continue to work for them as well as race. It's an office-based job in Leamington Spa and he works a couple of days there and a couple from home doing account management and dealing with customers. He says it wouldn't be what he was doing if he wasn't racing.

Tom's love of speedway means he's keen to do his bit for the sport whenever he can. He'd given up his previous Sunday to travel down from Coventry to man Kent Kings' stand at the 92nd anniversary event at Paradise Wildlife Park. He's also volunteered for the Ben Fund meeting at Scunthorpe in March. He agrees that it's disappointing that not all riders do.

'The Ben Fund, as a cause, is fantastic for riders. Especially for me, starting a bit later in the sport, it's very difficult to find any private insurance if you're hurt. When speedway becomes your main source of income between March and October and you get injured, it's very difficult. We still have bills to pay and a life to live outside speedway and, all of a sudden, your earnings are stopped. When I broke my back last year, I was very grateful for the collection that the Redcar fans did and the support I've had from the Ben Fund because injuries really impact your earning ability.'

There are no set wages in speedway. It's up to the rider – and his club – to agree what's in their contract. 'Some people, if they score no points at all, will earn absolutely nothing. Some people will be on a three-point guarantee or a set-money guarantee. In speedway, you work for yourself, so you negotiate your own contract. Points, pay, any guarantee, if you're going to get a tyre, if you're going to get any contribution towards oil or fuel and what you're going to get paid per mile for travel.'

While a new bike can cost as much as £10,000, a lot of riders build one from kit or parts and buy someone else's engine. 'Moving to Kent, I needed a second engine so I bought a totally new one. I've obviously paid for it so a lot of your outgoings are before the season, building new bikes and things like that, and then you look to earn it back.'

But it's the upkeep of a speedway bike where the cost really comes from. 'Every meeting, it's new oil, new tyre, new clutch plates – that's before replacing anything that's broken. Then after around 36 or 40 races, I'll send my engine to be serviced. It's a bit like driving your car for 40 minutes and then it needs a service. You can see how the costs mount up.'

Sponsors are 'incredibly important'. Tom says he has around ten who vary in size and in what they do, from product sponsors to those who offer financial support. He also has a support team; his dad – who is his mechanic, driver, mentor, 'everything really' – and another mechanic, Brian, who comes to every meeting with them.

Despite his two broken backs in the previous two seasons, Tom is remarkably phlegmatic about his hopes for the new season. 'Staying injury-free is never one of my targets. It's not something I focus on. If it happens, it happens and there's nothing you can do about it. My main aim is to carry on progressing as I have. Every year my average has improved and remember, I haven't actually been riding that long compared to a lot of people. All I want to do is show people what I'm capable of and hopefully improve as much as I know I can.

'A move into the Premiership at some point would definitely be the aim; I did three guest bookings near the end of 2018 and I scored well. I guested for Wolverhampton three times, was paid for eight points and won a race. I thought the chance would come last year but then I got injured. That's definitely the aim for this year; ride as well as I can and put myself in the shop window.'

It all sounds really positive. No one's to know that many shop windows – both real and figurative – are about to have their shutters pulled down in a way no one has ever experienced before.

March 2020 – Lockdown

LISTEN TO those involved in British speedway on the eve of the 2020 season and there's real optimism. For a sport well used to beating itself up over its deficiencies, it's refreshing – and unusual. Alex Harkess, who's been involved in speedway for more than 30 years and, being Scottish, isn't one for unnecessary exaggeration, believes speedway has 'turned the corner a wee bit. We've a lot more youngsters in the pipeline and I'm more positive than I have been for the last couple of years.' Olly Allen, the co-manager of the Great Britain team, thinks there's the biggest feel-good factor in British speedway for a long time. He and Simon Stead have held a couple of training session weekends over the winter involving a young Great Britain squad. They've done fitness testing, team building and track days too. There's a test match coming up at Glasgow in April and the Speedway of Nations – speedway's main international team tournament – at Belle Vue in May to look forward to.

More generally, there's excitement about the big names returning to British league speedway for the first time in years. As well as Nicki Pedersen and Jason Crump, former Grand Prix rider Peter Kildemand will be riding for Belle Vue. Niels-Kristian Iversen – a current Grand Prix rider – is at Peterborough. It's not just the new arrivals that excite Rob Godfrey, the chairman of the BSP Ltd. He's looking forward to the new television contract with Eurosport, highlights on a Saturday morning on free-to-air channels for the first time, and more meetings and more local derbies in the 12-team Championship. The new season is only a few days away, with the Ben Fund meeting at Scunthorpe kicking things off on 14 March.

Two of the top British riders, Danny King and Steve Worrall, agree there's a real buzz around the sport ahead of the new season. Scott Frame sums it up on the *Talk Speedway* podcast in early March, talking to his co-host Graham Muncie.

'You know what, Graham? I'm excited, I'm excited! I normally try and get a practice session in somewhere where you can hear the bikes and smell the smell. I am buzzing for this season to start, buzzing.'

In many ways, it's not surprising there's not much attention, at the very start of the month, to what's happening in the wider world. Coronavirus has become a concern – the number of deaths has been rising and it's now reached other parts of Europe. But, remembering SARS, MERS, bird flu and other exotic diseases that failed to live up to some of the dire warnings predicted for them, the great majority of us carry on as if coronavirus – or COVID-19 as it'll come to be known – will be just another Asian-based virus that will somehow pass by all of us here in Britain. Official advice at the start of March basically means washing your hands while singing 'Happy Birthday' twice.

Any impact on speedway is, initially, focused on whether it will stop riders from Italy – where there's currently a worrying surge in both deaths and hospital admissions – racing in Britain in 2020. While there's talk of large public gatherings possibly being banned by the Government, few think this would affect speedway. On the *British Speedway Forum*, there's wry humour that most crowds simply aren't big enough to qualify. One correspondent is more concerned about how much of the fan base will be left after the 'lergie' has been and gone.

* * *

Josh Auty has spent much of the winter planning his testimonial, which is now just a few weeks away on Sunday, 22 March. While having your own meeting sounds attractive, not least financially, putting it together has meant a lot of work.

'The weather has worried me a bit but there's absolutely no point worrying about that because I can't control it. I've been getting on and doing the best I can, meeting new sponsors, trying to give them a package that's good for us. I've been blown away by the support I've got from them. Scunthorpe's a really close-knit community and they are genuinely really nice, hard-working people. It has been a privilege serving them for the last nine seasons. I've virtually organised it myself in terms of trophies getting picked up, sorting out the medical cover, hospitality for sponsors, race jackets, rider mementoes, stuff for the volunteers. You name it, I've done it all.'

Amongst all that he's had to do, the most stressful turns out to have been getting all the content for the programme. He says it's taken quite a bit of time because he's determined to get all the detail absolutely correct.

His testimonial has attracted some big names – current British champion Charles Wright and former British champions Danny King and Chris Harris among them. According to Auty, with typical northern understatement, his line-up's 'decent'. He's sceptical that everyone who has said they'll turn up actually will. 'Some lads will pull out last minute. I'm kind of bracing myself for the call. Riders have been pretty good to deal with. Some of them have decided to ignore me, which is fine, you know, if that's what they want to do. Others have been brilliant.'

In between organising his testimonial, he's been picking up jobs over the winter.

'I've been doing any work that I can find. I was working at a scrapyard and then did quite a bit of warehouse work over Christmas. Then I was doing two days a week general labouring at a sponsor's, which was good. But I would say late January, things weren't moving quite as quickly as I wanted with my testimonial so I stopped working then and everything's been absolutely flat out to get sorted.'

Talk to him about his targets for the season and his answer is typically down-to-earth. 'I want to stay number one at Scunthorpe. If I get, like, an eight and a half, nine-point average including bonus points, that will be a good solid season again. I don't know what my average was for last season, to be honest. I think it was just above eight including bonus points, which is a steady season. It dipped a little bit due to my away form, which wasn't good enough. But when you're doing all the driving yourself and you're a one-man band, don't expect me to bang in 15-point maximums.'

Josh, like many riders, is worried about rising costs. He says the higher up you go, the more you need to spend to be able to compete. But the income that can be generated isn't worth the cost. He describes it as a catch-22 situation.

'For me, if I was to get a doubling-up spot this season with a Premiership team, I'd probably turn it down because financially I haven't got the operation to be competitive at that level. Why should I bust my gut washing my own bikes and driving myself everywhere and then taking another team place when my scores for Scunny would suffer because I'd be burned out? The guys who are doing the best out of speedway at the moment are the engine tuners. They're charging £350 labour to strip a motor down and build it back up. They can do that in a day and if they do five in a week, they're earning more than the riders.'

We speak on Wednesday, 11 March. I don't ask Josh about coronavirus even though, by now, it's not just the elephant sitting in the room, but one that's juggling buns and blowing a trumpet to attract attention. Without being aware of what's about to happen – no one is – Josh says he does worry about where speedway is going. If it shuts down tomorrow, it shuts down. That's it.

'And I'd have to move on and do something else.'

* * *

By the following day, however, things – globally – are about to take a decidedly noticeable turn for the worse. In the United States, President Donald Trump declares a national emergency. The US actor, Tom Hanks, has revealed he has the virus, which seems to have concentrated minds. In Britain, Arsenal's manager, Mikel Arteta, tests positive too, prompting renewed calls for a shutdown of Premier League football. Prime Minister Boris Johnson is to hold an evening news conference where, against the backdrop of 32 COVID-19-related deaths in the UK, he'll outline the 'delay' phase of his policy, urging anyone with a new, continuous cough or a high temperature to self-isolate for seven days. Scotland's First Minister, Nicola Sturgeon, goes further, saying she'll ban gatherings of more than 500 people from the start of the following week.

I speak to Rob Godfrey on the Thursday afternoon, before the Prime Minister's news conference. He's recovering from a bad bout of flu – and, in the current circumstances, he's keen to stress it was just flu. 'I was in the office sneezing like mad and I said to my wife, Gail, if I was in London, I'd get shot for that. But I've got flu! I haven't got coronavirus. I've no intention of catching it. We're up north and we sort of think we're distant from it.'

But he's realistic about what might happen.

'Saturday's Ben Fund meeting is safe. The Government had a meeting on Monday. Contrary to the press, there were no governing bodies allowed to go, it was down to media people like Eurosport, BT and Sky. We had representation through Eurosport. The Government – at that point – was saying there was no need to stop any big events. You've seen the horse racing at Cheltenham going ahead with thousands of people attending. So, short term, I don't think there will be a problem.'

He's less confident about Josh Auty's testimonial later in the month, saying they've got to take it one week at a time at the moment. 'I've never known anything like this. It's unprecedented and there's nothing that's really comparable. I just hope predictions that it will peak in two months are right and we will be past it. China is now at the point where it's got 15 cases a day, down from thousands, so they're pretty much out of the water now. They're swimming now, not sinking, so we've got to hope that the same happens for us.'

Rob points out how speedway's low crowds – often a source of concern – might actually be an advantage. 'Because we don't get massive crowds like football does, hopefully we'll slip under the radar and be able to continue the season. If there are any guidelines and it's 5,000 and below, we should be okay. It depends what kind of numbers are set on gatherings. I suspect the Government has no answer. It's a massive balancing act, the economy against this virus, allowing people to go to work but telling them they can't do this and they can't do that. At this point, we can only react to what the Government tell us we have to do.'

But he does admit it could potentially disrupt the whole season. 'I read today that Denmark's been locked down so there could be Danish riders not riding in our league if they're stuck at home. We all read about coronavirus in China but unfortunately we didn't react early enough and close our own borders. It's going to affect us all.

'Listen, it's annoying me now because it was billed to be one of our better seasons and, at this point, it could be one of the worst seasons we've ever had. The Ben Fund meeting on Saturday? That could be the only meeting we'll see, I don't know. I really don't know.'

He pauses and tries to look for the positives.

'It'll be alright, I'm sure it will be alright. We'll use the northern mentality, it will be alright.'

* * *

There probably aren't too many people who regularly make the journey to Scunthorpe from Oxford. The university city on one of the major tributaries of the Thames and the industrial town in Lincolnshire symbolise, in many ways, the different extremes of life in the United Kingdom in 2020. Oxford, built on its centuries-long reputation as a global centre of academic excellence, thrives. Scunthorpe, a town that symbolises 'left-behind' Britain as the remains of its once-prosperous steelworks lurch from one foreign owner to another, struggles. But the journey from one to the other is one that Rob Peasley, the one-time Oxford speedway fan, makes pretty much every week from March through October. It's one he's making today – Saturday, 14 March. The reason? His love of speedway.

For a Friday evening meeting, he's got the journey down to a fine art, leaving around three o'clock to make sure he arrives for the half past seven start. He can recite his journey as if he's a London cabbie in the middle of 'the Knowledge', their three-year intensive training course.

He purposely avoids the M40, because that's a bad idea on a Friday afternoon, and instead takes the back route onto the A43 and then the M1. 'The M1 itself isn't that bad now because they've finally finished those 50mph roadworks, but you still don't want to be on it too long, so basically at junction 21A, you come off onto the A46. You almost drive past Leicester speedway. The A46 is a really good piece of dual carriageway. It's fairly new and, importantly for a Friday, it's fairly clear. If I'm ever running behind, I've basically got that stretch of the A46 where I can catch up a bit of time. Then it's onto the A15 at Lincoln, which is single carriageway. It's a great road, it's almost 20 miles, but you don't want to get stuck behind something going slow. Then you come off it and take the back roads to Scunthorpe up by the steelworks. That's what I've found best. And if something's blocked I do know a lot of the back routes and other ways to go. I've been told that, coming up from Oxford, I probably know the North Lincolnshire roads better than the locals do!'

Rob doesn't go just to watch the Scunthorpe Scorpions at the Eddie Wright Raceway. He's one of the many volunteers who help keep the sport going. Whether it's helping out in the car park, selling programmes or raffle tickets or being in charge of the riders at the starting tapes, volunteers are vital for speedway. Rob works unpaid, running Scunthorpe's communications as press officer.

His association with Scunthorpe came about like this. After his beloved Oxford closed – and he'd had his disappointing trip to Coventry – Rob really disliked speedway. 'Goodness knows why I carried on going to it, to be honest.' Nevertheless, the following year, 2009, he sat down to plan out meetings he could go to and spotted that Scunthorpe were doing double-headers – two meetings, one after the other – on bank holidays. He'd been to Scunthorpe a few times before and enjoyed it: 'It's mega-wide, which is why it's such a fantastic racetrack.' He started to go up there for bank holiday double-headers, two or three times a year, because the racing was so good.

He got chatting to Richard Hollingsworth, the Scunthorpe team manager, who he knew from his Conference league days when Rob had been assistant team manager for Oxford. Richard knew Rob had written for the *Oxford Mail* and *Speedway Star* and wanted someone to do media work for him. He asked Rob if he'd like to be press officer for Scunthorpe. Rob's first reaction was whether he could really do that based in Oxford because he wasn't going to be coming to a lot of meetings. They discussed it and agreed that he'd have a chat with Richard after each meeting to get an idea of the real stories behind the bald facts of the scoreline. Rob's adamant that you can't write a match report just from the results. 'You need an update from the team manager to get their perspective.'

He then started going up to Scunthorpe on more than just bank holidays and, by 2012, he was going up more and more. That year, Scunthorpe reached the Championship play-offs against Somerset and won the league in his first year as press officer. Scunny won in a last-heat decider and after that Rob was up for nearly every meeting. His love of the sport had been reborn.

He's heading up there this morning. Not to do his normal job as Scunthorpe press officer, but as part of the unpaid Ben Fund team. He's – perhaps not surprisingly – involved in that too.

* * *

It's half past eleven on the same Saturday morning and I'm on my way north, most likely up the same stretch of the M1 as Rob drove along earlier. I pull into Leicester Forest East service station. Normally, this place would be busy with football fans from all over the country, breaking their journey on their way to the day's league matches. But today there are no replica shirts visible among the people milling around. All Premier League and English Football League matches were postponed on Friday. The coronavirus is finally hitting the

United Kingdom. Like a small dot that was visible on the rear-view mirror – real but far away – it's now suddenly accelerated and is about to cause mayhem.

Most non-league football games, apart from those in the National League, have also been cancelled. Premier League games have been – optimistically perhaps – suspended until 3 April. UEFA have postponed the following week's Champions League and Europa League fixtures, and games in France, Germany, the Netherlands, Portugal, Spain and the USA have also been cancelled. In rugby union, the Six Nations game between Wales and Scotland won't take place, nor Sunday's Premiership Cup Final. The London Marathon has been moved to October. Abroad, England's Test cricket series in Sri Lanka has been cancelled, golf's Augusta Masters has been called off and the opening Formula 1 races have been postponed too.

That morning's *BBC Sport* website helpfully lists the sports fixtures that, in the UK at least, have survived – Rugby League fixtures, Netball Superleague, basketball, five horse racing meetings, Olympic boxing qualifiers and badminton.

I'm on my way to a sporting event that, to no one's surprise, wasn't in the BBC's list. It's the opening speedway fixture of the season, the Ben Fund Bonanza at Scunthorpe. For the first time that I can remember, I'm delighted the BBC has ignored speedway. I'm hoping that, amidst all the cancellations and talk of banning large crowds, speedway can somehow evade scrutiny and continue during the summer.

* * *

Paul Ackroyd is, of course, already in Scunthorpe. He arrived at half past nine, having set off early from his home at Lytham in Lancashire. As the chairman of the Ben Fund, he's had a busy few days leading up to the event, not least discussing with Rob Godfrey whether it should still go ahead or not.

One of the original riders, Andreas Jensen, has been unable to travel over from Denmark because of the country's newly imposed

14-day lockdown. Edinburgh's James Sarjeant has stepped in – 'One phone call and he was there, which was lovely.' Paul tries to get four or five riders on standby every year just in case. Those riders are normally from the bottom league or the lower end of the middle league. 'You wouldn't get the very top riders saying, "Yeah, if you need me, just give me a call."'

They give the riders expenses, which covers their costs of getting there – even if they're from Denmark – but they'll try to get riders who are based in Britain. 'We always have some prize money that we generate from sponsorship as a way of saying thank you to them. But in comparison to what they earn normally, it's minuscule.'

The riders are the only ones who get expenses. The rest of those who help do it voluntarily and the referees have always done it at their own cost.

Paul's happy he's got 16 riders to make a decent line-up, but there are regrets. 'The biggest tragedy for our meeting is that it would have been a perfect opportunity for Team GB to have a day – free or paid for – of practice. They chose not to do that but it would have been a good PR exercise as well, to show how they're supporting the event. That would have added a bit of interest.'

* * *

When I'd left London, there were grey skies and drizzle. But Scunthorpe – belying its nickname as 'Never Sunny Scunny' – is bathed in weak sunshine. There's already a reasonable crowd inside the Eddie Wright Raceway.

As we go through the turnstiles, we're greeted by an eight-foot-high 'Benny', the mascot, with a plastic bucket for Ben Fund collections. He's busy too with most people stopping to drop in a contribution.

The Ben Fund programmes come with a 24-page brochure for Travel Plus's speedway tours to meetings in places like Poland, Sweden, Denmark and Russia in 2020. In the current circumstances, it does seem an overly optimistic gesture. There's no sign of what will become known as 'social distancing' with supporters, in warm jackets and woolly hats, sitting together on the shallow terracing and mingling freely in the bar. I see one man meeting an old acquaintance and, on being asked, 'Do we shake hands then?' saying, 'Sod 'em!' and taking his friend's hand and shaking it vigorously. Then again, I've never had to wait so long in a queue at a speedway toilet to wash my hands.

I'm meant to be meeting Rob Peasley and remember his email about him being in the 'Ben suite' during the meeting. I circle the Eddie Wright Raceway a couple of times looking for anything that might be termed the 'Ben suite' and struggle to find it. There's a bar and café but no sign for anything as upmarket as the Ben suite. I check the message again and realise I've misread it. He's actually said he'll be in the 'Ben suit, pratting about on the centre green.' I realise then that Rob – a true speedway all-rounder – is the man inside the 'Benny' mascot costume. I catch up with him on his tour – with bucket – around the stadium, although our conversation is greatly limited by the large expanse of fabric and foam surrounding his head.

British speedway is certainly well represented. From team anoraks, caps and programme boards, I spot supporters from all seven Premiership clubs, from Scunthorpe, Newcastle, Redcar, Berwick, Glasgow, Edinburgh, Leicester and Poole from the Championship, Mildenhall from the National League, Coventry, Boston and Workington from days gone by and even someone from Poland with an Unia Leszno team anorak.

One of those addressing the crowd during the opening presentation is a very self-assured and confident 16-year-old. What makes this even more remarkable is that the young man speaking had been critically injured and in a coma following a crash at Glasgow speedway just last summer.

In June 2019, Sam Norris was taking part in the third round of the British Youth Championships at Glasgow's Ashfield Stadium. In heat 23, he lost control of his 250cc bike and slid off on the first bend. A rider right behind him careered into him at 50 miles an hour. Sam was rushed to Glasgow Children's Hospital with serious brain injuries before being airlifted to the specialist unit at Cambridge's

Addenbrooke's Hospital near his home. In a coma for five weeks, he was blind and couldn't speak when he regained consciousness. His family, mother Claire and father Chris, were warned by neurosurgeons to prepare for the harsh reality that his recovery would be a long one.

The speedway world, as it so often does, raised £8,800 within days to help him, and the Speedway Benevolent Fund also got involved. It looked bleak but, over the months, Sam, with the help of various experts – speech and language therapists, psychologists and physiotherapists – staged a remarkable recovery. Claire describes her son as being 'very determined'.

The previous month, an amazing piece of video was posted on his Facebook page. Sam Norris, just over eight months after a truly appalling accident, was back on his bike. Underneath the video of Sam riding his GT140 bike was a message:

'What you are seeing is nothing short of the impossible coming true. Never would we have said that 8 months after Sam's horrific accident, which left him with lots of bleeds on the brain and brain damaged and in a coma, he would be riding a motorbike so soon. Sam's dream and inspirational determination to prove everyone wrong has finally been done by dreaming with his eyes wide open.'

There's still work to do on his recovery. Claire says that fatigue is Sam's main difficulty and when he's tired, his speech and thought processes are slower, which can affect normal things like walking. There's no sign of that, though, as Sam takes the microphone and thanks the crowd and the Ben Fund for their support. The applause at the end is long, sustained and genuine.

It's a joy to see speedway back again too, to hear the engines revving and to breathe in the methanol, even if it's not nearly as pungent and distinctive as it once was. We get to see some good racing too. While more than half of the winning riders come from gate four, there's a fair amount of overtaking too. The meeting is run briskly. As Josh Auty had said to me earlier in the week: 'Rob Godfrey really does like to get through the meeting. It's very simple but sometimes simple's good. People want to see the riders compete against each other, not a load of other rubbish. He doesn't want to drag the meeting through. He wants to get the entertainment done, get people on their way home. Job done.'

I'm unashamedly rooting for Josh and Tom Bacon, who are both riding. I find myself – like a family member – even more concerned about their welfare than I would normally be. It's Tom's first meeting back since his season-ending injury in June 2019. He has a tough first heat – not helped by what he'll say later are problems at the starting gate – and ends up with four points but says it was great to get a meeting on.

Josh, on his home track, fares better, winning three races on his way to 11 points and a place in the semi-final. He wins that with ease and ends up finishing third in the final behind winner Danny King. Interviewed on the centre green afterwards, he's practical as ever, saying he enjoyed the meeting, wishes he'd won and is looking forward to more racing.

But that's unlikely to be next week. Halfway through the meeting, Rob Godfrey takes the centre-green microphone. He thanks everyone for coming and talks honestly about the current situation. He compares the coronavirus to the Great Plague of 1665, which sounds dramatic. He says there will be an announcement about the start of the season on the following Tuesday, but it is pretty clear what's coming. 'If this was next week, this meeting wouldn't be on, I tell you that.'

My optimism that speedway could somehow continue, while other better-attended sports are cancelled, is turning out to be wholly unrealistic. I've been hearing throughout the meeting that other riders, many of them Australian, have already assumed there's no chance of the season starting on time and have decided to go home, Edinburgh's Josh Pickering and Kye Thomson among them. There's also talk that Jason Crump – that latest marquee addition to British speedway – has either returned to Australia or is about to.

There's something else too that I hadn't thought of. Every speedway meeting needs a medical team at the track in case of injury. At a time when the National Health Service is going to be under intense pressure to deal with the thousands of expected coronavirus cases, running speedway meetings and taking away even a few health professionals for a few hours just isn't going to be practical or morally defensible.

I drive back to London thinking I might well have been at this year's only speedway meeting. It's not a great feeling.

* * *

On the following Tuesday, just after noon, Rob Godfrey and the BSP Ltd announce the inevitable – the suspension of the speedway season until, at least, mid-April. You can feel Rob's sense of frustration and disappointment in a video interview released at the same time. He says they've had to make a sad decision to postpone the sport they love. 'There's a virus out there, coronavirus, that is affecting our way of life at the minute and we have to heed the Government advice, do the sensible thing and postpone the season at least until April 16th.'

Rob remains confident that there will be speedway this season. He's looking at China and how they've returned to some form of normality – if the figures can be believed. The BSP Ltd Director, Stewart Dickson, the Leicester Lions' team manager, echoes those hopes, trying to look on the bright side. 'I'd be very disappointed if we didn't get on track for at least June. Everybody was excited for the season but unfortunately when it comes to something like this, we're all frightened by it, because it is unknown, and we have got to do what we're told.'

But life moves – or rather – closes down very quickly and surreally from then. The following day, the Government announces that schools, colleges and nurseries will close at the end of the week. On Friday it goes further, with all pubs, restaurants, leisure centres and libraries told to close their doors that evening. Three days later, on 23 March, 28.2 million people watch the Prime Minister's televised address to the nation when he – effectively – orders a lockdown. He tells people to stay at home unless they are key workers, those whose jobs are vital to health and public safety. The rest of us are only allowed out to shop for food or medical supplies or take one permitted bit of exercise near our home. The following Sunday, the deputy chief medical officer for

England, Dr Jenny Harries, warns that the lockdown could last not just three weeks but six months. Life, as all of us knew it barely two weeks earlier, has been turned on its head.

In such circumstances, when people are dying and health workers, delivery drivers, postal workers, public transport workers, shop staff and refuse collectors are all putting their health and lives on the line, it seems petty to complain about cancelled leisure arrangements. Mine, for the next few months, largely revolve around speedway. I have tickets booked for the Speedway of Nations at Belle Vue in May, the British Grand Prix at Cardiff in July and I've persuaded my wife – a non-sports fan but someone who says of speedway that 'at least you can tell what's going on' – that this summer is a good one to go and visit Poland, taking in a few speedway matches while we're there, of course. I've pencilled in meetings at Edinburgh, Redcar, Scunthorpe, Sheffield, Ipswich and Belle Vue. Given what has happened in the last few weeks, it's unlikely any will now go ahead.

On the first *Talk Speedway* podcast after the season's postponement, Scott Frame and Graham Muncie discuss the pandemic and why the decision to cancel was the right one. The first issue is the medical cover required for a speedway meeting which, at a minimum, is one ambulance, one doctor or paramedic and six first-aiders. There's concern over public safety in that some people will go to a meeting regardless, so the decision needs to be taken out of their hands. Rider availability, with riders due to race in Britain this season now stuck in Poland and Denmark, is another consideration, particularly given the risk of contamination as they travel between countries or even around Britain. Finally, there's the reality that so many speedway clubs are hand-to-mouth businesses. There's no way that clubs could run meetings behind closed doors because, in normal times, if just 50 regular spectators don't turn up, that creates serious problems for the clubs.

Lee Kilby, the Swindon promoter, says he's working on a couple of alternative fixture list formats depending on when any season could actually start. But he admits it's hard to know what long-term effect this will have on all of us.

That, of course, is scant consolation for the riders themselves. In many ways, the lockdown – not just in Britain but across Europe – couldn't have come at a worse time. Leading up to a new season, riders have to invest in new equipment – bikes, engines, tuners – as well as vans and travel and hotel arrangements. That's all before any money comes in from meetings, which now seem unlikely to take place anywhere for several months.

* * *

Paul Ackroyd is counting his blessings that the Ben Fund meeting managed to go ahead before the lockdown. 'We were incredibly lucky to get it on, because had we not done it then, it would have been unlikely we'd have been able to restage it this year. If and when speedway does begin again, the priority will be for the leagues and not for us.'

Even so, the threat of the coming pandemic did have an impact on the attendance. A crowd of 1,000 turned up; Paul reckons half from Scunthorpe and half from around the country. But without the coronavirus, he would have expected to have had double that. A lot of people had decided not to travel and that will affect their income.

He says they always use the Bonanza meeting to get some cash flow in so that they've got money for the season. 'We have some projects going on at the moment with the paraplegic riders and the money that we made from Scunthorpe will cover that. They live in a kind of permanent lockdown. Life hasn't changed for them, which is a sobering thought. But because riders aren't getting injured in racing accidents, we're not paying out as we ordinarily would.'

But, despite the current circumstances, the Ben Fund won't be used to help unemployed riders who are struggling financially. Paul says it's been discussed but the legal constitution isn't set up for that, so they won't go down that route.

He points out that it's the same for everybody. Although he's personally retired – 'allegedly', he adds – his food wholesale business, which his son and daughter now run, has had to close, as have many other people's.

'The Benevolent Fund would never see a rider stuck in whatever way. However, the current situation is affecting the whole world, not just speedway riders. We would have to rewrite our constitution to implement some acts of kindness, if that's the right word. The public who have given that money have done it to help injured riders, not to help riders who can't race because of the coronavirus.'

Paul is also realistic about what the current crisis might mean for speedway in the longer term. 'There'll be some speedway supporters who'll say, "I haven't really missed it. I won't bother going again." Equally so, the hard core will be busting a gut and want to go twice a week. But there could be, for example, a mechanic who might think, "I can't afford to live like this anymore, I'm moving on." It's going to be a whole new world.'

* * *

In that new world, more cancellations are announced in the last week of March.

On the 24th, the 2020 Tokyo Olympics are moved to the following year. A week later, Wimbledon is cancelled for the first time since the Second World War, and UEFA announce that all Champions League and Europa Cup ties will be 'suspended until further notice'. The Fédération Internationale de Motocyclisme announce that one of speedway's flagship events – the Speedway of Nations Final at Belle Vue over the first May bank holiday weekend – has been postponed. All parties are studying alternative dates. The following day, the BSP Ltd release another statement. With the Government advising high-risk groups to stay at home for 12 weeks, the promoters say it is unlikely that there will be any British speedway before 15 June, at least.

On 26 March, Poole Pirates' owner, Matt Ford, says that in recognition of the incredible work being done by health workers, any NHS worker will be allowed, free of charge, into their 2020 meetings on production of their ID card.

Headlines from the *Speedway Star*, resolutely publishing as normal, reflect speedway at a standstill in a world of confusion: 'Planning ahead', 'Keep the faith', 'On hold', 'On the job hunt', 'Waiting game'.

While most speedway clubs still have rent to pay on stadiums and maintenance costs to cover, they don't have to pay their riders until meetings take place. So they're not facing the same financial pressures as lower-league football clubs. Rochdale, in the fourth tier of English league football, are one of the first to go on record, with their chairman warning that the future of the club depends very much on getting people through the turnstiles – unlike the Premier League, whose teams get so much from domestic and overseas television rights.

It's the two other groups that make up British speedway that might be more seriously and immediately affected. Chancellor Rishi Sunak has, by the end of the month, extended his state furlough support scheme for millions of the country's workforce to the self-employed. It's generally thought to cover the many gig-economy workers, mobile hairdressers, freelance theatre staff and the like. With most speedway riders either self-employed or running as a limited business, it means there's some kind of safety net in place. But those riders, realising they may well not race at all this season, could decide speedway no longer offers a viable living for them and their families and might find something else to do, however difficult that's likely to be in the current environment. Then there are the fans, a dwindling number to begin with, who might find it hard to get back into going to speedway once they've got out of the habit.

For a month that began with such high hopes for British speedway, the turnaround has been dramatic and demoralising. The only sure thing? Nothing will be certain in the weeks ahead.

April 2020 – Fear and frustration

APRIL 2020, both living through it at the time and with the benefit of hindsight, may well be the strangest month many of us ever experience. Confined to our homes, unable to see family members – children, parents, grandparents – and friends whenever we want, except through awkward video calls. Normal life no longer possible. Everyday venues like pubs, restaurants, theatres, cinemas and sporting venues all closed. Queues to go into the supermarket and restrictions on what we can buy when we get there. Keeping at least two metres away from anyone outside our own 'bubble'. The unexpected comfort of the weekly Thursday evening communal claps for carers. Add in, for several million people, the worries of being made redundant or their business having to close for the immediate future. Or for those key workers in hospitals, care homes, transport, retail, delivery and refuse collection, the real danger of actually catching the virus and putting their own and their families' health at risk. For many of them, the inconvenience of staying at home would be something they'd accept in a heartbeat if their work or financial commitments allowed them to do so.

It's a month dominated by a disparate collection of Fs: Fear. Frustration. Flattening the curve. Furlough. Watch any TV news bulletin and it's full of overworked, under-pressure and under-resourced hospital staff battling to cope with the surge in COVID-19 patients. Event centres up and down the country are turned into emergency hospitals, with volunteer staff told to anticipate seeing many deaths while they're there. The Prime Minister, already diagnosed with the virus, is taken to hospital on 5 April after 'persistent symptoms' that lead to breathing difficulties and three nights in intensive care. He recovers but the thought is there – if the Prime Minister can catch it, anyone can. No matter he'd spent much of March shaking hands with all and sundry against his own Government's advice. When he returns to work, there's talk that he has banned discussions of any 'exit strategy' and that a lockdown will last until 2021 to prevent a second wave of infections.

But that brings its own dangers. The Office for Budget Responsibility predicts that if the lockdown extends into the summer, Britain will face its biggest economic slump since the Great Frost of 1709.

There's not much to cheer people up when each day now seems indistinguishable from the one before. For those fortunate enough to be able to spend time in their garden, the weather's unseasonably warm and dry – the sunniest on record. Or there are those books to catch up on, *Tiger King* to watch on Netflix or that jigsaw to finish, although maybe not too quickly because Amazon reports that they're in short supply.

Easter is particularly strange. Church doors shut, streets empty, pubs closed, families apart and celebratory festive lunches curtailed. With good weather forecast, the Government's daily news conferences are dominated by pleas for people to stay indoors and protect the NHS. This is backed up, to varying degrees, by police forces up and down the country, shaming groups and individuals who they believe to be flouting the new rules. The good weather arrives, as promised, with temperatures up to 25°C in some places. But the weekend's news bulletins show that the Government's advice is generally being taken to heart. Brighton's seafront is largely deserted and parks sparsely populated. Clearly the majority of people are abiding by the rules. Some will later claim that the Government has done too good a job in scaring people into staying at home.

Given all that, the fact there's no speedway seems, frankly, a minor wrinkle. Life itself is more important. But the Easter weekend is traditionally one of the busiest for speedway in Britain. It's when the season really gets underway, with a rush of meetings and, where possible, local derbies arranged to boost crowds.

It's more than a little ironic that this Easter's weather is so glorious. Compare that with the start of the 2018 season when, of 41 meetings scheduled between 1 and 12 April, more than three-quarters – 32 – were either postponed or abandoned because of torrential rain.

Grand Prix rider, Niels-Kristian Iversen, due to ride for Peterborough this season, sums up the mood when he tweets: 'Great weather for racing #dreamon.'

But there seems little prospect of any racing soon. *The Times* reports an American epidemiologist saying that thousands of people in close proximity in a stadium will be 'very, very dangerous' until a vaccine is developed to combat coronavirus. It infers from this – given current timings for a successful vaccine being found – that when sporting events resume, they could be played in front of empty stadiums. Even with the vast majority of speedway meetings in the UK taking place in front of hundreds rather than thousands, it's hard to see how the sport could be exempted in the current climate. Something fundamental is happening, something much bigger than the enclosed world of speedway.

* * *

At a time when Premier League footballers are under pressure – some say unfairly – to take a 30 per cent pay cut, the contrast with speedway riders couldn't be starker. With no income at all, it's about earning money and doing things they would never have otherwise contemplated at this time of the year. Sam Jensen is back working as a blacksmith in Denmark rather than riding for Glasgow. Rory Schlein, who was due to double-up for Wolverhampton in the Premiership and Somerset in the Championship, is working 12-hour shifts, five days a week, for Hermes, delivering parcels. Ellis Perks, also due to double-up for Leicester and Swindon, is a courier for DPD in one of its warehouses sorting out parcels. Berwick's Aaron Summers is working for one of his sponsors, Border Eggs. Sheldon Davies, based in Barnsley but down to ride for Plymouth, has started work on the front line as a porter at his local hospital. He says he'd rather be doing something to fight back against coronavirus. Jordan Jenkins, bound for Redcar and Kent, is working in a Tesco supermarket.

Other riders are at home, like Danny King – the Ben Fund winner – who posts a video showing how he's juggling childcare, home schooling, domestic duties and exercising with Joe Wicks while his wife, Clara, goes off to her job as a deputy head teacher. Whatever they're up to, every rider will be worrying about the money they've spent on their equipment ahead of the now delayed – and possibly never to be started – season.

British champion Charles Wright speaks for many when he says that the loss of income will run into hundreds of thousands for the entire sport. He tells *Speedway Star* that it's going to mean many riders all over the UK and Europe on the breadline. He says he would have expected to have raced 30 meetings by 15 June, the earliest date speedway in Britain can resume, and will never get that money back. He's not sure what will happen to clubs either, as promoters will also be finding it hard with stadium rents to pay. He says speedway is on a par with non-league football clubs, dependent on ticket revenue to survive and pay all the bills. He's just not sure that many people in the sport can survive four months without any income.

* * *

Tom Bacon knows that, compared to most people in Britain at the moment, he's one of the lucky ones. When many have lost their jobs or have been 'furloughed', he's working full-time from home. His employers specialise in safeguarding for teachers and, with schools closed and teachers at home, he's actually been busier than normal.

But he's still frustrated. This isn't what he was expecting to be doing in April. Financially, it's quite a big difference from what he'd budgeted for and speedway is what he loves doing. He'd also spent those months recovering from injury.

'I'm still doing a lot of running. I train at home as best I can. It's not ideal but you can still stay in shape.' He says the main problem for riders is maintaining their bike fitness. 'You use muscles when you ride a speedway bike that are very hard to train specifically. I worked really hard to get my bike fitness to be good for the start of the year. What you're doing on the bike is very hard to imitate without actually riding, because of the vibrations. It's your forearms, your grip strength, just getting relaxed so you're not gripping too hard and you're not working so hard on the bike. A lot of people struggle with bike fitness early in the season because it is different to your general fitness. I'd ridden a lot leading up to the season. Obviously, all of that has been a waste of time because when I get back we'll have had quite a long time off the bike again.'

Tom's team for 2020, the Kent Kings, have their own WhatsApp group, but he says it's all been very quiet. He thinks everybody's doing their own thing and keeping themselves to themselves. 'We hadn't even had any get-together as a team yet. Obviously, we all know each other from riding together at different times, but it's almost as if the team aspect hasn't happened yet, which is a bit bizarre.'

The fact that it's been an unusually dry and sunny April hasn't, for the speedway rider, been welcome. 'It's hard. When it was meant to be our press day, it was beautiful sunshine and I thought, "I can't believe it's like this." Or you think back to your first meeting in previous years, when it's been wet and cold and dark and horrible, and now it's beautiful sunshine and you're sat inside. It makes it worse.'

* * *

Up in Stalybridge, on the outskirts of Manchester, Tom's frustration is also keenly felt by Scunthorpe's Josh Auty.

Josh lives with his girlfriend, Olivia, whose grandfather is Jack Lee, former team manager at Buxton, Birmingham and Sheffield. It's not just the speedway he's missing. Josh hasn't seen either his parents or his gran and grandad, with whom he's really close, since before the Ben Fund meeting in the middle of March. He's been doing FaceTime calls but says it's not the same. Like so many in Britain, he's been doing what the Government advise: stay in, protect the National Health Service and save lives.

'I've missed lots of things. Not seeing my family's been a killer. I've not been able to be anywhere near my grandparents the past five weeks. It's worrying times. I don't think there will be any speedway this season, I honestly don't. Everybody's in the same boat and nobody really knows. I'm frustrated, everyone just wants to get out on their bike and meet up with friends as well. The social aspect of life has been totally taken away from everybody.'

It's particularly difficult for Josh because he'd put so much work into his testimonial meeting scheduled for 22 March.

'I knew at the Ben Fund the week before that it wasn't going to go ahead. You could see in the media that this virus was going to be pretty serious, so I asked Rob Godfrey what was going on. He said the promoters were going to have a meeting on the Tuesday and speedway was basically going to shut down indefinitely. I probably didn't even need to ask him. It was common sense because every other sporting event was getting shut down.' Josh says he was gutted but adds that it was equally disappointing for Stuart Robson and Todd Kurtz, riders whose testimonials were also cancelled at the same time. 'It just sucks at the minute.'

He wisely hadn't budgeted proceeds from his testimonial into his season. 'Obviously, I wanted to raise a bit of money for myself, but I just wanted to put on a really good event that Scunny could have been proud of. It will happen although we're going to be looking at 2021 now. I think if speedway does resume, we're not going to be able to fit these testimonials in because we'll just get straight into league fixtures. If we can get 20 meetings in and get a league completed, that would be a major success.'

As well as being stuck at home, Josh, like a lot of riders, isn't working and isn't earning any money. Luckily, he says he's got a bit of savings that he's been living off. 'The jobs that are about are all warehouse work so you're going to be with a lot of people. I don't really want to do that because this virus obviously spreads and I don't want to be with loads of people. But obviously if we're three, four months down the line and things haven't changed, I might have to.'

But there's no suggestion he'd think about doing something else permanently. 'I miss competing at racing and I think the other lads miss it. You get a good feeling from winning and riding well and being part of a team. Every now and then you get annoyed if you're not doing as well as you should and you're sick of washing your bikes, doing the same routine, stuff like that. But, in isolation all I've been doing is going for walks or having a little kickabout by myself. It's just difficult to replace competing for me.' He pauses. 'Competing at anything really.'

* * *

Under normal circumstances, Rob Godfrey would have spent Good Friday at the Eddie Wright Raceway watching his Scorpions team take on the Redcar Bears. But these are different times so he's sitting in his lounge at home answering questions from fans on the British Speedway Twitter channel. The BSP Ltd has often been criticised by fans for not opening themselves up to supporters' opinions. That's something Rob wants to change. 'I've always been transparent, contrary to what people think. I like transparency because if we do something, there's always a reason why.'

Perhaps surprisingly, only a couple of the near 20 questions that are asked are about the coronavirus lockdown and when speedway might get underway again. Rob now says that the first of July is the earliest feasible date, although there's only so much anyone can say about the future right now. Rob is hopeful that all clubs will survive financially through the crisis and says he's had no indications otherwise.

Instead, the bulk of the questions are some of the perennial topics raised whenever British speedway is discussed. Why isn't there an independent body running the sport? Why is the current management team the best equipped to lead the sport? Will there be Championship speedway on TV? What power will the newly announced track curators have in taking action against clubs whose tracks aren't well enough prepared? Even confined to short, Twitter-length replies, Rob is keen to underline his confidence in the long-term prospects for the sport. Asked where he'd like to see it in ten years, he says he'd like to emulate Poland. 'We'll work very hard to try and achieve this. We must set our goals high.'

One question that receives a lot of interest from those on the Q&A forum is around the fate of former clubs like Weymouth and Reading and keeping their names alive. Both clubs have been without a home track for several years but have run teams at other tracks in the lowest-level development league, below the third-tier National League. But that's no longer permitted. Rob replies that it's part of an ongoing 'tidying-up process' whereby teams will be allowed to run under those names for one-off meetings but not in full-time leagues. That leads to comments that it's a shame they've done this, that 'tidying up is a pathetic excuse' and that what the BSP Ltd has done is a 'spiteful act'. Speedway loyalties run deep.

Later, Rob will say that he wouldn't mind doing another online Q&A. 'I would have liked to have injected a bit more fun into it, to be honest. But it was quite serious questions and you got honest answers.' He'd also done a podcast with former world champion Greg Hancock and had hoped to inject humour into that. 'I wanted to tell funny stories but I never got the opportunity. I'm going to one day, and I'm going to make everyone laugh because they need to laugh.'

Particularly at the moment, given that the figures Rob is keeping his eye on at the moment aren't race times or team scores but the daily COVID-19 death statistics released each afternoon. Like everybody I speak to in speedway this month, Rob's first thoughts are not of the sport he loves but those who've suffered a family loss as a result of the virus. But he's hoping the figures will start dropping and some kind of normality can return. He's looking ahead and has asked the Speedway Control Board if the speedway season could extend into November if needed.

When we catch up later in the month, he's still positive. 'I personally think that in the next few weeks there will be some kind of lifting of restrictions because this country can't sustain the amount of money that's going out and not coming in. I don't know where all the money that's been promised is coming from. We were promised help but, so far, as I sit here today, I haven't had one penny off the Government. I can speak for the other promoters – because I liaised with most of them this morning – and nobody's had a penny. At some point, we are going to need help and I'm anticipating that we will. I have had emails from the council but, as yet, we've had nothing. I just hope, whether we've got league speedway or not, that the stadium can operate with some capacity very soon, maybe in the next month or so if the lockdown does lift. With 50 or 100 people or more, we can start to get some revenue coming back – we need it.' He talks about things that supporters wouldn't normally consider, like how they've got about £3,000 worth of beer at the Eddie Wright Raceway that's going to go out of date soon. 'That's just one problem that we've got. It is a worry but I'm not worrying, if you know what I mean. We've got to stay positive.'

He jokes about hoping to get the stadium operating again soon because he and his wife, Gail, are running out of jobs to do there. They've been doing maintenance jobs at the Eddie Wright Raceway, like tending to the grass and weeds. The stadium's looking very smart at the moment but there's nobody around to see it.

Then, when I ask him how he feels six months into his role as chairman, he says something which surprises me. 'It was a job I never really wanted. I love the job now, don't get me wrong, but I didn't want it. Years ago, you'd say something and no one listened to you. You say things now and people do tend to listen to you. I don't like the negativity from the supporters where you can't do anything right. But the genuine supporters who appreciate what we're trying to do, they take that on board. We've just had a big kick in the bollocks with this COVID-19 because it was going to be such a great year, with Eurosport and all the other good things.'

He reveals they were very close to announcing a long-awaited league sponsor to run along the new five-year TV contract just before the season was suspended.

'But we will come through it. It is inevitably going to take a little bit of time. I've got a good team behind me, the other directors. It is a team effort. We're doing the best job we possibly can.'

* * *

At seven o'clock on Saturday, 11 April, the Glasgow Tigers should have been opening their season with a Scottish Cup tie against their old rivals from along the M8, the Edinburgh Monarchs. Instead they're releasing *In the Red*, a 90-minute documentary looking at their 2019 season.

Given that it was commissioned and paid for by Allied Vehicles – the Glasgow Tigers' owners and main sponsors – it would probably fail the BBC's current affairs guidelines for being independent and objective. But, even so, it's an excellent advert for the sport, beautifully shot, nicely edited and full of the characters – on and off the track – that make speedway the sport it is.

It was filmed, edited and produced by a young filmmaker, Patrick Rooney, who only graduated from the SAE Glasgow Institute film school in 2017. He's already directed several short films and documentaries and it's clear an immense amount of work has gone into this. Following the Tigers home and away resulted in around 120 hours of material, with a lot of time and editing needed for the finished film. It receives a deservedly enthusiastic reception from those who watch it as it chronicles the Tigers' ultimately unsuccessful journey to the Championship Grand Final, where they lost to Leicester. There are several highlights – Rasmus Jensen and Craig Cook joining the travelling fans on the terracing at Somerset for selfies after winning the Championship Pairs; Sam Norris, whose near fatal accident happened at Glasgow, joining – and being serenaded by – the Glasgow fans on the terracing of the first leg of the final at Leicester.

It's also illuminating in the details it gives of the company who run and sponsor Glasgow – and what that says about speedway's financial well-being in Britain, even before the coronavirus crisis.

Allied Vehicles got involved in Glasgow speedway in 2014 and, it's fair to say, have not only saved them from closure but developed them into one of the biggest teams in the second level of British speedway. Before then, Glasgow had lived a nomadic existence, starting off at the old White City Stadium, where Bert Harkins had first seen them, before moving around Glasgow – from Hampden Park to Coatbridge to two venues in Blantyre, to an unsuccessful season in Workington and then two periods at the Shawfield greyhound stadium before settling in Ashfield, the home of the local junior football club. The stadium is situated in Possilpark, one of the most deprived areas of Scotland. Allied Vehicles is a local – and successful – employer in the area, with 700 people earning their living supplying adapted and special-purpose vehicles. Co-owner, Peter Facenna makes clear at the opening of the documentary that they are not in speedway for the money.

'Speedway's not a wealthy sport. It's a sport that struggles to survive. Our initial investment was £3 million – which we were happy to give as a gift. For us, speedway was about giving something back to the community. It was about saving Glasgow Tigers, which meant we also saved Ashfield Junior Football Club that's been going over a hundred years.'

It's clear that while *In the Red* refers to the Tigers' colours, it also reflects their financial status. 'We want the business to stand on its own two feet. It's not, it's still losing six figures a year, and whilst, again, we can afford to do that, we don't want to do it long term. It's not in our nature to lose money running any business.'

And yet, if Glasgow can't make it pay, then who can? They're well known for an innovative social media approach and make real attempts to reach out to a wider audience. But home attendances last year were just shy of 1,000. They still lose money.

Perhaps the most poignant moment from the documentary is an off-track one. It shows, vividly, how much speedway means to those who watch it – and how it can reach out and help those fans when they need it.

George Steven is a Tigers' fan. If you're in any doubt, he'll show you the 'Glasgow Tigers' tattoos on his arm. A joiner by trade, he used to go to every meeting with a friend. By his own admission, all they did was 'drink beer and go home pished'. He knew his life wasn't right and he was going off the rails.

When Allied Vehicles first got involved in 2014 and Gerry Facenna was visiting the stadium, he looked up at the stand and saw a couple of men sitting drinking beer. He asked the then owners who they were and was told that it was George, the Tigers' number-one fan. He was told George lived at the stadium, did all the handy jobs and then sat in the stand and had a few cans of beer. When they met, George told Gerry he loved the club and wanted to help them, the new owners, repair the stadium. Many people would have told George that things were different now and, thanks all the same, but it was time to go. But to his credit, Gerry said that was fine and that as long as George turned up and didn't let them down there would be a place for him. Just one thing, there would be no drinking in the stadium.

George took Gerry at his word. He turned up at seven in the morning until eight at night, working with the Facennas and their team to do up the stadium. After three months they gave him a maintenance job at Allied, which he's done ever since. It's a job George loves – 'a brilliant job' – and one that has changed him completely.

As Gerry Facenna says in the documentary: 'I dread to think where George would be if we hadn't come in because I think he was a wee bit lost at the time, but he's a great guy.'

He's continuing to work for Allied in their facilities team, helping to prepare the building for life after lockdown by putting up screens in the call centre booths to make sure that social distancing and work can go together.

It's a real, true-life story. One that illustrates that speedway – at its heart – makes a place for the little guy who's down on his luck, in a way that a lot of other sports simply wouldn't.

* * *

For the moment, with no prospect of live action, the speedway world is doing what many other sports are doing and delving into its archives. People enjoy a dose of nostalgia and a shared cultural experience at any time, but it's more keenly felt now. Eastbourne, Edinburgh, the Isle of Wight, Birmingham, Berwick and Poole are the first clubs to make classic matches from the past available on their social media channels. The BSP Ltd, which has been criticised in the past for being slow to embrace the digital world, does its bit too, running online quizzes on a Friday night and meetings on a Monday night.

Rob Godfrey reveals that they'd been expecting somewhere between 200 and 300 for their first quiz and ended up getting 2,500. 'We're working a lot on the social media side. It gives people something to do and keeps reminding them what speedway is. The numbers are encouraging because we want, at some point, to start streaming matches and it's good to find out how many people will watch and, if necessary, pay. There's certainly an appetite for it and that's encouraging.'

I'm one of those sitting down at their laptops on Easter Monday to watch both legs of the 2012 Championship Grand Final between the Somerset Rebels and the Scunthorpe Scorpions. Speedway commentator Nigel Pearson introduces the action with pre-recorded links from what looks like his bedroom, a location that would have sounded bizarre just a month ago but seems perfectly reasonable now.

I decide that as well as watching the action, I'll follow the other viewers' comments on the YouTube chat forum. Most of us are keen to see some speedway, however old it is. One fan says he's really missed it: 'It's been that bad, I've been standing outside throwing shale in my face.'

For a few – and it is just a very few – others, it's a chance to have a moan. I get a sense of what it must be like to be a promoter or someone involved in speedway management. The first leg at Somerset comes in for criticism from one person in particular, who states that the video quality isn't high definition and the commentary is unacceptable –

both seem fine to me; he claims the meeting is terrible with little overtaking – it's not, there's lots.

I suspect most of us watching know very well who wins in the end, but nobody's letting on so as not to spoil it for anyone who doesn't. The second leg at Scunthorpe, with the home team having to claw back a five-point deficit, really is a classic, with the overall lead swinging wildly back and forth. I make it that our audience on YouTube peaks at 1,546, with probably more over on the Facebook page where it's also being shown.

Rob Peasley, in his dual role as Scunthorpe fan and press officer, gives us his insights during the meeting on the chat forum. He reveals that the pits had been under water when he'd arrived and the meeting had only gone ahead thanks to the work done by the track staff, which included Scunthorpe promoter and owner Rob Godfrey. It's hard to imagine Premier League managers mucking in on pitch preparation for a key, end-of-season finale.

On the chat forum, Rob Peasley is explaining how Scunthorpe really thought everything was going against them, beginning with an incorrect decision to rerun heat 8. 'Crap refereeing is part and parcel of the sport,' says Rob Godfrey with typical northern candour when I ask him about it later.

In heat 14, Scunthorpe's Ashley Birks is excluded after coming off on the fourth bend. Rob Peasley ramps up the tension again: 'That's it, surely. Scunny have no chance now.'

But, of course, they do. After a tense heat 15 when Somerset's Richard Hall tries – and fails – to sweep up by the fence to get past the home side's Nick Morris and Josh Auty, Scunthorpe are presented with the trophy.

Everyone seems to have enjoyed it, including Gary Irving, one of Scunthorpe's reserves on the night. His verdict? 'Enjoyable throwback, that. Good times.'

Certainly compared to what we're all going through at the moment.

* * *

When you're six and three-quarters, your seventh birthday is a big deal. Amelie Klindt is no different. Except, when your birthday's on 25 April 2020, in week five of a national lockdown, it's not going to be a 'normal' celebration. No party for starters. No large family gathering either. But her dad, Nicolai Klindt, is determined to make sure Amelie's birthday is still memorable. On the day itself, he posts a photo on his Twitter account of Amelie on a shiny new Apollo Cherry Lane bike, her head – protected by an equally smart turquoise and pink cycling helmet – bent over the handlebars, ready for the off. Amelie loves watching her dad on TV on his speedway bike. Chester, the family labradoodle, is pictured beside her, not looking quite so primed for action, which leads one Twitter wag to post that the start marshal looks a bit ruff.

Nicolai Klindt is a Danish rider based in the market town of Shifnal between Wolverhampton and Telford. He'd been due to ride for Ipswich in the Premiership as well as for teams in Poland and Denmark.

The lockdown has come at a bad time, not just for him but for his girlfriend, Sarah, who's been on maternity leave after the birth of their four-month-old daughter, Maeve. Nicolai says they've had chats about how bad it could get. 'It is a nightmare. My head has been spinning round because I don't know what I'm going to do if we're not going to ride at all.'

Nicolai had spent a lot of money, around £50,000 – 'more than I wanted to' – on equipment this year. He'd invested in a brand-new van for the next five years and it hasn't left him with much money in his bank account. He's cut spending back to just the bills that he has to pay. He has a mechanic abroad whose wages he's had to cut by 50 per cent because there's no income. As he explains, it doesn't matter if you're riding in the Premiership or the National League, it costs exactly the same. 'You have to pay for fuel, a mechanic, there's wear and tear, oil, tyres, clutch plates, everything. Speedway riders are not on a weekly salary like other sportsmen. I would say we are one of the harder-hit professions.'

But he's trying to remain positive and is glad to be getting more time with his family than he normally would. He admits that, in the past, he's had a problem with being too negative. He's taken action to help himself – seeing coaches and sports psychologists – to build up his mental strength and try to look at the positives as much as possible. 'Then you get the benefits.'

Not just for himself either. Earlier in the month, he was one of several Ipswich riders who made time to phone up the club's season ticket holders, some of them elderly, just to see how they were doing.

Nicolai will be 32 in December. He's one of the most recognisable speedway riders in the country thanks to a thick, brown beard, which certainly wouldn't shame a ZZ Top tribute band. He was European Under-19 champion in 2007 and second in the Danish championship in 2012 but has, by his own admission, not lived up to some of that early promise. In 2018, after a series of injuries and setbacks, he messaged every club in Britain but only two wanted to sign him – Berwick and Workington in the Championship. He took stock and decided to start the second part of his career. He still has dreams and he's invested money to achieve them.

'Do I want to be Nicolai Klindt, the league rider, or do I want to be Nicolai Klindt, the Grand Prix rider? Well, I want to be a GP rider and so I have to put money into it. When I finish my career, I don't want to look back and think, "Maybe I could have done this or maybe I could have done that." But it costs a lot of money.'

To be a Grand Prix rider, you have to race outside Britain. It's something, he says, Sarah's found difficult in the past because he can often be gone for a couple of weeks at a time. It comes with costs too; Nicolai reckons around £10,000 a year on flights, not counting hotels and car parking at airports. 'I try to be organised and plan as far ahead as possible. Because I'm riding in Denmark and Poland this year, I'd already booked most of my flights and hotels. That's a lot of money to spend before the season started, which I'm now claiming back. But most of the airlines and hotel chains will not do a refund anymore, just a credit voucher.' At a time like this, when he's not earning and has an extra mouth to feed, having the money in his bank account would help enormously.

'Luckily I've had all my financial sponsorships come through, which has helped, so I'm not totally skint. I don't really want to spend the sponsors' money on day-to-day stuff, but that's what I'm having to do at the minute because I don't have an income.'

Then there's the worry about what might happen with sponsors if there's no speedway season at all in 2020.

'Let's say we get half a season out of it, then we obviously have to negotiate sponsorship deals in the winter. If we don't race, then we have to sit down and see if we should just roll over into next season with what they've already paid for. That's probably going to hit hardest because, if we don't ride this season, I'll be in a position where I won't have the capital to start the 2021 season. I'm trying to cut corners and hope for the best.'

Actually, Nicolai's doing more than that. He's got himself a temporary job as a delivery driver for Tesco, which will cover his bills for the house and take some of the immediate financial pressure off. He applied at the start of April. Tesco rang him up, he's been on training courses and will be working a five-day, 38-hour week delivering groceries and food to people's homes. While he says it's not great money, 'I'll enjoy it because I'll be on my own spending a few hours of the day driving around. It'll also take my mind off things because all I do every day is think about when we can start riding again.'

A week later I see on Twitter that Nicolai's started his job, which he says is lots of fun with great colleagues – 'a bit different to what I normally do!' I suspect he'd much prefer to be doing the day job though.

* * *

Scarlett Farrell, a King's Lynn fan, sums up the feelings of many in speedway in April when she tweets: 'Proper miss going to speedway and seeing my favourite people.'

The problem is that not everybody will be rushing back even when the lockdown is eased. That's clear when you listen to Len Silver, the promoter of Championship side Kent Kings, Tom Bacon's new team.

If there's anyone in British speedway who's either older than Len – he was 88 in February – or has been involved for such a long time (he first rode back in 1953), then they're keeping themselves well hidden. Len was a rider for ten years and then moved into management and promotion, running tracks at Hackney, Rye House, Rayleigh and Kent as well as managing the Great Britain/England team between 1973 and 1975. He's seen a lot in his time in speedway, but nothing like this. At the end of March, the Prime Minister had announced that 1.5 million people in the country – the most clinically vulnerable – should stay at home for 12 weeks. That included Len.

'I'm one of the people who must not get that virus because if I get it, I'll be pushing up daisies. I can't afford to get it; if I do, I'm dead. I have got no immune system,' Len tells Peter Oakes in *Speedway Star*. He says the sport has never encountered anything like this, even during the Second World War. 'I expect that many of our fans will be living as I am, at home and not mixing with others. I exhort you all to follow the Government guidelines, stay away from others. Let's stop this virus in its tracks together.'

Kent are the first club to announce they'll be reimbursing supporters for pre-paid season tickets. If and when speedway does begin again, Len feels many of its supporters – maybe not quite as elderly as he is – won't be keen to rush out. He reckons 30 to 50 per cent of Kent's crowds are old age pensioners. He doesn't think that's exceptional.

'It's impossible for speedway to run behind closed doors, no one takes enough money from sponsors to do that. We have to have people in the stadium but I think they will stay at home because they will all be nervous. I'm going to be nervous myself.' Len would want to keep away from people, which – no matter how careful he is – is almost impossible to do if he's running a speedway club.

Len's at one extreme. Rob Godfrey – accepting that some people will be scared to come out, but remaining as positive as he can be in hoping that speedway will return at some point this year – is at the other. Which will be correct is something that only the coming months will determine.

May 2020 – The speedway bubble

MARK LEMON, Belle Vue's Australian manager, tweets on the first of the month: 'Has anyone else felt that this April has been the longest month ever?'

Welcome to May, Mark.

As it's a new month, there's a new letter for everyone to focus on: 'R' for the rate of infection. Or, in plain language, the number of people one infected person will pass the virus on to, on average. A rate of under 1 is good, a sign that the virus is under control and that some kind of normal life might soon resume. If 'R' goes above 1 – as it clearly had during March and April – then all bets are off and lockdown Britain will continue.

But before we say goodbye to 'F', there's a worrying reminder of it in the first day of May's news headlines. A survey for Ipsos MORI, the polling company, says that fear is still an overriding concern for most British people, with many saying they would be reluctant to leave home even if the Government did lift restrictions in a month's time. More than 60 per cent would be uncomfortable going to bars and restaurants or using public transport. For a sport like speedway, where 50 people deciding not to turn up makes the difference between covering costs and losing money on a meeting, this is bad news.

One scientist on BBC Radio Four's *Today* programme – Sir David Spiegelhalter, Professor of Statistics at Cambridge University – puts the opposing case. He says the risks for most people, particularly those in the younger age group, are very small and that the media is partly to blame for emphasising the occasional healthy, young person's death from COVID-19. In his view, it's made many people over-anxious and he's calling for a campaign to persuade those least at risk from the virus to get out and start living again once the lockdown is lifted.

On the same morning there's another item of news of interest to those running speedway. Rugby League has become the first UK sport to be bailed out by the Government. With its season suspended on 16 March and wage cuts already in place, clubs' survival – from Super League down – is in doubt. The Government has made £16 million available in the form of loans to tide the clubs over. The rationale given is that Rugby League is a special case because of its social value in mainly northern communities and the real risk of it being wiped out. You can't help thinking that, at another time, speedway might have been afforded the same financial benefit. But not today.

Instead, with more talk of football starting up later in the summer without crowds, the BSP Ltd are adamant that won't be happening in speedway.

Rod Godfrey doesn't mince his words. 'There's not a chance of speedway being run behind closed doors. We haven't got the millions and billions that football has. It's wrong, it should never happen. No matter how much money they've got, without spectators you haven't got a sport. If football is really that desperate to do it, then good luck to them because all they're doing is cutting their nose off to spite their face. Football is nothing without spectators. It's just not right.'

Tom Bacon had mentioned that he could see his football team, Coventry City, live in midweek for £10 on the EFL's iFollow streaming service. He thought it was worth considering for speedway as long as they were sure they'd get enough people paying to watch. They might even attract more than would have gone along to the meeting.

In fact, those in charge of running British speedway had been set to experiment with streaming meetings live, for the first time, this coming season. Stewart Dickson, team manager at Leicester and a BSP Ltd director, confirms plans had been put in place to trial-stream Somerset against Glasgow. They wanted to get two tracks as far away from each other as possible so as not to impact the actual attendance. But with no prospect of running meetings at all, this is postponed for now.

Ian Jordan, one of the directors at Eastbourne in the Championship, offers a realistic view on what clubs can and can't do, in a question and answer session on the club's website.

With no TV deal for clubs at Championship level, Jordan agrees with Rob Godfrey that racing behind closed doors would be a non-starter. He doesn't rule out streaming. 'But, as it stands, if we were to run a live speedway match and stream it, we'd reckon to sell 200 or 300 units at £5. That would not even pay the rent.'

He says Eastbourne had already paid out between £15,000 and £20,000 ahead of the season in insurance and regulatory items. Each meeting costs around £4,000 to stage, which includes stadium rent per match, match insurance, medical cover, tyres for both teams, referee's fee and other costs involved in getting a meeting on. A huge slice, 95 per cent, of their day-to-day turnover comes from gate money. They also have to make sure revenues from that home match cover the cost of the corresponding away match points money, with rider travel costs, home and away, on top.

He's clear about the minimum requirements for Eastbourne and, indeed, most clubs in the Championship. 'Most teams would have a break-even figure of between 600 and 800 supporters. If Boris Johnson announces in August that you can hold sports events with crowds of 500, we couldn't run because every time we opened the gates, we'd probably lose £5,000–£8,000. Remember, you've got maybe 100–140 people in there to run the meeting before you even let a supporter in.' He says they can't really consider running until the Government's permitted figure reaches 1,000.

'My gut feeling is the best-case scenario would be to run a few open meetings in September and October. I've already got an individual meeting mapped out, like the Championship of Sussex, with seven Eastbourne riders and eight or nine top GB riders.'

Eastbourne are unique in the top two divisions in fielding an all-British team for 2020. Given the possible difficulties in the new world of air travel and countries imposing travel restrictions, this is looking like a wise move.

Eastbourne is well known for having an older population who have moved to the coast to retire so the club may well have a number of supporters who are not comfortable with coming out. Ian's keen to make sure the club takes their views on board and is putting together a survey to find out how they'd feel about being in a crowd. At a time when the Government's messages – and our own sense of self-preservation – tell us to be wary of our fellow human beings, that familiar spot on the first bend might not seem quite so appealing.

But he's confident, even if this season can't go ahead in any form, that Eastbourne will be ready for the 2021 season. 'We lease the stadium, which is potentially going to sit unused for a year. As a business, I am very confident we can cope with this. The query is what the structure of the sport looks like next year if, God forbid, some clubs don't come through.'

There is some positive news from north of the border. Edinburgh's co-promoter, Alex Harkess, needs it. Like many people running their own business, he's 'struggling a wee bit at the moment'. He works in the motor trade; the part that makes and repairs motor car radiators is ticking over slowly, but the other half, which makes number plates for the motor trade, is absolutely dead. He and co-promoter, John Campbell, have already surveyed their fans. They're surprised by the findings – 85.7 per cent say they'll attend if speedway is staged in 2020 with Government approval or measures in place.

It's given Alex a boost. 'The survey has come out a lot more positive than I ever dreamt it would. I told Rob Godfrey to tell the other top league teams at their meeting today about it. There are always people being a bit negative. The next thing I know I had a phone call this morning from British Speedway who want to put it out because it's the most positive story they've had for some time.'

* * *

The lockdown is proving tough for Redcar Bears' promoter, Jitendra Duffill, both personally and professionally. As an optometrist, he lost his work early on but he's not feeling sorry for himself. 'It's just the way it is for a lot of people.'

In some ways, he's more despondent about the prospects for his speedway team. They're having to pay rent on the Media Prime Arena Stadium, even though they're not running any meetings. The land is owned by the council and, while they still have rent and rates to pay, they've been awarded a grant from the Government, which should allow them to cover that.

'We'll do our best to get through it. We're quite lucky that we've got two directors who are really passionate about the club. It wouldn't be the first time they've had to put their hands in their pocket if it came to that.'

As I'm hearing all too often, Redcar are yet another speedway club that doesn't make money over a season – or even wash their face. 'It costs us money every single year. Last year we did better than we have in a long time because we worked really hard on the sponsorship side and that improved our finances quite significantly. We're better sponsored than a lot of, if not most, clubs in the Championship. But we've made no secret of the fact that we lose money at Redcar. It's a very expensive hobby for our directors at the end of the day.

'Last year we were pretty successful on the track and I think that brought a lot of people back who'd stayed away. But we're still not at the level we need to be. I'm a pretty positive person and I still believe in speedway as a sport. I wouldn't be doing it if I didn't. We're just trying to work on getting the club to where it should be.' He says his aim for the year – not an ambitious one, he admits – had been to try and get the club on an even keel and get it paying for itself. He believes they could have done that if the lockdown hadn't happened.

'It's not just guys like myself, Jade Mudgway [co-promoter] and Jamie Swales [a former rider who joined in March as a third co-promoter]; there are a lot of volunteers working hard for us behind the scenes. There are very few people at Redcar speedway who get paid for what they do. We were all working towards that goal and this is going to set us back, as it will everybody. God knows what's going to happen with the sponsorship as well, because a lot of those people are probably going to find their purse strings will be tighter now. The situation is quite worrying for a lot of businesses. It's a pretty scary time for everybody.'

That includes the riders. Jitendra knows many of them are struggling. He mentions current British champion Charles Wright, who was due to double-up for both Belle Vue and Redcar this season. 'I know he's invested pretty much everything he had into his equipment for this season. And then, come the eve of the season, his means of earning a living are taken away from him and that's left him in a pretty difficult situation.'

Jitendra also talks about Erik Riss, another Redcar rider and the current National League Riders' champion. He's German and has been living in Jitendra's house, renting with his Australian fiancée, Maddie Campton. They'd been planning to fly back to her home in Australia but, two days before their flight was due to leave, Australia locked its borders to non-nationals, which meant Erik couldn't go. They then looked into going to Germany but this time it was Maddie who wasn't allowed in. 'If they wanted to be together, they had to stay here. But neither of them had an income.' As it turns out, Erik ends up returning to Germany by himself after Maddie decides it's time to go back to Australia before a total lockdown is imposed by her home country. Jitendra pauses. 'Charles and Erik, just two small stories really that I'm sure are reflected elsewhere with other riders across the country. But all of them are self-employed and they're going to struggle.'

Every year, Redcar Bears traditionally collect money for Easter eggs, which their riders then personally deliver to sick children at the James Cook University Hospital in Middlesbrough. It's their way of giving a little back to the community. Clearly, this year the lockdown has prevented them doing it as normal – but the collection still went ahead, thanks to two of the club's volunteers, commercial manager

Ian Drinkel and Claire James. Jitendra says they were pretty persistent. They liaised with a local charity that works with the hospital who were quite happy for it to go ahead as long as it was done carefully. They usually ask for eggs but this year they asked for actual donations. They raised around £1,100 within days, which Jitendra considers an amazing effort in light of all the uncertainty that everybody is facing at the moment.

It's one bright spot in a testing time that shows little sign of easing. 'It's a little demoralising really. You put in all that hard work and you just feel as though it's been swept away and you're back at square one. I try not to think about things too much. We'll just wait for this to pass and then see where we are and try and rebuild from there. I don't really know where it's going to leave us – or the sport in general.'

* * *

As May continues, there's confusion over when, or indeed if, Britain's lockdown will be eased. It's an indication of how much our daily routines have shrunk, that the thought of queuing to get into a garden centre or visiting a council tip – socially distanced, of course – can be dangled in front of us as some kind of reward for two months of self-sacrifice.

While the numbers of those dying from COVID-19 are on a definite downward trend, daily totals are still in the hundreds. The front pages of national newspapers on the first Thursday of the month had been full of over-optimistic headlines about lockdown effectively being lifted on the following Monday. But when the Prime Minister does speak to the country it's to clarify his Government's new 'stay alert' slogan, which has been described as nonsensical and rejected by the devolved governments in Scotland and Wales.

There are signs of sport beginning again in other parts of Europe. In Germany, the Bundesliga restarts in the middle of the month behind closed doors.

But for speedway riders, it's still a matter of what might have been. On 17 May, Swindon's Adam Ellis tweets that today should have been his 31st meeting of the season. He's been counting. While the BSP Ltd remain confident that there will be speedway this season, possibly in August, there are others who think that the Ben Fund meeting back in March will be the only one.

There is, however, the strong likelihood of competitive league speedway in June.

Just not in Britain.

* * *

There's a lot of talk about speedway needing to reach a much younger audience. One of the ways to do that is clearly through social media. Speedway, it's fair to say, was a late convert to the digital world. But that is changing. All clubs have an active social media presence and, when it comes to which club leads the way, the name which often comes up is that of Glasgow Tigers. Their number of followers on Twitter – nearly 21,000 – is, while not likely to cause Kim Kardashian any sleepless nights, the highest of any speedway club in Britain. It's the same with Facebook likes and Instagram followers.

Much of that is down to the work of 27-year-old Robert McFarlane. He'd always wanted to get into sports marketing and got a job at Allied Vehicles, Glasgow's owners and main sponsors. He admits he hadn't actually heard of speedway at that point. But when someone was needed to work on marketing for Glasgow Tigers, Robert put his hand up. He became the go-to person and, after a year and a half, he convinced them to make the role full-time. He's been there just shy of two years although, like many, he's furloughed at the moment.

Robert's – and Glasgow's – approach to bringing more people in through the gates isn't just based on the actual racing.

'We realised that if you want people to come and watch 15 races, that might be enough for someone who's been for years and who loves their speedway. But if you're wanting kids to come along, you have to try and get them involved and make it more of a spectacle. We think that sets us apart from a lot of teams. We maybe take a bit longer to run a meeting, but then it's more of a night out for people my age.'

Robert's friends do come along but only because of his connection. 'None of them had heard about speedway before, apart from wondering if it was something that used to be on Sky.'

Trying to market to different individuals and age groups is something that Robert and Glasgow have thought about very carefully. It's a question of tailoring content, much of it done through Facebook advertising. 'That way you can be very specific. Some people going for a night out want to buy alcoholic drinks, but that might not appeal so much to parents, so you let them know they can have their kids running about in centre-green races.'

That's where Glasgow's mascot, Roary the Tiger, comes in. 'The kids love it because they get to go on the centre green and race against him. There's a couple I know who come along and all their daughter talks about is, "I want to come along and see the Tiger!" She's not really bothered about the speedway. What's good about Glasgow is it's very broad. You've got kids running about, with their mums and dads. You've got old people too. You've got boys from a biker club who come along to watch or guys who just come along for a few beers. It's really varied.'

What Glasgow are doing has been noticed by the rest of the league. Alex Harkess, whose Edinburgh team enjoy probably British speedway's most keenly felt rivalry with Glasgow, says the Tigers spend more money on speedway in the Championship than all the other clubs added together. 'They spend and lose a fortune but they can afford to do it, so they try to get it right. They'll spend more on advertising a weekly match than most teams spend in a season. They accept that you've got to try and attract the younger generation. A very high percentage of pensioners come to speedway and they're not going to be there indefinitely. They do these races on the centre green and they get a lot of kids to come, so good on them for doing that.'

In a city known the world over for its keenly felt and often hostile rivalry between its two football teams, Glasgow Tigers make a point of sailing a conciliatory middle course. 'We have people who come along in Celtic tops, people who come along in Rangers tops, even amongst the management. We try and have a wee joke about it, but we do try and distance ourselves from it. We'll pitch ourselves as: "See if you can't be bothered with the whole drama and politics of supporting a football club in Glasgow? Then come and watch the speedway." I think our supporters buy into that as well. "Who's your team – Celtic or Rangers?" Neither, it's Glasgow Tigers.'

Then Robert brings up the topic of what he calls the 'speedway bubble' – and how it can, inadvertently, get in the way of spreading the sport's appeal more widely.

'I think people who are involved in speedway – and this isn't a criticism – are caught in a bubble. When I look at what the volunteers were doing on our social media before, it was great but it was all very focused towards speedway fans. It was preaching to the converted. The older people are going to come along anyway, they're your bread and butter. But to get other people along you've got to try and open it up. If somebody arrives on your Facebook page, for example, they have to be able to see something within the first two posts which they can understand. If you've just got the scores up, you've lost them. I only managed to work out how the whole bonus points system worked about six months ago.'

It's true. For a sport that should be simple – four men racing round an oval track for four laps on 500cc bikes – its workings can be deceptively complex for the newcomer. As a result, Robert says they do funny videos or something daft that a rider has said or done to make it more user-friendly for anyone clicking through to their Facebook page.

And while I, and many others, had been excited by the off-season activity in British speedway, Robert's not so sure. He doesn't think the Nicki Pedersen and Jason Crump signings were as big as people think. He understands that it'll bring older people back who might have drifted away from the sport, but he brings it back to the bubble. 'They're both big names for people who know speedway, but if you go outside that, people just don't know who they are.'

Robert apologises for being pessimistic but what he says is true. Crump and Pedersen's signings were big news for *Speedway Star*. For the *Daily Mail* or BBC Radio 5 Live? Not so much.

* * *

Like many people stuck at home throughout the unseasonably warm and dry spring, Dave Tattum has been doing things he should have done 20 years ago, like sorting out cupboards, painting around the house and creosoting the shed.

Dave had been looking forward to the new season. Although he does admit to feeling a bit down that Stoke weren't going to be part of it, he did have his new role at Newcastle to look forward to. 'The new promotion had cheered everybody up and people can see that Rob Grant means business. It was all good and then this happens and – gosh, it's terrible.

'My heart goes out to all the people involved in speedway. To be really cruel to us, it's the best spring we've had in years. It's been great speedway weather.'

If there's one consolation, it's that Newcastle don't have to pay rent while the season's postponed. New promoter, Rob Grant, had secured a deal where he only pays if he runs a meeting. Dave, at Stoke, would have had to pay some rent at Loomer Road had he still been there.

Ask him what he's heard from his old riders, and he'll reel off what they're up to, like a proud headmaster looking back on his recent school-leavers. Most of his Stoke riders from 2019 work anyway: Joe Lawlor does tree surgery work, Tom Perry works for Barclays Bank, Connor Coles helps to manufacture chimney pots.

'I speak to folk regularly and it's a bit frightening. It's like we're all running around with very dark glasses on not knowing when the lights are going to be turned on. I think Len Silver's right in what he's saying about older supporters. The majority of our support are senior citizens. Are they going to want to come out and stand shoulder to shoulder with somebody after this? Most speedway people like to stand in one spot, don't they? By the starting gate or wherever. Will we even be allowed to do that now? They'll be cautious and rightly so.'

The lockdown has stopped demolition work – for now – at Loomer Road. Dave makes occasional visits to have a look and he's upset with what he's seen. 'It has been wrecked. I have someone who flies a drone round a couple of times a day who reports back to me if there's any kids playing or anything untoward going on. They've absolutely wrecked Loomer Road. You wouldn't believe that maybe one or two teenagers could do as much damage as they've done. Every window in the grandstand's smashed to pieces. The referee's box – smashed to pieces. The interior of the bar is just absolutely smashed to smithereens. If you'd paid somebody to do it, they couldn't do as good as they've done.

'It's a hard pill to swallow when you know you've put in thousands of pounds to make it nice. It was an absolute money pit at one time. It's very sad. It was going to be knocked down but that isn't the point. It bugs me to think another human being can do what they've done to someone else's property.'

On 13 May, a few days after we speak, Stoke's stadium is indeed demolished. At the end of the month, it'll be revealed that Loomer Road is to be turned into a £16.8 million warehouse scheme. Peveril Securities has applied for permission to redevelop the site to provide up to 300,000 square feet of warehousing space.

* * *

When you're used to a family home with 24 acres of grounds, being cooped up in a small flat must come as a bit of a shock. Particularly when you've had to leave your wife and two young daughters behind with no idea of when you'll see them again. And you're effectively quarantined in the flat for two weeks and not able to go outside.

Even so, Tai Woffinden doesn't want his new circumstances seen as any kind of sob story. In the current climate, he's fully aware that everyone's suffering and the current reality is something everyone has to accept.

He's left his home in the East Midlands for a rented apartment in Wrocław. Poland, with its much more lucrative TV contracts, can afford to run league meetings behind closed doors and is aiming to restart in the middle of June. But in order to do so, Tai – along with every other foreign rider arriving from outside Poland – has to fulfil the terms of his contract and go into quarantine. It'll be a routine of Zoom calls back home, Netflix-watching, loading and unloading the dishwasher and exercise wherever he can manage it in the flat.

It's meant some of the top riders who, unlike Tai, were due to ride in the British League are now in Poland – Jason Doyle, Robert Lambert, Dan Bewley, Niels-Kristian Iversen and Nicki Pedersen. There's some doubt – given the current restrictions on travelling in and out of Poland – as to whether they'll even be able to return to England, or indeed Sweden or Denmark, should the leagues there start up again. But given there's no prospect of that at the moment, it's not a pressing issue.

Doyle, due to ride for Swindon in 2020, has been put up in a five-star hotel by his Polish team, Częstochowa. He jokes that it's pretty much just below being in jail, telling Nigel Pearson and Kelvin Tatum in their weekly podcast that the highlights of his day are breakfast, lunch and dinner. He'd posted a video just before leaving, outlining why he was going to Poland and saying how tough it was going to be leaving his wife, Emily, and family back in England.

That wasn't the only consideration for the riders. With meetings going ahead behind closed doors, there have been tough negotiations with the Polish Ekstraliga authorities. New sanitary regulations will be implemented when the season starts. Riders won't be allowed to shower at the stadium after meetings or change in the dressing rooms. Social distancing will be in force in the pits and there's to be a limit on the number of mechanics allowed, with masks mandatory between races. But, with no crowds in the stadium and far less revenue, the authorities have insisted on changing the riders' original contracts. And that's taken some time to agree. Before the pandemic and subsequent lockdown, the maximum signing-on fee for a rider racing in Poland's top league was 250,000 PLN (just under £48,000), with the maximum payment per point being 5,000 PLN (£963). After negotiations with the riders' union, reduced figures have been agreed at 200,000 PLN in signing-on fees (£38,500) and 2,500 PLN (£480) per point – a 50 per cent reduction.

Even with those new rates, pay in British speedway still comes nowhere close according to Edinburgh's co-promoter, Alex Harkess. 'There'll be nobody in Great Britain getting paid that kind of money, £480 per point. One or two will be on a guarantee where it doesn't matter what points they score, they're going to get the same amount each week. Poland's the only country that's paying that sort of rate.'

While not every rider in Poland will be on the top level of pay, it's obvious why the riders have accepted the pay cuts and, potentially, opted to leave their families for five months. Speedway careers are short and riders need to maximise their earnings when they can. Poland, as it has been for some years, and continues to be now, is far and away the best place to do that.

* * *

It wasn't always this way. But Poland's position at the pinnacle of the speedway world is worth reflecting on because, in some ways, its strengths reflect the current predicament that British speedway finds itself in, even before the COVID-19 crisis.

Its rise has been gradual. Poland ran domestic speedway leagues after the Second World War and enjoyed international success – their national team won the World Team Cup four times in the 1960s and Jerzy Szczakiel was individual world champion in 1973. But it was just another country where speedway took place. After the fall of communism in 1989, the Polish leagues gradually opened up to foreign riders and, over the last 20 years, led by their second world champion, Tomasz Gollob, Poland began to dominate international competitions and become the place where the world's best riders competed.

Last year, the newly crowned world champion, Bartosz Zmarzlik, was voted Polish Sports Person of the year, ahead of Bayern Munich's star striker, Robert Lewandowski. Crowds in the top division are generally close or full to capacity – pre-COVID – with anywhere between 7,000 and 16,000 fans. Lublin, in the eastern part of Poland, sold out every season ticket for the 2020 season back in November.

The crowds aren't just bigger but generally younger too. Visit Rybnik, a city of 140,000 near the Czech border, and you'll see young schoolchildren wearing speedway caps and T-shirts. Away fans – now largely an endangered species in British speedway – are visible and vocal in their segregated pens. The atmosphere is intense, much more akin to a football match.

That makes a big difference to the kinds of sponsors the sport can attract. Joe Parsons is the director of marketing for Monster Energy drinks, a big sponsor of both Polish speedway and the Grand Prix series. In Jenny Gow's *Speedway* podcast, he explained that wherever speedway tracks exist in Poland, sales of Monster Energy drinks go up. The sport and the number of people it attracts works for them.

Every top league Ekstraliga meeting is televised live and the amount of money dwarfs what British clubs get. Leading Polish speedway journalist Tomasz Lorek revealed details in the 'Future of Speedway' issue of *Speedway Star* in November 2018. In that year, every top league club received just over £10,000 every time they were live on TV, meaning that, on average, they earned nearly £250,000 over the course of the season. Even more money can come from local sponsorships, with Lorek saying that an average Ekstraliga club might receive around £550,000 a year from local companies like car dealers, construction and insurance companies and small banks, figures the like of which British clubs can only dream.

Even in the troubled times that everyone finds themselves in just now, Polish Ekstraliga clubs had half a million zloty, just short of £100,000, transferred to them from sponsorship and TV deals in April to help ease them through their own lockdown.

It all means that riders, if they want to get to the very top, need to be racing in Poland. Tai Woffinden has said that he probably gets paid many multiples more than he would if he did the exact same job at home. Not everyone's a three-times world champion, of course, but Britain's co-manager, Olly Allen, rode in the Polish league for nine years and says it's something else. 'As a rider, the pressure is five, six times what you're experiencing in England. The lows can be lower but the highs are much higher. Obviously, it's much better financially as well. I would say ten times higher per point.'

There is a downside to riding in Poland. Because of the rivalry amongst teams, fans just wouldn't accept one of their own riders turning out for another club, particularly one in the same area. So Polish clubs, which last operated a British-style points limit on teams in 2013, operate with squads where riders can be rotated in and out of the starting seven depending on form and injury. That means they're not guaranteed to race in every match – or to be paid every week either. They're only part of a squad and a couple of bad matches can mean they're sitting, often unhappily, on the sidelines.

If we're being picky, it's fair to say that Polish speedway is stronger and more popular in some areas than others. In the same way that there's no speedway in London, there is no speedway club in Poland's capital, Warsaw, either. Polish speedway also struggles to get coverage in the national press. While five different commercial TV channels cover meetings, there's little coverage on the free-to-air network. But that, as we've said, is being picky.

To return to the advantages that speedway clubs in Poland have over their British cousins, look at the support they get from their local councils. For many Polish municipalities, particularly in medium-sized or smaller towns, direct grants to speedway teams are seen as a way of promoting their name nationally. For some clubs in the top Polish league, the council funds more than 30 per cent of a club budget.

Earlier this year, it was reported in *Speedway Star* that Rybnik had to pay back one million zlotys – around £200,000 – to their local council. The reason? They hadn't spent it. A problem your average British speedway club would love to experience.

It's not just financial support. Councils in Poland have helped clubs build purpose-built speedway stadia. The MotoArena in Toruń is one of the most impressive venues around. Built in 2009, with a capacity of 15,500, it's used by the local speedway team, KS Toruń, for one of the Polish rounds of the Grand Prix, for stock cars and concerts. But, because playing football matches there would mean putting a pitch over parts of the shale speedway track, that's not allowed. Speedway takes precedence, which rarely happens in multi-use stadia in Britain. In addition, in Toruń, after the old stadium was bought by private investors, the council financed the construction of the new one.

Contrast this with Great Britain. Manchester City Council is the exception. It played a big part in the construction of the National Speedway Stadium for both the Belle Vue club and Great Britain international matches. Otherwise, council association with speedway generally tends to be limited to turning down initial planning applications or imposing curfews because of noise and disruption.

Adam Isherwood, Stoke Potters' team manager during their last season at Loomer Road, said there didn't seem to be the willpower from councillors in the area to get behind other sports. In his view, football dominates. Cradley fans would no doubt agree.

Then again, maybe it's hard to criticise councils for failing to support their local speedway teams after a decade of austerity and with possibly worse to come. Take one of those councils that does have speedway in its area, Newcastle upon Tyne. Earlier this year, *The Guardian* reported that the council, one of the hardest hit by years of relentless cuts, had lost some £300 million in the past decade in Government grants. That had led to the closure of youth clubs, libraries and children's centres, and the neglect of parks and other facilities. While they were able to raise council tax by two per cent and received £16 million from a Government cash injection in 2019, that only covered the rise in the minimum wage. The city now had to slash another £20 million from its budget and cut deep into its provision for social care – again, before the impact of COVID-19. In that environment, helping a local speedway track clearly doesn't figure as a priority.

But Poland shows what can happen when clubs and cities do work together. Joe Parsons, from Monster Energy drinks, highlights the key differences using Wrocław as an example. The city owns the track and grants it to the club in the form of a sponsorship. In Britain, with a few notable exceptions, clubs rent tracks from private owners who don't have any intention of improving facilities. In time, the land that these tracks sit on becomes so valuable that the landowner sells out to build flats or houses.

'Those sports with noise are getting pushed out and away. In Poland, what they did a long time ago was put all these tracks where there weren't big cities. The cities ended up getting built around them. But in the UK, property got too valuable. Had the speedway community back in the late 70s and 80s bought those properties, speedway in England would probably be just as strong as it is in Poland.'

It's a view with which many in British speedway would, sadly, agree.

June 2020 – Closed doors

AFTER WHAT we've all lived through over the last ten weeks, the start of June offers some relief. The Government is relaxing its lockdown rules, those everyday guidelines that would have seemed ludicrous three months earlier, but which are now an accepted part of the new world. Much of what's announced is open to interpretation – both in what it means and who it applies to, particularly given widespread public anger over revelations about special adviser Dominic Cummings' trip to Durham during the early stages of lockdown. The main points of this new easing are that, from Monday, 1 June, groups of six can meet outside; more shops, car showrooms and outdoor markets can open; and, most importantly for the frustrated sports fan, both sporting and cultural events can resume – but with conditions.

'This guidance provides the safe framework for sports to resume competitions behind closed doors,' says the Secretary of State for Digital, Culture, Media and Sport, Oliver Dowden. 'It is now up to individual sports to confirm they can meet these protocols and decide when it's right for them to restart.'

Given that the Bundesliga in Germany has been running for two weeks without any apparently linked rise in COVID-19 cases, this seems a sensible move. The Premier League announces it will resume matches in the middle of the month, with the Championship set to follow a few days later. No spectators will be permitted but, crucially, every single game will be televised on a variety of channels – Sky, BT, BBC, Amazon. This is not an option available to speedway. Nobody is offering hundreds of thousands of pounds for the right to screen Wolverhampton against King's Lynn.

Rob Godfrey, though, remains upbeat. He reckons speedway could get underway in August assuming that – like every other sport – it can satisfy the Government's 'phase three' guidance.

Speedway's first steps towards a return to action will begin this month with behind-closed-doors practice sessions at tracks like Scunthorpe, Leicester and Berwick. Godfrey says that if everyone follows the rules, they can then move on to the next stage – in July – which would involve open practices and amateur meetings. A few weeks after that, he's hopeful they can get the professional leagues up and running.

Being able to start in August will still allow time for a shortened and meaningful league season, although its exact format and play-off system is still to be finally agreed. Rob's also in constant touch with Eurosport, whose first year, of a five-year contract, this was meant to be.

And so, on the first of the month, British sport's ten-week hibernation ends with snooker in Milton Keynes and horse racing at Newcastle. But, for speedway, the day brings two disappointing developments – one expected, the other not.

The first comes from the Fédération Internationale de Motocyclisme. It says that the British Grand Prix, scheduled for Cardiff's Principality Stadium at the end of July, has been cancelled, 'due to ongoing health concerns and UK Government restrictions regarding COVID-19.' No one is surprised by this, given that every other Grand Prix scheduled up to this point has also been cancelled. But seeing the news in black and white is further confirmation that, while lockdown may be easing, nothing is returning to normal quickly.

Later the same afternoon, Glasgow Tigers release a statement. Given how rarely news in the speedway world – signings, closures, fall-outs, rumours – remains secret, this does come out of the blue. It's from their owners, Gerry, David and Peter Facenna.

'Having thought long and hard about the 2020 speedway season, we regret to inform you that the Tigers will not be taking part this year.'

They say there were many factors behind their decision, very similar to the ones facing just about every other speedway track in the country.

First is the health and well-being of supporters, volunteers, staff, riders and officials. While restrictions in Scotland are different to those in England, Glasgow say it would be virtually impossible to safely control social distancing in the stadium and they're not prepared to put people at risk where this isn't possible.

Equally, it wouldn't be financially viable to restrict the number of people they can allow into the stadium as, unlike other sports that enjoy additional income streams, Glasgow's revenues are primarily down to ticket sales.

Then there's rider availability. Five of Glasgow's seven riders are currently overseas, with two in Denmark, two in Australia and one in the USA. With possible travel restrictions for August unknown at the moment, they feel it's understandably quite a lot to ask riders to come back to take part in a vastly shortened season, after having already been here and gone home earlier in the year, all at their own expense.

They also point to the fact that, especially in Glasgow, the weather's not the best in October. 'If we were to take part in a shortened season, it would be likely that we would be running right up until the end of October, with no doubt a few rain-offs along the way.'

Then, finally, a factor no one can be sure of. 'We're also not convinced the appetite to come and watch speedway will be where it was last year, especially if it's a shortened season and with many people not having received full wages for the last few weeks, let alone those who will sadly lose their jobs. We also need to consider our supporters and the confidence they'll have in attending populated live events, given that many are in the "at risk" category as far as Covid-19 is concerned.'

They hold out the slim possibility of one-off individual meetings before the end of the season – but, while saying every club will need to make their own decisions, Glasgow are now looking forward to the 2021 season.

Reaction is almost universally positive and understanding, whether that's in replies posted on the Tigers' Twitter feed, the *British Speedway Forum* or the friendlier, more nostalgia-tinged *Friends of Speedway* group on Facebook. The general view is that Glasgow have made the right move and been open and candid. It's unusual to find such unanimity in the British speedway world.

But it is just the speedway world talking about their withdrawal. I'm surprised, given Glasgow Tigers' activity in promoting and marketing themselves to a wider audience, particularly in the west of Scotland, how little coverage their announcement gets, even in the Scottish media. After all, there aren't many teams who have pulled out of a season because of COVID-19.

Rob Godfrey releases a statement in response on behalf of the BSP Ltd. He says they've been aware of Glasgow's concerns in recent weeks and respect their decision. He stresses that the majority of clubs still wish to press ahead with a season if this is possible. 'Despite Glasgow's decision, there remains an air of cautious optimism throughout British speedway.'

In the following days, several clubs – Leicester, Poole, Sheffield, Edinburgh and Ipswich among them – release statements underlining their intention to run some form of league speedway in 2020.

The only other club to partly follow Glasgow's example are Newcastle, who announce that their Gems' team will not run in the National Trophy. The Championship Diamonds team will still take part if circumstances allow.

But as the month goes on, and with the likelihood of a 14-day travel quarantine on recent arrivals to the UK threatening rider availability, there's a creeping feeling that the British season might not go ahead in any form. For the first time, there's more discussion about teams starting afresh in 2021 with the same squads they had for 2020.

* * *

Every so often an event occurs that has repercussions way beyond anything anyone could possibly have imagined at the time. Such an event is George Floyd's visit to a grocery store in the Powderhorn area of Minneapolis on Monday, 25 May.

His death, after one police officer kneels on his neck and three other officers either restrain him or fail to intervene to save him, results in protests across, first, the United States, and then many other parts of the world. It's sadly not the first time that American police have been culpable in the deaths of African Americans, but it's clear that this has sparked something deeper and more permanent.

It goes wider than street protests and the pulling down of statues. By June, businesses in Britain – from the Bank of England to the pub group Greene King – are forced to re-evaluate their past and apologise for links to the slave trade. Even *The Guardian* newspaper is pulled into the debate, with claims that its founder, John Edward Taylor, profited from a cotton plantation that used slaves.

Several big names from the world of entertainment are also forced into saying sorry for what are now deemed to be errors of judgement. The producers of *The Simpsons* announce that their famous Indian character will no longer be voiced by a white actor. Comedians Ant and Dec and David Walliams and Matt Lucas apologise for historic sketches where they've impersonated people of colour.

The world of sport is, inevitably, also brought into the debate. In the United States, the Washington Redskins, under pressure from corporate sponsors, announce they are to change their name. In Britain, football comes under scrutiny, more for what it's failing to do now. The Premier League receives billions of pounds a year in broadcasting revenue and is called out for contributing just £300,000 to Kick It Out, the anti-racism campaign. Penalties on clubs whose fans are guilty of racial abuse are also criticised for not being harsh enough.

The Premier League restarts behind closed doors on 17 June with Aston Villa against Sheffield United. Players' names on the back of their shirts are replaced with 'Black Lives Matter' and all on the field – including the referee and his assistants – take the knee in a gesture of solidarity. But that doesn't prevent criticism of football's record in recruiting black managers. Black footballers account for 30 per cent of the Premier League's players but only one manager – Wolves' Nuno Espírito Santo – is black. In June 2020, just six out of the 91 managers in the top four leagues are black. By the end of the month, the Premier League, the English Football League and the Professional Footballers' Association have come together to set up a new scheme to increase the number of black, Asian and minority ethnic coaches.

In cricket, the former England batsman Michael Carberry says racism is 'rife' in the sport and that not enough is being done to combat it. Formula 1 is to set up a foundation to fund apprenticeships and scholarships to increase diversity in the sport.

But what, you may ask, has all this to do with British speedway? The reason? To give context around what follows.

It's fair to say that speedway, in general, would not score highly as a 'woke' sport. Its noisy and dirty bikes are powered by methanol, not as polluting as petrol or diesel but still considered a volatile organic compound and, hence, an air pollutant, by scientists. Start-line girls hold up lane boards at several British tracks and at Grand Prix events and Polish league matches. The row that saw their counterparts removed from Formula 1 grids a couple of years earlier largely passed speedway by. One of Britain's top riders of the last 20 years, Chris Harris, is nicknamed 'Bomber'. It was given to him when he rode at Exeter because of his habit of 'dive-bombing' underneath riders from behind. But it's more widely known as the nickname of Sir Arthur Harris, who oversaw the controversial RAF policy of saturation bombing of German cities during World War Two. Somerset Rebels did have the Confederate flag on their club badge until 2016 even though the 'Rebels' refers to the rebel uprising at the Battle of Sedgemoor in Somerset in 1685. Promoter Debbie Hancock decided it should be replaced, given events in the United States, and changed it to the mythical Wyvern, the Somerset county symbol.

If you think 21st-century Britain is a multicultural society then, against that background, British speedway does not reflect that at all. It is – undeniably – a white sport. Look at the team photos in the *Speedway Review 2019* – the sport's new annual records bible – and every face among the riders is white. Spectators attending speedway are, as well as generally being older, almost exclusively white as well. Some would say that isn't a problem, but it does cut the sport off from a source of both riders and supporters at a time when it clearly needs more of both. A correspondent on the *British Speedway Forum*, at the height of the 'Black Lives Matter' discussion, wonders how much scrutiny the sport would be coming under with its lack of diversity if it was better known.

But, at a time when other sports are under attack for exactly that and for failing to give black athletes real opportunities, British speedway isn't in the firing line. There are no demands for British speedway to change its ways and open up for black or Asian riders.

There have been two black riders who have competed in British league speedway over the last 40 years, the most prominent being Antonio Lindbäck. Abandoned as a baby in Brazil, he was adopted, and moved to Sweden when he was four. He raced for Poole Pirates and Belle Vue in Britain, but has mainly concentrated on riding in Poland and Sweden. A regular in the Grand Prix series since 2004 – he was 12th in 2019 – he was once dubbed the 'Tiger Woods' of speedway.

The other black rider was Paul Muchene. Born in London, Paul raced for Arena Essex at Lakeside as well as for Scunthorpe and Oxford from 1984 to 1989. A popular rider, Paul sadly died in July 1989, four days after an accident at Hackney when he fell and was hit by an oncoming rider.

But no one should equate that lack of black riders with British speedway being racist or closed to BAME riders. Nobody I speak to during the year of researching this book says anything other than that everyone – whatever their colour, age or gender – is welcome.

Rob Godfrey insists that speedway is there for everybody and that they're always reaching out to other communities. 'Ultimately, we are a family sport and we're always evolving, but we can only evolve with what's in front of us. At the moment we have no multiracial speedway riders, but if they were to come along it would be absolutely great.' One of his predecessors as promoters' chairman, Alex Harkess, backs that up. 'I don't care what colour you are, we're all the same, that's my attitude. Everybody's welcome! We have a complete shortage of riders worldwide and anything that opens the door and gives us new blood, then fine, let's go with it.' That is echoed by Barry Bishop, co-promoter at the Isle of Wight. Barry grew up on the multiracial housing estate of Blackbird Leys in Oxford. He's keen for speedway to have a more diverse rider base and fan base. 'We have to look at how we spread the word and what groups we aim for. Our entire philosophy on the Isle of Wight is that we want to entertain you whether you're five or 95, and that should apply equally across people's ethnicity too.'

Jitendra Duffill is the only BAME promoter in British speedway. His father is English, his mother Indian and, being half-Asian, he has come across racism in his life. 'There's always going to be a certain minority of the community that are ignorant or uneducated, unfortunately. There are just some idiots in the world.' But that's not happened in British speedway. 'If someone's perceived me as being different, it's never come across. That would be the same for anybody of any race in speedway, whether they're of Asian descent, black descent, it really doesn't matter. I don't think it would be tolerated in this sport, same way as it shouldn't be anywhere. We would welcome absolutely anybody at Redcar speedway and I know I speak for my colleagues at the BSP Ltd and our co-promoters and our riders too. I certainly wouldn't keep friends or riders who showed any signs of intolerance towards anyone else because of the way they looked.'

Jitendra freely admits that it's a difficult issue to talk about in the current climate. 'It's a bit of a relief that this hasn't crept into speedway and we've not had to comment. In speedway, everybody's welcome. I don't really know why there aren't any Asian speedway riders or even, if you look at our support, many black or Asian supporters coming through the gate. Maybe it's a cultural thing in that motorsports aren't as widely spread in that community?'

That's something I hear often. I'm told there's no reason whatsoever why black people shouldn't prosper in speedway but that it's not really the kind of sport they get involved with.

Indeed, if you look at some of those other sports – motor racing, superbikes, even professional cycling – you'll find the occasional article bemoaning a lack of diversity. If one of the criteria for being a speedway rider is getting used to being on a bike, then it's clear that being white is – for whatever reason – an advantage. Various studies over the last 15 years have shown that even in British cities like London (where one in three people identifies as black, Asian and minority ethnic), the overwhelming majority of cyclists, for example, are white.

Various theories have been put forward. That cycling just doesn't have the grassroots appeal to non-white communities or it might be considered low status in recent immigrant communities compared to owning a car. Or with ethnic minorities more likely to live in smaller or more densely occupied homes or flats, this might – practically – mean a lack of storage space.

Back in 2009, the Olympic Team GB cycling coach, David Brailsford, said that breaking down barriers to wider participation from black and ethnic minority groups remained the great unconquered goal for British cycling. Judging from the various British cycling squads for 2020, there's still work to be done in professional cycling too.

There are other practical considerations. Given that speedway has fallen out of general public consciousness since its golden periods – with the majority of Britons of whatever race now unaware of its continued existence – it's perfectly feasible to assume that it's passed by those first and second-generation immigrants as well. Many people involved in speedway today were introduced to the sport by their parents or grandparents. BAME groups lack that speedway-going heritage. Most riders who come into the sport today either have family histories with speedway or some previous involvement in other kinds of motorsports like motocross or grasstrack. Putting it bluntly, more parents – white or black – might want their children to go into the glamorous world of Formula 1 rather than become involved in a sport that involves careering around a dirt track at 60mph without brakes, where the risks appear greater and the rewards on offer much less.

Whatever the reason, speedway is not on any target list for black activists wanting to arrest historic or present inequalities. While that may be something of a relief for those involved in the sport – who have more than their fair share of challenges to be getting on with – it's ultimately a shame that a sizeable section of British society either can't or won't get to enjoy what, on its day, is one of the most thrilling sports taking place in this country.

* * *

Back in the world of COVID-19 restrictions, the Government is under pressure to reduce its guidance on social distancing from the current two metres to one metre. Restaurants and pubs in particular say they just won't be financially viable without that less restrictive distance, which is now permitted in many other European countries. If the crowds flocking to Bournemouth beach this month as the good weather continues are anything to go by, many people have decided to go with their own gut instinct anyway. For many, particularly younger people, fear of catching the virus now seems a very remote possibility.

While the point is made that most speedway stadiums already operate at no more than 25 per cent capacity at the best of times, there's no likelihood of that being put to the test any time soon. Instead, British speedway fans have to look abroad because action is getting underway in countries where governments took lockdown actions earlier and, as a result, lifted them more quickly too.

The first speedway meeting in Europe in the 'new world' is the Czech Republic Individual Cup Round 1 in Pardubice on Wednesday, 3 June. The limit on paying spectators is 150. But when the Polish Ekstraliga starts the following weekend there are no spectators inside the stadiums. Permission to operate with 25 per cent capacity crowds won't start until the following weekend.

Nevertheless, it's speedway, with the top riders, and it's clear that a lot of British fans are watching Premier Sports' live coverage. The star of the first weekend isn't anyone on the track though. It's Dave Goddard, who's commentating remotely from Britain. Dave doesn't have a co-commentator to bounce off or to give him time to gather his thoughts. Nor, certainly for the first few meetings, does he have the luxury of any advertising breaks either. Instead, when the host broadcaster cuts to studio interviews in Polish, Dave has to improvise. He reads out the many tweets sent to him from British viewers, which allow him to reminisce about long-gone tracks or riders from the past. To some this might be the equivalent of a local radio presenter filling in time because the newsreader hasn't turned up for the top-of-the-hour bulletin. To me, it's another sign of that speedway community. It may be relatively small but even if it can't currently meet up in the grandstand at Poole, it can keep in touch – and revive fond memories of long-gone tracks – through the medium of televised speedway from Poland.

Of the three Britons taking part in the first round of weekend races, Robert Lambert and Tai Woffinden score well, but Dan Bewley, likely to be the third member of Great Britain's international team for the Speedway of Nations, looks off the pace. Those running Polish speedway also seem to love grading their tracks, and if you're someone who's missed watching tractors spraying water, then all your stars have aligned this weekend. The start-line girls – a feature of all Polish Ekstraliga meetings – look completely different with their mandatory masks matching black catsuits as if they've wandered on track from the set of a David Lynch film. Overall, the opening couple of weekends are a bit of a mixed bag in terms of entertainment. It's like looking forward to seeing someone you've not met for ages and then discovering that you don't actually have that much to chat about after ten minutes or so.

Inevitably, the weather plays its part too. After Poland had enjoyed the same dry, sunny weather that had marked the initial months of lockdown here in Britain, the start of the speedway season coincides with rain. Several matches are postponed.

By the third weekend, even with clubs now allowed to have 25 per cent crowd capacity to give some atmosphere, I don't think I'm alone in wondering what all the fuss in Polish speedway is about.

There are the occasional good races, but they're the exception. Even Dave Goddard admits in one early meeting that if you're off gate four, you've basically got no chance of winning. The tracks are dusty, never a sign of good, competitive racing. I find myself pausing the action and returning to the screen half an hour later so I can fast-forward through the replays to get to the live action. As I'm doing so, I realise – or rather remember – something that's really important about speedway. If I spin up to the very start of a heat and miss who's lining up in which lane or helmet colour, then the race that follows has less appeal. Admittedly, quite a few of the riders – particularly the young Polish reserves – are names even the most diehard speedway fan would struggle to recognise, but that's not the point. Knowing who the riders are before the race, anticipating who's going to win, who might miss the start but then work his way through from the back, is all part of the joy of watching speedway. I'm reminded of my first season watching Edinburgh Monarchs in 1982 and how the seven riders – Dave Trownson, Benny Rourke, Ivan Blacka, Chris Turner, Eric Broadbelt, Brett Saunders and Ian Westwell – hardly changed from week to week. I got to know their individual riding styles and, as a result, I got hooked. Without knowing who's who and getting that connection, we can lose interest; never a good sign for any sport.

Seeing speedway for the first time in several months has also underlined one of those key differences between speedway and other sports. We want to be entertained. If I go along to watch my favourite football team play then, above all, I want them to win. If they play well and score a few goals in the process, that's even better. But grinding out a dull 1-0 win and getting the three points will do. If I'm a true fan, I'll most likely be back for the next game. Speedway's different. Yes, I want my team to do well, but I want to see the other team make a decent match of it. Watching a succession of 5-1s, where your riders finish first and second every time, is – frankly – dull. You could say us speedway fans want to have our cake and eat it. We want our team to win but, ideally, can we do it on an exciting last-heat decider please?

Collections for injured speedway riders at the Ben Fund Bonanza in March 2020

The chairman of the British Speedway Promoters Limited, Rob Godfrey, was open to questions in a Twitter Q&A on Good Friday

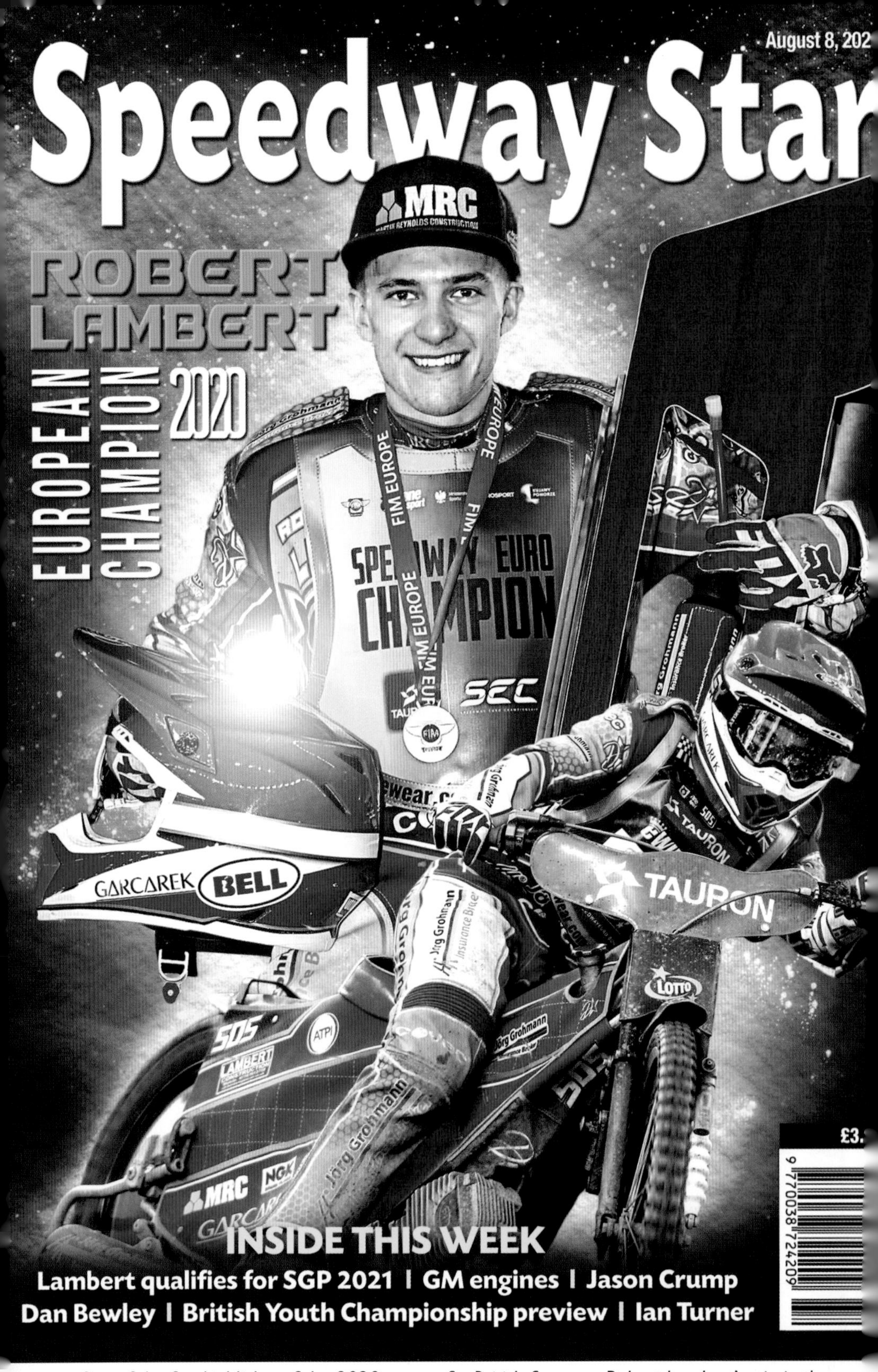

One of the few highlights of the 2020 season for British fans was Robert Lambert's win in the European Championships

July's Downing Street COVID-19 briefing by DCMS Secretary Oliver Dowden which – in the end – led to the cancellation of the British speedway season

Young riders prepare to take to the track at Redcar for an August practice

The new world greets spectators for the first speedway meeting since the outbreak of COVID-19 at Scunthorpe in August 2020

GB Young Lions manager Neil Vatcher takes some of the riders in the British Youth Championship through social distancing protocol

Races between Britain's Tai Woffinden (left) and Poland's Bartosz Zmarzlik (right) were the highlights of the 2020 Grand Prix series

Sixteen-year-old Katie Gordon is determined to become the first woman rider in the top leagues of British speedway

The British Final – finally – went ahead without spectators but was streamed live

Jason Crump in the red helmet leads in a heat of the British Final at Belle Vue on 28 September 2020

Edinburgh speedway takes place 25 miles outside Scotland's capital city at Armadale in West Lothian

Robert Lambert, Drew Kemp and Dan Bewley in their GB kevlars – complete with new sponsors – ahead of the 2020 Speedway of Nations in Poland ***(Taylor Lanning Photography)***

With 90 points up for grabs over 15 heats of team speedway, the last thing that will tempt someone back the following week is anything close to a 75-15 whitewash.

That's particularly true when you're not supporting either of the teams, such as when I sit down to watch Zielona Góra face Grudziądz on the third weekend. The meeting had been postponed on Friday because of rain and, to be frank, conditions aren't that much better by the time Saturday comes around. The track looks slick and there's precious little passing of any sort. My daughter's partner, who's been staying with us during lockdown, is a sports fan but hasn't come across speedway and has become interested in what I'm writing about. He sits down to watch this meeting, which turns out to be a bad choice. After a couple of heats, he makes the not unreasonable observation that whoever gets to the first corner in the lead ends up winning. It's hard to disagree. I find myself making excuses – there's been a lot of rain, the track's not ideal, if it wasn't on TV it might have been postponed – to try and keep his interest, but it's to no avail. He wanders off.

And, as a result, he misses one of those speedway fixtures which, at the opposite extreme, proves why, once we're gripped, it can be compulsive viewing. It's the first fixture the next day – Robert Lambert's newly promoted Rybnik versus world champion Bartosz Zmarzlik's Gorzów. It's a close meeting throughout and there's exciting racing and passing galore, exactly what we all want to see when we go to speedway. While Lambert's races are all worth watching, the highlight is one he's not in, heat 12. Rybnik are reduced to just one rider after an exclusion and no one expects much from their rider, young home reserve Kamil Nowacki, of whom I know nothing. He's up against two more experienced riders and hasn't taken a point from his first two races. But Nowacki leads from the gate and I find myself willing him on, despite frenetic and repeated attempts from the visiting riders to take the lead. He wins – to the delight of the home support. It's an exhilarating and wholly unexpected minute of pure speedway drama. Even without dramatic passing and overtaking, it showcases the best the sport can offer.

As a result, the slightly ho-hum nature of the previous three weekends is banished from my mind. Roll on next Friday.

* * *

One of those keeping a close eye on the meetings in Poland – and the progress of the British riders in particular – with special interest is Rob Painter, the managing director of GB Speedway. With the impact of coronavirus and the subsequent lockdown, he, his partner, Vicky Blackwell, and team managers, Simon Stead and Olly Allen, are looking at a 'significantly reduced calendar'. Their focus is the team Under-21 Championship Finals in Denmark in September and the Speedway of Nations in Manchester, which has been rescheduled to the end of October.

While the lockdown has been frustrating, they've not been standing still, by any means. They had two face-to-face camps earlier this year at the University of Southampton and Leicester speedway, which have been followed by online sessions with the squad every few weeks. Rob says it's something that they'd never planned to do and it's something positive that's come out of a bad situation. 'We've been able to build a real bond between us and within the rider group because they're not getting out and about – or up until recently certainly they weren't. They would come together every two weeks and train on the Zoom call and we'd also do work on mindset and riding techniques and really break down what it means to be an elite-level speedway athlete.'

Rob adds that they've created a support network for the riders in the British squad, the under-21 squad and the GB Academy. 'It can be a longer process to educate the riders who are slightly older because this is very new to them. They might be many years into their professional career, whereas the younger guys, this is all they've really known. Some of them are taking their first steps into the under-21 squad, and with that has come the new regime, and that's been received very well. What is very clear is that the riders of this generation and the next will be the best they can be. That isn't to say that we're going to produce multiple world champions, but what I'm absolutely sure of is they will have the opportunity to fulfil their potential whereas, in past generations, that hasn't been the case.'

The lockdown, though, has got in the way of off-track commercial development and sponsorships. GB Speedway's income comes, 100 per cent, from commercial partnerships. Without that, as Rob says, the wheels – literally – stop turning. He says they were going to make a significant announcement in March that they've had to postpone. 'You work hard for six or 12 months before you can begin a commercial partnership. It's an ongoing process but one that's moving in the right direction. In an ideal world, we'd be able to click our fingers and the vision that we've got for where we're going to be in four or five years would be here right now. But you can't cut corners. It would be fantastic if we were to have a commercial partner come in who could unlock the door to the future quicker, but that just isn't the case. We do have to build because we are doing something that's new. I'm not very patient. I wish that we were two or three years further ahead. But in terms of where we are right now compared to where we thought we would be, we are on track. I'm pleased with that. I just wish we could go a bit quicker.'

It's a refreshingly professional approach, in difficult circumstances, which says a lot for where the Great Britain international team is headed, both on and off the track.

* * *

In the last decade, two completely new speedway venues – the National Speedway Stadium in Manchester and Beaumont Leys in Leicester – have opened. Manchester's ambitious stadium, much appreciated for its facilities and the quality of its track, owed much to welcome support from Manchester City Council – £7 million to date – who were looking to regenerate the eastern part of the city. Leicester's stadium was more basic, built on spare land behind the Beaumont Leys shopping centre and next to an industrial estate, just a few miles from the M1. It meant that speedway returned to the East Midlands city after its original track was sold for housing in 1983.

So while it's easy to get caught up in the seemingly never-ending list of tracks closing – Buxton, Workington, Lakeside – it's important to remember that tracks can, given the right circumstances, re-emerge. That's why June is notable for not one, not two but three potentially promising pieces of news.

The first isn't entirely unexpected but it's still welcome. Oxford City Council, following their consultations back in December, have approved the local plan until 2036, following the recommendations of the planning inspectorate. It means, if you're a speedway fan, that Oxford Stadium should be retained as a leisure facility for the next 16 years, while allowing for 100 homes to be built on the main stadium car park. The chairman of the Save Oxford Stadium, Ian Sawyer, says it's a fantastic step forward for their campaign. He says it doesn't mean they've won but it does place another major obstacle in the way of anyone wanting to redevelop the stadium into housing. As is the way, nothing is expected to happen immediately. Rob Peasley, wearing his Oxford campaigner's hat, says they're waiting to see what the stadium's current owner's (Galliard Homes) next move is. With their plans to build housing seemingly thwarted for now, it's believed several people have come forward offering to buy the site. He describes it as a 'waiting game'.

If that's a step in the right direction, there's even better news from Bradford. Odsal Stadium once housed more than 100,000 people back in the 1950s for a rugby league match. It's a vast, natural, cavernous bowl of a stadium that has been used for a variety of sports and hosted two speedway World Finals back in 1985 and 1990. Today, though, it's empty. The rugby league team, the Bradford Bulls, moved out on cost grounds last autumn.

But now, according to the local newspaper, the *Telegraph and Argus*, speedway could return to the venue as early as April 2021. Steve Rees is primarily a stock-car promoter, but he's looking to put together a joint venture – which includes the Bradford Bulls and a speedway promoter – to bring sport back to the venue. Rees says the only way to make it viable for the Bulls to come back is to generate an additional revenue stream. He believes that can be done subject to further discussions with both the Rugby Football League (who hold the stadium lease) and a prospective speedway promoter. 'I'm now more than encouraged – I'm enthusiastic because it is definitely doable.'

But it's the third initiative, one that seems to come out of nowhere, which might yet be the most likely to come to fruition. Peter Oakes reveals in *Speedway Star* that Southampton – which hasn't staged any kind of speedway since its Banister Court home closed in October 1963 ahead of, you guessed it, being sold for housing – may stage racing again in 2023. Plans are well advanced: a small group of campaigners – Bring Back Southampton Speedway (BBSS) – have spent five years looking for a suitable patch of ground for a track. They've found land just outside the Southampton city boundary and close to the M27 motorway. Not only that, purchase of the land has been agreed in principle subject to interim planning permission. This would likely have already gone ahead had it not been for the COVID-19 lockdown. Given that the location is on infill land in a sparsely populated area, campaigners hope there will be no objections from local residents.

What's different about the plans for Southampton is that the initial aim is to build a track and basic stadium for amateur racing, to promote grassroots speedway and provide an opportunity to help the development of home youth talent. League racing is a longer-term ambition, but first they have to get the track open for people to use.

With two 'amateur-only' tracks already running at Iwade and Lydd in Kent and concern about the costs of running professional speedway in Great Britain, perhaps the campaigners in Southampton are pointing the way to a more sustainable – less professional admittedly – future for the sport.

There's also heartening news from Plymouth, where work has carried on through the lockdown on building a new 500-seat grandstand. Their application to move up to the Championship may have been turned down last November, but it hasn't stopped Plymouth making improvements. The grandstand has been dedicated to the

NHS – the seats in club colours feature 'NHS' and two hearts – and is a hopeful sign of the club's intent not just to continue running speedway but to do so at a higher level. At the other end of the country there's new hope for Workington, with Andrew Bain keen to run some kind of league racing at the Northside training track, although he's not putting any timescale on his plans.

But if there's promising news from Workington and Plymouth and Oxford and Bradford and Southampton, it wouldn't be British speedway if there wasn't a disappointment to set against all that. Earlier in the year there seemed to be realistic hope of speedway returning to the Greater London area with the reopening of Rye House in Hertfordshire. But, as Peter Schroeck, who'd continued to run training sessions there up until March, had hinted during our recent call, that might not be the case after all. The lockdown has hit the owners hard. Peter's view? 'It's run by a really nice guy but, at the end of the day, he needs to make it pay.'

And, when the long-awaited new plans for the site are released, those fears are confirmed. The existing speedway track will disappear, to be replaced with a 4G football pitch. The stadium owner, Ricky Musk, bought the site in May last year and feels the football pitch is a better fit as a leisure and sports facility. He'll tell *Speedway Star* that he's '90 per cent' sure speedway won't be returning.

'I don't think it is the way I want to go. It doesn't earn any money. It's not the sort of image we are trying to give.'

It's a sad indictment of the state of the sport that a 4G football pitch is thought likely to generate more revenue than leaving the existing track for speedway.

Musk says, quite rightly, that he can't run a business if it's not making him any money. But the same views of speedway as a noisy and dirty activity that the Stoke estate agent had mentioned to Dave Tattum are apparent here too.

'If it made money, I would still be semi-reluctant to do it [speedway] because it's a bit messy and I am a bit of a clean freak,' says Musk. 'I like things looking neat and tidy. We are putting some really nice-looking buildings up and I think they will get all grimed up with the speedway bikes going around there.'

The prospects for the sport returning to London – for better or worse, the country's biggest and most influential city – look even bleaker than they ever did. The memory of those five tracks running one night after another look set to remain just that.

July 2020 – An elite sport

MANY PEOPLE have found new ways – comforting and familiar – to occupy their time over the last few months. It might be gardening or reading or clearing out cupboards or sorting out photos. Rob Godfrey, when he's not running his garage or spending hours on calls around his chairmanship of the BSP Ltd, has spent his time lovingly restoring a 1980 Ford Capri. He's spent a total of about 370 hours on it. But he makes time, like millions of others, to watch the Government's daily coronavirus briefings. This evening – Thursday, 9 July – it is led by Oliver Dowden, the Secretary of State for Digital, Culture, Media and Sport (DCMS). As the minister speaks, Rob feels increasingly upbeat, euphoric even. He won't be ashamed to admit later that there are tears in his eyes as he listens. Dowden has been given a 'good cop' brief this evening. He's announcing a further easing of restrictions. Nail bars, swimming pools and outdoor theatres and arts venues can open later in July. More importantly for speedway, he says recreational sport can resume from the weekend, with five-a-side football, basketball, hockey and countless other sports to follow shortly after.

Rob has had four months of seemingly endless Zoom calls with other promoters, Government representatives, local MPs and councillors and Eurosport. He and his team have pretty much had to start from scratch with MPs given the demise of the All-Party Parliamentary Group for speedway. But tonight's announcement seems to make it all worthwhile. Some kind of speedway season can go ahead. Sports will need to publish specific guidance approved by

Government officials, but the BSP Ltd members have been working on that so it shouldn't be an issue.

But, when full details are released on the DCMS website that evening, Rob's worried. He begins to doubt what he'd heard earlier. The statement makes clear that the easing of restrictions applies to competitive grassroots sport. Speedway, in the Government's eyes, is an elite sport. Its athletes, the riders, are paid and therefore professional. As a result, it's being classified in the same bracket as Premier League football and Premiership Rugby Union. There's no green light after all. It's Rob's lowest moment of the summer.

That's reflected in the promoters' statement released the following day. In contrast to the previous, confidently worded announcements, this one introduces the first element of doubt that league speedway will take place.

It says, pointedly, that 'we believe the biggest risk to riders is the natural danger element of racing motorbikes with no brakes.' While there are heartening words about being within touching distance of being able to start a reduced season in a safe and enjoyable manner, 'we acknowledge the clock is ticking and if we cannot begin league racing in August there is every chance the season will run out of time.'

With infection rates heading down, various tracks, including Rob's own at Scunthorpe, have already opened up for practice sessions for riders keen to get back on their bikes after weeks of confinement.

It's all strictly controlled, with the number of mechanics allowed in the pits limited, hand sanitisers aplenty and areas safely cordoned off. Medical teams are available too, in contrast to earlier in the year when part of the reason for stopping anything sport-related was to avoid extra pressure on the NHS. For a club like Leicester, practice sessions are vital. Like Scunthorpe and King's Lynn, they own their own track, but that means having to cover fixed stadium costs. Being able to make even a little back on running training sessions helps with that.

But, in Leicester's case, the boost of added income has been short-lived. On the last Monday in June, the Health Secretary, Matt Hancock, announced that, because the city's COVID-19 rates were rising again, Leicester would become the first area to be put back into local lockdown. While the rest of England enjoys having pubs and restaurants open again from the first Saturday in July, Leicester's non-essential shops and schools close again under the Prime Minister's new 'whac-a-mole' strategy. The city is effectively cut off except for what's deemed essential travel.

It might be the prospect of other local lockdowns following Leicester. Or it might be that the long-awaited reopening of pubs and restaurants – with all their new restrictions – isn't the joyous occasion it might once have promised to be. Whatever, there's undoubtedly a glum resignation across the country as the pandemic enters its fifth calendar month. At the start, when it was new and there was genuine fear of the unknown, there was a sense of all being in it together, sharing the same burden for a common goal and, for some, experiencing unexpected excitement at being a small part of it. Now? While small steps are being taken towards restoring daily life as we know it, there's also an awareness that lockdown could be reimposed at a moment's notice. There's a long, slow grind ahead for everyone, with real normality far beyond the current horizon.

It doesn't help that it's increasingly hard to keep up with what's allowed and what isn't when it comes to Government advice. Trying to follow any logic is a fruitless exercise, as Rob Godfrey underlines. 'I can let you into my stadium and sell you a pint and a burger, but I can't let you watch any speedway while you're eating and drinking. It is massively frustrating, I have to be honest.'

On the same day as Dowden's announcement, the Prime Minister appears to reverse his opinion on the wearing of face masks as he's photographed wearing one for the first time in shops in his constituency of Uxbridge. A week later, he announces that sports' stadiums can open from 1 October with, more importantly, trial events with restricted crowds taking place from the end of July. The three – cricket, horse racing and snooker – are Surrey against Middlesex at the Oval, the Glorious Goodwood Festival and the World Snooker Championship in Sheffield. There's no mention of speedway.

British promoters, meeting for their regular Tuesday morning conference call and juggling various fixture lists in the event that some truncated league action does go ahead, can only look on at the rest of European speedway with envy. In addition to the Ekstraliga, the Polish first division has also restarted. There's league racing in Russia, challenge matches in Germany and individual meetings in the Czech Republic, Hungary, Italy and Sweden. It's announced that Swedish league racing will start on 11 August. With different government restrictions in place in Sweden, meetings can go ahead with a maximum of 50 spectators. TV money is nowhere near that in Poland, but each Swedish club has received the equivalent of £48,000 from the state to cover missing income from March through June. Teams will be reduced from seven riders to six and the standard of the league will be considerably lower than normal. But there will be league racing.

Hopes are raised here when it's announced that stock car racing at Ipswich's Foxhall Stadium – where the speedway Witches ride – has been given the go-ahead for the end of July. Amateur speedway meetings are put in the diary for tracks at Scunthorpe and Lydd in Kent, although no spectators are allowed at either. The date for the Lydd event isn't being disclosed, to try and ensure that no one actually turns up. I have to read that twice to make sure I've got it right.

But choosing whether to run professional speedway, even if the Government does give elite sports the go-ahead, is not a simple task. For some clubs, the decision isn't theirs to make. Poole, for example, rent a council-owned stadium that is operated independently by a separate company. Newcastle are in a similar position and, with the stadium staff currently furloughed, Dave Tattum says they'd struggle to host meetings.

It's clear too that there isn't unanimity amongst the promoters about the wisdom of rushing back into action. Sheffield co-promoter Peter Mole, who had been looking forward to a season back in the Premiership with star signing Nicki Pedersen returning to British speedway, admits that he has personal reservations about taking part in a shortened season.

He tells *Speedway Star* that the club's long-term future is his priority and that any return to track action must be practical and financially sustainable. He also poses some important questions.

'We are tenants. Will our stadium landlords be supportive of changes to make stadia COVID-secure for enough spectators to cover our meeting costs? Would reduced spectator numbers give sufficient financial security to run a meeting? Can pit areas and other designated areas be accommodated for social-distancing requirements? Are PPE requirements and testing procedures within budget? Would riders be available/allowed to travel and wish to compete in a shortened season themselves? Will sponsors be able to stay on board due to their own financial situation? Are local medical back-up and NHS hospital facilities supportive, including county ambulance back-up? Are all fans of all ages fully supportive and willing to turn out in sufficient numbers?'

All legitimate questions without immediate answers for the many riders who, like British champion Charles Wright, have been kicking their heels. He admits the uncertainty is mentally stressful for all of them as they don't know whether to twist or stick. He says one of the toughest things is wondering whether he's trained all winter and spent a lot of money getting his equipment ready for nothing. He's never watched the news so much to find out what's happening and adds that, for most riders, it's difficult not knowing whether to commit to a full-time job or wait in the hope that some sort of positive decision is made.

* * *

Innovation is not a word normally associated with the world of speedway. That's not meant to be a criticism – sometimes change for change's sake doesn't always work – but it's a fact. 'Tried and tested, same again' is the approach most in the sport tend to go for much of the time.

But that's not something that Barry Bishop, co-promoter of the Isle of Wight Warriors in the National League, believes. Which is why, on the first Thursday evening in July, several hundred of us are sat in front of our laptops and iPads watching something called 'Virtual Skid'.

During lockdown, many clubs have done their bit to keep fans engaged. In fact, it's becoming one of the positives of the whole summer, the way in which they've developed their uses of social media. They range from online question and answer sessions with riders to special auctions or replays of old meetings. While the Isle of Wight do show weekly classic meetings, Barry has taken it a stage further and injected a welcome element of suspense.

While 'Virtual Skid' is still based on video footage of old meetings, the vital element of 'who wins' is maintained for even the most devoted fan by the simple twist of randomly selecting heats from different meetings. Tonight's online contest is between Oxford and Swindon. Barry has access to Oxford's four home meetings against Swindon between 2004 and 2007. He's invited two speedway celebrities – former Oxford rider Spencer Timmo and Swindon co-promoter Lee Kilby – to 'manage' the two teams. This involves each of them, in turn, selecting a random heat to be shown from one of the four years – hidden as A, B, C and D. Spencer, as the 'home' manager, chooses D from the four heat one choices, which turns out to be from 2007. Fortunately for him, it results in a 5-1 for his Oxford team. For heat two, Lee gets to pick A, B, C or D, again without knowing which year is which. If a team falls more than six points behind – as Swindon frequently do during the action that follows – a manager can ask to see either team's pairings to give him, he hopes, more information and a better chance of choosing the one that will bring his team the most points. A full meeting is broadcast, but made up of random heats from four different years.

If it sounds a bit complicated to explain, it's actually really easy to follow. It helps too that there are some cracking races selected and it's a good hour and a half of speedway escapism. Andy Hague does an excellent job on production, cutting from recorded video action to the live video streams from Spencer and Lee. I've seen national broadcasters make a much less professional job.

Barry himself is our enthusiastic host for the evening, appearing on camera to make the introductions at the start, taking part in the live text chatroom during the meeting and offering his congratulations at the end. He's wearing his Isle of Wight Warriors polo shirt but is, unashamedly, rooting for Oxford, who win 49-41. Barry grew up close to Cowley Stadium and still lives near Oxford. His job, surely unique in British speedway, is working for a German software company, writing algorithms that enable financiers to trade on the stock markets.

'Virtual Skid' isn't the first innovation that Barry has come up with. Earlier this year, he sent out boxes of four model speedway riders to primary schools on the Isle of Wight. He was hoping that children would ask what they were playing with, and that someone would say they were speedway riders and that the island had its own team. The Warriors were one of the event sponsors for the World Championship Darts at Alexandra Palace in January, Barry liking the crossover between darts and speedway. He's arranged discounts and sponsorships with Isle of Wight ferries. And the Isle of Wight was the first speedway club in the UK to produce face masks – primarily for charity but also for marketing.

'We try and look at how we can get our brand outside the island. If people think about Isle of Wight speedway, I think most people would say, "It means a great day out. We get there, we have good fun, we get entertained and we're looked after. We don't feel we're overcharged, the food prices are reasonable," and so on. That's our brand. We want to take that further. I want people to talk about us, the smallest club in speedway, on a bigger scale.'

Barry has promoted speedway on the island with his partner, Martin Widman, since 2016. He says they studied how speedway on the island hadn't worked previously and tried to find a way to make it successful this time. The two of them are different, a contrast that works.

'Martin's a quiet and reserved man. He was in the RAF. I was in the Royal Navy, a submariner. I'm loud and extrovert so we complement each other really well.'

Barry says he goes into a different mindset on race day, focused completely on what someone will think when they walk through the gates. He wants every person to be entertained. 'Win, lose or draw, they've had a great night.'

There's no chance of the Isle of Wight doing what Workington did and overspending, if Barry has anything to do with it.

'One hundred per cent won't happen. My family are more important to me so there's absolutely no way I would risk any financial security of my own for a speedway club. We always cut our cloth. That is the right way to do it. Martin and I don't take anything out of the club. We never have done and we're really proud of that. Everything that we make we reinvest. I think the Championship is a great league. We could participate in it but we have excellent nights of speedway in the National League.

'Why would I want to lose money to entertain you? I don't want to do that. I want to invest my money and break even and have a club that succeeds. Every club should have that vision because if you're prepared to throw loads of money at it and just lose it then maybe the vision isn't right.'

Barry is a true believer in speedway, in many ways an old-fashioned showman promoter. He thinks it's a fantastic product but one that needs to be talked up, not down.

'If you look on most clubs' social media sites, there's negativity all over the place. If you look at ours, we hardly ever have negativity. I say this at every single speedway meeting I do, I say it at every 'Virtual Skid' that I do and I say it at every single speedway school that I stage: "If you've loved this, if you've had a great time, tell the world about it, tell everybody. If there's something you didn't like or something you want us to improve, then tell me or Martin because no one else can change it. There's no point you splattering it all over Facebook for a bit of attention."'

And while not everyone in the sport would agree with him, Barry knows what he wants to see from an evening's racing. 'I'm really not interested in whether the track record gets broken. I couldn't care less. You might sit back as a proper speedway fan and say: "That was absolutely superb, he didn't make a mistake the whole time round."

But then what would you rather see? A race that's three seconds slower and someone diving around the rider on bend four to get in front of them at the finish line or someone who wins by half a street but breaks the track record? I know what I want. I want characters, I want elbow-to-elbow racing, I want passing, I want incident, I want entertainment. That's what we need to have as a speedway product. That's how we have to change.'

With no final decision yet on when – or indeed if – there will be British speedway this season, Barry has his own views on what could have been done. He admits it's easy to say, with hindsight, that he'd have approached it in a different way but, with so many issues around running a league season, he'd have run an open competition – a 'King of Great Britain' – at whatever tracks could stage it.

'It would have been a safer and more logical way of doing it because then we could have gone to the Government and said, "Look, we can't do anything this year, all our clubs are not going to receive any income, but thank you very much for the grants and everything else but we really need further support." Instead of us keeping hanging on. Because that's what every other sport has done. Our cricket club have received a grant from the England and Wales Cricket Board and they are purely Sunday league.

'I'll be very surprised if we do run. I wouldn't want to risk the health of anybody who comes into my stadium. We all have to seriously consider if we do run speedway that, sadly, we live in a litigious society right now. If, with track and trace, you're found to be the cause and you don't have everything spot on as regards COVID-19 … I fear the worst for how our world works at the moment.'

* * *

The 27 October 1978 was a long time ago. Prime Minister James Callaghan, despite being ahead in the opinion polls, had rejected calls for a General Election that year. Margaret Thatcher was Leader of the Opposition. On that evening, far from the corridors of Westminster, the city of Bristol staged what would turn out to be its final speedway meeting at Eastville Stadium. But, nearly 42 years on, there's still a Bristol Speedway Supporters' Club.

Club secretary Brian Mead will add a qualification to that though. He'll tell you, 'They exist and they don't exist, if you see what I mean.' The club used to run a team in a local skittles league up until a few years ago, but members have passed away and they've not managed to replace them. Brian's role is to act as a contact for anyone with old Bristol Bulldogs memorabilia and to organise the annual coach from Bristol to Cardiff and back for the British Grand Prix.

Despite the lack of members, Brian manages to fill his coach for Cardiff with 53 people. They get interest from all over the country. I was supposed to be one of them this year. But with this month's Grand Prix now cancelled, my plans to catch up with Brian and another club member, John Short, are taking place on the phone rather than on the coach.

Brian's relationship with speedway is probably typical of many one-time active supporters of the sport. He started going to speedway locally in Bristol and, when that ended, he used to travel to Oxford and Reading. Both of those tracks have since closed. He did travel the 40 miles or so to Swindon when they had a bus that went from the stadium at the end of the meeting back to the train station. But that doesn't run now. As a result, the only meeting he goes to is the Grand Prix at Cardiff.

'Speedway was one of the sports, back in the 70s and 80s, where you could actually go, mix with your opposing fans and not have to worry about getting attacked or beaten up – compared to football. That was what attracted me to it. That and the racing obviously.'

Brian thinks speedway in Britain isn't as good as it used to be. He says he gets confused by the rules because they change them every year. But the main reason is that the top heat leaders don't race over here anymore. 'We're missing some of the top Grand Prix riders in the world. If it's £20 to get in and you're taking the family and spending £50–60, then you want to watch the best. That's quite a bit of money for a night out.'

Brian had been keen for me to speak to fellow member, John Short. John is 77, 'one of the so-called vulnerable' he tells me when we speak. He's still active though. John is a master of ceremonies for wrestling, his last engagement in Scotland at the end of 2019. And he still goes to speedway, although he's keen to stress that he's not fanatical.

'I've been to every league track that's run in the country since, I think, 1966. I've been to over 100 tracks in this country and a total around the world of 251 in 27 countries, including the Czech Republic, Slovakia, Romania, Australia, the United States, the Ukraine – it's quite a long list.'

When I ask how many meetings he got to last year and he tells me that he's 'dropped down quite a lot lately', I'm expecting him to say a handful. But no. 'I think I did about 40 meetings last year.' It turns out he'd also been at Stoke's final meeting, having made the journey specially. The most he did in one year was 95. He talks enthusiastically of one trip he did with the supporters' club where they went to Reading in the morning, Wimbledon in the afternoon and White City in the evening. All three tracks are now long gone. 'As I say, I do have other interests, I'm not fanatical.'

Like Brian, John points to the sociability of speedway and its participants and supporters. 'One of the attractions is the friendliness of the crowd – and the riders, for that matter. In speedway, everyone from Jason Doyle down to the novice at the bottom of the tree, they'll always chat, assuming you get them at a sensible time, obviously. You don't speak to them when they're on their way out to the first race. Most promoters – not all but most – are like that too.'

Ask him about the possibility of new tracks opening up – a revival at Exeter is the latest to be mentioned this month – and he's sceptical. 'We hear this every year. The silly season has just started a bit earlier, that's all. I've seen it all before.'

John's certainly not expecting speedway back at Bristol. The city's first track at Knowle closed in 1960. It's now a housing estate. It took until 1977 for a new venue to be found at Eastville Stadium, the then home of Bristol Rovers. John says the opening meeting in 1977 got

– depending on whose figures you believe – anywhere from 17,500 to 25,000. 'Cars were driving along the M32, the elevated motorway that runs above the stadium, stopping on the hard shoulder to watch and were being booked by police.'

But Bristol City Council never seemed to share that enthusiasm for the sport and went to the High Court to have it stopped on noise and nuisance grounds. Curfews and restrictions were put in place but worse followed in December 1978 when an injunction was issued shutting it down for good. John was amongst two coachloads of SOB79 – Save Our Bulldogs – supporters who delivered a petition with 10,000 signatures to Downing Street. John says it was Bristol speedway's winter of discontent. Unfortunately, James Callaghan and the country itself were experiencing their own, more serious, version by then and the supporters' efforts failed. Bristol Rovers played at the ground until April 1986 and greyhound racing continued until 1997. Eastville is now the site of an IKEA store.

Proposals to stage speedway at a site in the Avonmouth area were put forward in 2010. But they came to nothing over objections about its possible impact on birds flying up the Severn Estuary to the Slimbridge Wildlife Centre. John clearly doesn't think the council were ever behind the sport. He says he saw Bristol's mayor at the time and asked him about the outline planning permission for speedway. 'His reply – and he was 100 per cent serious – was, "What's speedway?"'

Not surprisingly, John has his own views on where British speedway has gone wrong. He believes it's not advertised properly, particularly nationally. That, in his view, comes down to the people running the sport. 'It's only a personal opinion but there's too much infighting between the different promoters. Perhaps they should look in the dictionary and see what the word promote means. There are some very good promoters. I would single out Len Silver at Kent. There are also promoters who are only interested in themselves. I realise it's a business, but it would be a better business overall if different promoters cooperated. What it really needs, in my opinion, and that of quite a lot of other people, is an outsider to control things.

At the moment, it's all controlled by the British Speedway Promoters' Association – or whatever they've chosen to call themselves this year. They're obviously not independent. It needs an independent tsar to oversee it all.'

For someone who's spent more hours than most following it, his ultimate verdict on speedway is damning.

'In this country, speedway is basically dying, committing suicide.'

* * *

Another complaint from British speedway fans is the lack of a league sponsor for the Premiership. There hasn't been one since Sky Sports ended their coverage at the end of 2016. Rob Godfrey has talked about being very close to securing one at the start of this season, until coronavirus struck. Much of the work to secure that has been done by Sadie Wrigglesworth, the former head of commercial for the Sahara Force India F1 team. Godfrey has spoken of how important Sadie was in helping to land the five-year Eurosport TV deal.

That absence of a main league sponsor has been exposed in the current environment. The Polish Ekstraliga has support from Polish electricity giant, PGE, while one of the reasons that the Swedish Elitserien can run behind closed doors with a maximum of 50 spectators is partly explained by having the backing of multinational DIY chain, BAUHAUS.

Britain's top speedway league has had its share of sponsors over the years. Before Sky Sports' sponsorship ended in 2013, Gulf Oil had been the longest-running sponsor for six seasons from 1974, with Sunbrite and Homefire smokeless fuels sponsoring in the late 1980s and early 1990s.

In terms of individual club sponsorship, it's now very much a case of local companies – garages and haulage and boiler service companies. In the past, car manufacturers were active sponsors too, although it wasn't the BMWs or Mercedes of this world. During the 1980s, just before the fall of the iron curtain, it was eastern European car manufacturers who targeted British speedway. FSO Polonez from

Poland supported Mildenhall; Lada did the same for the Newcastle Diamonds; Škoda sponsored Peterborough Panthers.

Today there are still large businesses keen to get involved in sponsoring speedway. One good example is the global travel management company, ATPI. Not, perhaps, a household name but a company with an annual turnover in excess of £1 billion.

Much of the impetus from ATPI's involvement in speedway comes from current chief executive, Ian Sinderson.

His first experience of speedway came back in the mid-1970s when he was growing up in Sheffield, going on Thursday nights with his father. Then he moved to London and drifted away from the sport until, in 2007, he was at a loose end and went down to Cardiff to watch that year's British Grand Prix. He was impressed and felt the sport had moved on significantly from when he'd gone before.

Ian admits his non-speedway colleagues needed a bit of persuading to get involved with the sport. 'Not because they wanted to go anywhere else but because it was something new that we were trying to do. We wanted to be involved at a level which allowed our ATPI brand to become fairly endemic within the sport. We then use that in our own promotional campaigns to show what we do within speedway so we can attract second-tier sports who have a lot of travel requirements.'

ATPI began speedway sponsorship in 2009 with the Grand Prix and Jason Crump. After that, they became more involved once the new Belle Vue stadium was built. 'We needed the theatre to be able to do that and the trouble with a lot of speedway tracks is that they're not sufficiently upmarket. The old Belle Vue stadium was falling to bits so there was no way you could build a credible hospitality programme to show to anybody. But in the new stadium we've set up the sports lounge there. At the end of the day, you're never going to be able to go to Manchester United and say, "We can build a hospitality experience for you," because they've got tons of people who can do that.'

Ian points to sports like archery or wheelchair basketball, both well-sponsored sports, which don't have the infrastructure or the resources to set up their own hospitality programmes for corporate sponsors. A lot of what ATPI does in speedway is done for free in order to showcase what they can do. 'We're then in a position where we can sell the services that we provide for free, if you like, to a number of other sports and that can bear fruit for us.'

The ATPI Sports Events business works closely with high-profile businesses and federations. Amongst its clients are Manchester United, Southampton, Everton, the Dutch Olympic Federation, the Canadian Olympic Federation, the Equestrian Federation, Heineken and Volvo. But speedway plays an important role amongst those big names. 'ATPI's pretty well involved in all aspects of speedway for a very modest sum. It's a very cost-effective way of doing it compared to something like football or cricket or rugby union.'

And, even in these tough and uncertain times, Ian sees no reason why ATPI's sponsorship of speedway won't continue in future.

* * *

Had British speedway carried on as normal in 2020, tributes would have been paid at many tracks to Danny Ayres, who died at the start of February. A special charity meeting in aid of Danny's dependants would have taken place at Mildenhall in June. Instead, with COVID-19 restrictions forcing its cancellation, it was replaced with a 'Do it for Danny' event where supporters and riders were encouraged to rev their motorbikes for two minutes and send in the video to raise funds.

The inquest into Danny's death is held in Ipswich in July and his partner, Jodie, releases a statement to *Scunthorpe Live* news that reveals more details of the battles that she and Danny faced.

She doesn't seek to blame anyone but says Danny had been let down by the health system. She describes how mental health is not only about being depressed or suffering from anxiety. In Danny's case, he'd told doctors how he couldn't relax and that his mind and body never switched off. For Jodie, it was obvious that Danny was suffering from something like ADHD – attention deficit hyperactivity disorder.

'He was so hyperactive, impulsive and full-on, everything was just full throttle and that's what I absolutely adored and loved about him, as did everyone else. It made him exceptionally talented on a bike. It was his strength with his career as a speedway rider, but his weakness off the track and, devastatingly mixed with a cocktail of alcohol and drugs, his undoing.'

Danny had been told by a doctor that there was no such thing as ADHD in adults and his diagnosis was given as drug dependence, although Jodie emphasises that Danny wasn't an addict. 'He didn't go near anything when he could focus his mind during the season on his career.'

Jodie says she wants to become a life coach involved with speedway riders, particularly those in similar situations to Danny. 'As unique as he was, I'm sure there are others out there within the sport that can relate to Danny's struggles and it's them I intend to help.

'He absolutely thrived and loved speedway and for me it saved his life more than once. When he was on a bike, he literally felt normal and had a sense of belonging. Speedway was our life together as a family and I will always hold the speedway family very close to my heart.'

* * *

The inevitable confirmation that there will be no league speedway in Britain at Premiership or Championship level finally comes just after noon on Monday, 21 July, in a BSP Ltd statement. The sport's elite categorisation combined with the Prime Minister's statement that crowds won't be allowed back into stadiums until October doesn't leave enough time to run any kind of league season. Rob Godfrey thanks sponsors who have stayed loyal and there are reassuring comments from Eurosport's Jamie Steward that the broadcaster remains committed to the sport and is already working with the BSP Ltd on plans for 2021.

It's big news, important enough for *BBC Sport Online* to not only cover it but make it the lead story on its motorsports section. Rob Godfrey makes himself available for interviews and admits that the last few months have been one of the worst times of his life. He's felt like he's had the world on his shoulders and talks of how it's almost a relief that a decision has been made so everyone knows what's happening. Rob believes clubs will survive this but adds there's no guarantee they all will.

He says they've gone through all sorts of avenues – local MPs, ministers, everything – to try and get some exemption for speedway. 'I feel so sorry for the riders. We've all been in it together and they've been sitting there waiting, believing, as we did, that the day will come when we can get started. Sadly, it's not going to be this year.'

One of those helping Rob has been Swindon's co-promoter, Lee Kilby, who'd been tasked with putting together various fixture permutations if and when some kind of a season could be staged. He was on his seventh or eighth version when the season was finally called off.

Lee believes the promoters' regular conference calls during the lockdown have helped to bring them together. The son of former rider, Bob Kilby, he has only been in his current speedway position for the last couple of years and is aware of the promoters' past reputation.

'I think we've probably talked more as a group of promoters than we ever would have if this hadn't happened. Everyone seemed to start sharing best practice and said the same thing, that there was a real collective working towards positives out of this really big negative.'

That elite tag was never, for the promoters, in doubt. 'We never looked at it in any other way. We didn't think we could sneak through the back door with any amateur-style set-ups. Because, to us, we are an elite sport. If you can attract 35,000–40,000 people to an event at Cardiff every year, that's a huge attraction for people. Yes, there are differences with other elite sports, but we see ourselves as a sport which has professional riders and is a professional organisation.'

Reaction amongst current promoters is best characterised as resigned disappointment – although there are some grumblings about the way news of the cancellation is communicated. Some promoters are told just an hour before the official announcement.

While there's to be no league speedway in 2020, there may still be some racing. Several clubs want local council permission to stage meetings with spectators at National League level. Unlike the Premiership and Championship, this is regarded as amateur – grassroots – rather than elite and so meetings could take place from August. Scunthorpe throw their hat in the ring straightaway, with Rob Godfrey saying he'll definitely be running meetings. He's more than happy to be a guinea pig for the new COVID-19 world. He talks of his hopes for a British Final later on, in October, in addition to the grassroots meetings.

Statements from various clubs reveal some of the different views that have been expressed in private meetings over the last few months. Belle Vue are scheduled to host the two-day, season-ending Speedway of Nations tournament, which will go ahead at the end of October – with or without spectators – due to its television deal. Tracks that have staged practice sessions – like Leicester, Berwick, Redcar and Plymouth – are amongst those wanting to run meetings. Eastbourne director Ian Jordan says they've already contacted riders who could make up a competitive National League level side. While admitting the situation is not ideal, he feels any speedway is better than none.

Some clubs are non-committal on their plans, but others come out straightaway and say they will not be running until 2021, Championship side Birmingham among them. Their co-owner and former rider, David Mason, says they've considered running amateur racing but non-league fixtures don't attract much of a crowd.

Debbie Hancock, the Somerset co-owner, won't be running either. She says they're heavily dependent on the holiday season through June, July and August, and the longer the season delay went on, the more doubts crept in about racing going ahead at the Oaktree Arena. 'It would have been a massive gamble to go down the route of a few weeks' racing this year to jeopardise the immediate future of the club and threaten our participation in 2021.'

Those hopes of running even National League fixtures disappear when the Isle of Wight, Kent and Mildenhall all say they won't be running. Barry Bishop says it's the hardest decision he and Martin Widman have had to make but, unfortunately, they can't see a way of racing without putting riders, fans, sponsors and the wider public on the island at increased risk.

For the remaining three months of the season, British speedway will be confined to junior racing, with the possibility of open meetings for established riders in October, if and when spectators are allowed into stadiums.

For the riders, former British champion, Danny King, talks of how it's been a rollercoaster, with racing looking likely one minute and then unlikely the next. He's confused by the logic that allows stock cars to run at his Ipswich team's Foxhall Stadium but not speedway. He talks too about how it's been a tough time for him, those carefree early days of that lockdown video looking after his two children at home now seemingly a lifetime away.

'I won't lie, I am very stressed at the moment. My wife is a schoolteacher, so I have had to have the children throughout lockdown. I have been a stay-at-home dad, which has been testing in itself. I had a little bit of hope that we could get racing, but it doesn't look that way now.'

For the fans, Scott Frame summarises his view in the first *Talk Speedway* podcast after the announcement. 'It's frustrating because you want to think of speedway as an elite sport but I think anyone listening to this or involved with the sport would happily agree that it's not an elite sport at this point. We're not talking cricket or football. There's probably more people in the Metrocentre in Newcastle on a Saturday afternoon bumping into one another than there would be at any sporting venue.'

* * *

If British speedway fans are feeling deflated after the cancellation of the league season, there's some consolation in the last week of July.

On the face of it, the individual European Championship sounds like it should be second only to the World Championship in terms of prestige. That's not always been the case. Originally part of the arcane and confusing system of qualifying rounds for the individual World Final, it struggled to find a role in the Grand Prix era, with the continent's top riders largely absent from it and the title, as a result, devalued.

In 2013, backed by the Polish company One Sport, it was revamped and given a higher profile. But British riders found themselves caught up in a row between BSI, the promoters of the Grand Prix, and One Sport. This year, a form of speedway détente has broken out and the winner of the European Championship will, for the first time, qualify for next year's Grand Prix series. As a result, even though some of speedway's top riders are still absent – Tai Woffinden among them – there's a real purpose to this year's championship.

The only British competitor is Robert Lambert. For speedway fans, it's hard to believe that Lambert is still only 22 as he's been around British tracks for 13 years. His father had ridden for Mildenhall and, so committed were the family to furthering Robert's career, they took out a 500cc licence for him to ride in Germany when he was 14, a year earlier than he could have done in Britain. Since then he's made good progress, moving on to become a Great Britain regular and one of the best heat leaders in the Premiership with King's Lynn. The GB Young Lions manager, Neil Vatcher, says Lambert is probably the single most professional young speedway rider he's ever worked with.

Last season, though, was one where he probably didn't make the progress expected. That was due to two factors: injuries, most notably in the Speedway of Nations tournament in Russia when he collided with team-mate Craig Cook; and a punishing schedule of commitments to race for teams in Britain, Poland, Sweden and Denmark as well as reserve appearances in the Grand Prix.

This season, though, is different. He's been in impressive form for his Polish team, Rybnik, and starts the reorganised, five-meeting European Championship series as one of those tipped to win. Nicki Pedersen is in the mix too, but the main competition comes from Denmark's Leon Madsen, who was runner-up in last year's Grand Prix.

Madsen wins each of the opening three rounds, the first time anyone has done that in the competition's history, to lead Lambert by six points. It looks like the best the Briton can manage will be second.

But then, in the fourth round at Gniezno, the tournament turns on its head. Madsen, by his own high standards, has a bad night, scoring just nine points and failing to make the final. In contrast, Lambert is imperious, scoring 17 points out of 18 and turning that six-point deficit into a two-point lead. Heat 14 typifies his performance. Drawn on the outside gate, Lambert – for once – isn't first away. But he's got the speed of both thought and ability to spot that the three riders inside him are heading wide into the first bend. In a split second he spots his opportunity and cuts inside, effortlessly gliding ahead of all three by the second bend to lead, where he stays for the rest of the race.

The final round, at Toruń, sees both Madsen and Lambert in a head-to-head tussle that swings back and forth. Lambert goes into his final heat knowing that he has to finish first or second or else Madsen will be champion without having to win another race. Lambert wins and goes into the final two points ahead of his rival. It means he can finish behind Madsen and still be European champion. But he doesn't settle for that, bursting from gate two to win and take the title by three points.

Afterwards, in the post-presentation interviews, Lambert, normally calm and reserved, seems genuinely and understandably caught up in the moment, particularly when thanking his family for all their support. It's the biggest achievement in his career to date – European champion and a place in 2021's Grand Prix.

Sadly, it's not celebrated in the British media. You find yourself wishing that the sport was better funded to employ a PR agency on a coordinated campaign of phone-bashing to get the good news out there. The only national coverage for what is, after all, a Briton winning a European title, in a sport officially categorised as elite, is in the *Daily Star*. Peter Oakes, one of the few national newspaper journalists still covering speedway, says that big names mean something to sports editors and sports staff. He can almost guarantee he'll get a story in the paper about Tai Woffinden because they've heard of Tai Woffinden; Robert Lambert, certainly at the moment, doesn't do it for them.

That's not the only thing gnawing at the minds of British speedway supporters. With Lambert now joining Tai Woffinden in the Grand Prix – and knowing that too many meetings in 2019 had very likely held back his progress – there's immediate speculation that Lambert's continued participation in the British leagues is in doubt. He's very diplomatic, saying that he'll only decide after this truncated season is over.

But it's once again obvious that, just as it unearths another global star of speedway, Britain might well lose him to domestic league racing.

August 2020 – Some kind of normal

EVEN AT quarter to nine on an otherwise quiet Sunday morning, the South Tees Motor Sports Park is a busy and noisy place.

It's in the Cargo Fleet district of Middlesbrough, the town's old port area, about a mile and a half from the Riverside Stadium. The largest section of the park is the Teesside Autodrome, billed on its website as the longest kart circuit in the world. Its 2.1km track is filled with a never-ending stream of drivers, making it impossible to work out who's leading and who's lagging at the back. Further up the hill is the Iron Works Moto Park where young motocross riders propel themselves and their machines up into the Teesside air as they negotiate the course's many jumps. Finally, to the left of the main entrance, at the end of a long car park, is the Media Prime Arena, home of speedway's Redcar Bears.

It may be a noisy place but its existence doesn't seem well known to everyone in the town. That was made clear when I stopped off for breakfast at a McDonald's a couple of miles away. I got chatting to one of the staff who was trying to make sure everyone used the hand sanitiser on arrival and followed the new ordering system inside. I said I was off to speedway and he knew what it was, a friend of his father having travelled all over the country years earlier following the then Middlesbrough Tigers. But he didn't know that speedway still took place in the town. When I mentioned the Motor Sports Park, he looked at me blankly.

This morning is the first of six scheduled Teesside Championship amateur meetings. No spectators are allowed so it's the least busy of the park's three locations. But, under the watchful gaze of Jamie Swales, the Redcar co-promoter, they'll get through more than 50 races during the day. Berwick's Leon Flint, one of the country's most promising riders, is here to prepare for Friday's European Under-19 semi-final in the Czech Republic. The first round of the British Youth Championships, scheduled for Scunthorpe in the afternoon, has reduced the number of attendees, but it's still good to see bikes back on track in competitive action after so long.

The money from staging amateur meetings, while not huge, is vital for those running Redcar speedway, as Jitendra Duffill explains a few days later. He mentions the stress that he and his two co-promoters had been under, wondering whether they'd get the season underway without knowing the full financial implications. He's relieved that they haven't been asked to pay back money from sponsors and season ticket holders. It would have been a significant amount, one which has helped keep them on an even keel. The money from staging amateur meetings and training schools pays the rent which, Jitendra says, is their biggest outgoing at the moment.

He says he can't speak highly enough of the speedway community for keeping Redcar going. 'Our income is from season ticket holders, fans who come through the gates and from sponsors. We know we can't survive without supporters and we made it quite clear this year that we wouldn't run behind closed doors.' He says sponsors are equally important, although most do it knowing that it won't result in people flooding through their doors. They very often don't even have businesses that are open to the public.

'The sponsors see it as doing their bit, which is amazing because the club's not their responsibility. They understand that we're not the most financially secure sport in the world because we don't get the crowds that we need. They've got their own businesses and financial worries so for them to give their money – for no reward essentially – is pretty amazing. The sponsors love the sport as much as we do and they're the ones who put their money where their mouth is. Speedway is a really special place. It's been quite humbling really.'

The lockdown has also seen a change of role for Jitendra. British speedway no longer has a co-promoting optometrist. He says that all the PPE, visors, masks, gloves and aprons just weren't for him and he fancied a change. Which has certainly happened. He's starting work a week on Monday in infrastructure finance, working for Redcar's main sponsor, Agilia. Their head office is in Middlesbrough and they work on major projects like roadbuilding, railways and sewage systems; not the sort of sponsor who'd be expecting an impulse buy from a speedway fan on the drive home from a meeting.

Jitendra is confident that when the country bounces back from the lockdown, he'll be in a good place. He says it's nice to have a little bit of security. 'There's been a lot of uncertainty recently.'

* * *

Although there have been a handful of amateur meetings behind closed doors, today's British Youth Championship round at Scunthorpe is the first where a paid crowd will be allowed. Many of us arrive well in advance of the scheduled five o'clock start, presumably keen to smell the methanol that's been denied us over the last five months, relish the sound of motorbike engines revving and just enjoy being at speedway again. There's a strict limit of 500 adult tickets – £6.50 each – with accompanied children permitted as well.

Speedway's elite classification has, as ever, divided opinion but, as far as Rob Godfrey's concerned, it's for the best in the long term.

'We now have a presence with the Government through the Department of Culture, Media and Sport, which is something we've lacked in the past. It may open other avenues to us. We've done it through hard work and sheer determination to get our voice heard. I said when we started communicating with them, if they don't know what speedway is, they will do when we've finished. And by God, they do! Hopefully, in future, when this crisis is over, it will give us a bit more recognition within world sport.'

It's clear that Rob, his wife Gail and their many volunteers have spent a lot of time making the Eddie Wright Raceway COVID-19 compliant. There's hand sanitiser available on tables outside the toilets, signs underlining two-metre social distancing and yellow and black tape on every second seat in the home-straight stand. There's also a strict entry and exit system in place in the clubhouse, as I discover when I put my head round the door to see who's inside, turn around to walk out the way I've come and am politely told to continue ahead. That aside, I'm carefully following the rules, like most people are, as if we're all on our first morning induction at a new job. After the initial visual changes, it's not that much different from a normal speedway meeting. It's certainly a world away from the photos of packed bars, beaches and parks that have been all over the front pages of today's papers as lockdown-weary Britons make the most of what is the hottest weekend of the year so far. There's even an ice-cream van on site – with socially distanced queuing, of course.

As we're outside, there's no requirement to wear a mask and probably around one in five people are. One man has both a plastic visor and a cloth mask, but his caution is very much the exception. I watch as Neil Vatcher, the manager of the GB Young Lions team, calls the different groups of riders together for their pre-meeting briefing in the pits. They're given a friendly warning about keeping two metres apart as the meeting is being filmed to be shown on British Speedway's YouTube channel the following day.

This is the first round of the championship although, as Vatcher makes clear in his briefing, there are – as yet – no further confirmed rounds. It's entirely possible that whoever wins this evening will be the British champion. It's unlikely that the young riders on show need any more motivation but it's an extra incentive.

In a normal season, the British Youth Championship wouldn't be a big draw for speedway fans. This year's external events have changed that, but it's clear from the work that Neil Vatcher and GB Speedway – along with devoted parents, grandparents and carers – have put in, that the sport has, at this level, a bright future. There are four categories of racing – 500cc engines for those riders who have, mainly, taken part in National League, third-tier racing, and who, if coronavirus hadn't intervened, would have been racing in the Championship. There are less powerful engine categories: 250cc and two 125cc groups for the youngest riders, like ten-year-old Caydin Martin from Fife.

Rob Godfrey is, as you might expect, as busy as ever. He's master of ceremonies on the centre green, delighted that speedway is – at last – back. 'The downside, and there is a downside,' he tells us, 'is that it's my music and I get to control it from here.' He presses his remote and heads off to the tractor to water the track to Michael Jackson's 'Killer'.

With 37 heats to get through – two and a half times the normal number – and knowing how prone speedway meetings are to delays, I'm wondering how long this one will take to run. I shouldn't have worried. Rob Godfrey is well known for powering through meetings. Track re-gradings are kept to a minimum and he's certainly not a man for race-the-mascot interruptions. We go through eight heats in the first half hour, with barely enough time to fill in the results of one heat before the four riders are lining up for the next.

The racing's good too, competitive and fair, and any young riders who fall do their best to get off the track as quickly as possible to avoid the race having to be stopped; a welcome contrast to what occasionally happens with some of their professional colleagues.

While most of the focus, and the best-known names, are in the 500cc class with the likes of Leicester's Thompson twins – Joe and Dan – who are expected to battle for the title with Scunthorpe's Jordan Palin, the best race is in the 250cc class, with 13-year-olds Max James and Luke Harrison passing and re-passing each other over the four laps. It's a reminder that a great speedway race doesn't need the most experienced or best-equipped riders to provide a real spectacle.

It's good too to see a couple of girls competing against the boys. Rebecca Weston picks up two points in the 125cc B group. Knutsford's Katie Gordon has entered the 500cc category amongst some of the brightest – male – prospects in British speedway. The previous weekend, the now 16-year-old had won the novice group at Scunthorpe's Summer Championship despite only riding 500cc bikes for four months.

In the crowd are her dad, Graham, and mum, Morag. It's normal for Graham to be there, less so for Morag who, according to Katie, doesn't really like to come and watch.

Most people, when they attend a speedway meeting, are simply after an afternoon or evening of entertainment. That could mean good, close racing, lots of skilful overtaking and their team coming out on top at the end. They may enjoy seeing a couple of spectacular crashes too, but ones where everyone involved simply gets up, brushes down their kevlars, checks their bike and gets ready for their next race, fit and uninjured. Nobody at speedway wants to see anyone get hurt.

I'd been going to meetings for a number of years without really appreciating what watching must be like for those whose husbands or sons or brothers or – in Katie's mother's case – daughters are taking part. Looking back now, it seems pretty thoughtless, as if I'd completely disregarded the risks that each rider faces every time they take to the track.

It was only when I was sitting in the grandstand at a National League meeting a few years ago that I understood what it must be like to watch someone you know and care about riding a speedway bike. A middle-aged couple sat in the row in front of me. They'd occasionally chat as they watched the racing and they seemed very much like any other spectators. Halfway through, I realised that I was sitting behind one of the mothers of one of the young reserves. Her whole demeanour changed whenever he was in a race. For this particular heat, she sat up straight, her back rigid and tense, fingers clasped together underneath her chin. There was no conversation between her and her husband. Her eyeline did not follow the two riders battling for first place, but instead her son trying – unsuccessfully – to get past the rider in third. Entering the fourth lap, he lost control of his machine and careered dangerously wide towards the safety fence. There was a short, sharp intake of breath from his mother and an involuntary jerk of her head backwards, as if she was on the bike with him.

At the end of the meeting, none the worse for his fall, he walked along the front of the small grandstand, acknowledging a few well-wishers before going and sitting next to his mother. As I remember it, he'd only scored a couple of points in the meeting. But that didn't matter. She gave him a big hug when he sat down, a gesture that said, without the need for words, that she was just glad he was in one piece.

Fortunately, this afternoon, there's nothing for Mrs Gordon to worry about. Katie remains on her bike throughout and certainly isn't out of her depth. Despite finishing last, she improves her times by a couple of seconds.

Katie can understand her parents' concern. She admits that speedway bikes are scary things, but says that if you have the passion for it, it's the best thing ever. 'When I get on that bike, I'm ready to go and race. There's so much adrenaline in you that it's just brilliant to ride.'

Graham says they'd entered the 500s knowing that she would struggle. 'I didn't want her to get disheartened by it because I said these kids you're going to race now are the cream of the crop in the country. She wasn't a million miles behind and I was dead pleased for her. All you can do is keep trying to progress.'

It's now a question of getting a bit more speed as well as improving her style. She's managed to do quite a lot of training during the summer at tracks like Scunthorpe, Redcar and Leicester. And she's adamant that she wants to compete with the men rather than, as happens with women's football, having separate teams. Rob Godfrey has talked about the possibility of women's meetings in future, but that's not what Katie wants.

'I understand it might be harder for women, but I feel like speedway's a sport that, if you have the talent, it doesn't really matter what gender you are. Creating a women's team would be great and having a league from that would be brilliant, but I still believe women should be able to ride with the lads.'

Ask her if she's annoyed that people – including me – don't just treat her as a speedway rider but as a female rider and she says everyone should be treated the same. People have been good to her during her short career, although there are drawbacks. When she goes to meetings, there's never a female changing room, so she usually has to use a toilet or a store cupboard.

Graham, who's her mechanic and driver, as she's still too young to legally drive on British roads, used to go to the old Belle Vue stadium in Manchester when he was younger – 'when Peter Collins and Chris Morton were in their heyday.' Then he put speedway to one side when he discovered girls, which is slightly ironic given what's happened since. When he was in his 40s, he decided to start riding grasstrack and Katie came with him. They started going back to watch speedway at the new Belle Vue stadium and it was Katie – rather than her dad – who thought she'd quite like to have a go at it herself. It's all developed from there.

Speedway doesn't run in the family though. Katie's older sister is a psychologist and her brother is an English teacher, and they don't normally come to watch her. Most of her friends didn't know about speedway and wouldn't have been interested if she hadn't been riding. 'I've had a lot of people come to watch me, not knowing what's going on, but in the end they've loved it.'

She's hoping for a National Development League place in 2021 as the next step towards her ambition of being the first woman to ride for a Championship or Premiership team. As she walks round the track at the end of this British Youth Championship meeting, several people approach her for an autograph or a chat. While enjoying the recognition, you sense this confident young woman would rather be in the afternoon's final race, the one deciding the round's 500cc winner.

It turns out to be the only race of the day where there's any kind of controversy. Lining up against the Thompson twins, local favourite Jordan Palin starts from gate four. Coming out of the second turn, he's forced wide by Dan Thompson and goes straight into the air fence. For a few seconds, it looks like a bad crash but, fortunately, Palin gets up and strides along the back straight towards the pits. The referee decides not to exclude any rider and Palin makes a clean getaway in the rerun. Although Dan Thompson is at his heels throughout – it's hard to believe we're watching two 16-year-olds – Palin holds on to win the first round. His winning time, 59.60, is faster than 14 of the 22 heats the adult riders had back at the Ben Fund Bonanza in March. While you'd expect tracks to be faster in the middle of summer, it still shows the pace that these youngsters are going at.

Afterwards Palin plays down the crash, saying it 'was a bit of racing' and that he'll no doubt be competing against the Thompson twins throughout his career, just as they have been since starting out on 125cc bikes. It's certainly a rivalry that promises good things for British speedway.

Rob Godfrey believes so. He'd signed Jordan for his Scunthorpe Championship side this season. He first saw him riding at a local training school on 125cc bikes. 'I watched him then, as you watch a lot of kids on 125s, and then, when he went to 250s and 500s, you just knew. What we saw in Tai Woffinden, I can see in Jordan Palin.'

All in all, it's a good two and a half hours of racing, which even some technical problems with the starting gate in the second half of the meeting can't spoil. At the end, Rob Godfrey pays tribute to North Lincolnshire council for allowing it to go ahead and talks of another meeting on bank holiday Monday.

As we file out, happy to have had our speedway fix after so long a break, I'm sure I'm not the only one wondering why, if just short of 500 people can pay to watch under-18 riders in a meeting, a similar number can't pay to watch a professional meeting? But then, logic long since seems to have gone out of the window when it comes to this post-lockdown world.

* * *

It's certainly something that puzzles Tom Bacon.

'What baffles me is what makes it professional and at what level does that make a difference? Is it the ability of the riders? Is it the fact you're paying the riders? When they said they were going to run

National League, I found that very odd. Is it that you just pay the riders less, in which case do you then ask some of the Championship guys if they want to race at that level but it's for a third of the money? Some of them might have said yes. I don't quite get what the difference is between grassroots and professional when it comes to speedway.'

Tom would love to ride competitively again. He's managed three practice sessions since the Ben Fund meeting. He rode with his Kent Kings team-mates at King's Lynn a couple of days before the announcement that the league season was cancelled. Tom says he had a good idea then because no one was particularly optimistic. 'I'm going to try and stay on the bike in case there are individual meetings later in the year. I'm definitely not putting it away. You don't learn anything sat on the sofa.'

On his and other riders' reaction to the cancellation of the season, Tom is phlegmatic. 'I think everyone was fairly understanding. Most people are obviously very frustrated, everyone was hanging on to the hope that we'd get something on. I don't think anyone's blaming anybody because you can't really. Nobody thought it was going to end up like it has.'

Tom is thankful that he's managed to continue working full-time over the summer, but he would have earned a lot more money racing, even if it had only been once or twice a week. He hasn't yet worked out how much the cancelled season has cost him but, like Jitendra Duffill at Redcar, he says sponsors have been a big help.

'They'd all paid up before the season and none have asked for any money back or to have it rolled over. One sponsor has continued to pay me monthly, which is absolutely fantastic. Now that it's looking more likely that we'll get no racing, I'll have to write to them about next year and see what they want to do. If they just wanted to keep the same sponsorship as this year, obviously I'd honour it, but I'd like to think some of them will help out with a bit more. We're still going to have costs this year and we'll have to get the engines done again before next season.'

Tom says it would really help if they could get some individual meetings on at some point, even though more clubs seem to be coming out and saying they won't run until next year.

But ask him whether this lost season has dampened his enthusiasm and there's no hesitation in his answer. 'No, not at all, definitely not. I'll be ready to go when we can go racing.'

* * *

If there are any silver linings to be found in the British speedway summer, then the growing number of podcasts is probably one of them. There's Ian Brannan's *Humans of Speedway* series, Mike Bacon's *The Speedway Podcast*, the *UK Speedway Tavern* and *The Speedway Chat Show*. The commentary duo of Nigel Pearson and Kelvin Tatum, kicking their heels on the speedway front until the start of the Grand Prix at the end of August, began their own podcast back in May. If there aren't meetings for fans to watch, there's no shortage of speedway talk for them to listen to.

One of the earliest podcasts was *Talk Speedway*, an unashamed 'labour of love' for two Scottish speedway fans, Scott Frame and Graham Muncie. Their speedway credentials are unquestionable. Scott's speedway CV includes blogging, working in the pits for several riders – including Grand Prix rider Max Fricke when he began his career in Britain – and presenting preview shows for the Edinburgh Monarchs. He's now involved with the Berwick Bandits. Graham is a freelance sports journalist, with two books on Formula 1 under his belt, who was co-host on a weekly radio show dedicated to speedway on RockSport Radio. He's the host for Edinburgh Monarchs' preview show and one of the series' running jokes is that he'll put 50 pence in a jar whenever he mentions them. Which is quite often.

Scott and Graham are both in their mid-30s and began the podcast three years ago but had to stop because of work commitments. Then, towards the end of the 2019 season, they both decided they were missing it and wanted to start again. Now, *Talk Speedway* is sponsored and one of the sport's most popular podcasts.

We chat on a Zoom call on a Friday evening, a few days before the release of their latest interview with former rider, David Howe. With a touch of typical modesty, they play down what they do. According to Scott, they're just fans who are lucky enough to know a few people in the sport so they can call the right phone numbers to get guests. Graham puts it like this: 'We're a couple of fans that dinnae mind putting the headsets on and gibbering away for an hour or so.' They welcome the growing number of speedway podcasts because the more there are and the more people talking about speedway, the better.

Their overall aim is to be topical and light-hearted, but they've not been afraid to experiment with formats. Earlier this season they tried to cover the Polish league, but that didn't prove popular. Instead, they've discovered that what really works with listeners is focusing on one rider's career, something they've called 'My life in speedway' and which has featured former world champion Mark Loram among several well-known names. They say they try and keep their questions and comments to a minimum because they want the riders to tell their own stories.

But while they're happy to give their forthright opinions on speedway – the enigmatic Polish rider Krzysztof Kasprzak, who's just qualified for next season's Grand Prix, is a particular bête noire – there's one area they won't talk about: the politics of speedway. They're happy to leave that to others. Graham points to the *British Speedway Forum*. 'You go onto that general section and every second day somebody's started a new post: British speedway's dead, blame the Government, blame the BSPA. On its day, for me, speedway's still the most exciting sport in the world. When you've got four guys at the tapes, on those bikes, ready to jump off, four guys toe-to-toe for 60 seconds, that's what we want to shout about.' Scott agrees: 'There's that much negativity surrounding British speedway, it's actually difficult to be positive about it.'

Even though this season has been cancelled, they believe there are good reasons for optimism. Graham says this year could actually be a reset for British speedway. 'What I hear when I speak to promoters – and I don't think it's just lip service – is they've never worked more closely with each other. Yes, there are some who are peeved about what happened with the season this year. They'd offered solutions, felt other things could have been done or were maybe out of the loop a little bit. But overall this year might just have a unifying effect.'

And, unsurprisingly for two true speedway fans, they feel that the doubling-up of riders has to disappear. Scott says he can accept a rider appearing for another team if someone's injured or missing due to an international event. 'But if they're away riding for another British team, that's difficult to accept. How do you explain that Craig Cook is not going to be riding at King's Lynn because he's got a commitment for Glasgow in the league below? It's the most insane thing. I understand why doubling-up is there, but the rules are not being followed correctly.' He feels the Championship has been the most competitive league in Britain for some time because they've diluted the top level so much.

They both feel the sport in Britain has to attract younger fans. 'We have a sport that, at a world level, is marketed so well and attracts millennials and generation Ys,' says Graham. 'Yet you go to British tracks and you'll see a 70-year-old guy with 100 badges on his Wulfsport jacket. That's not having a go at that guy, because he's a fan, spending his money, but why is that the demographic at league speedway when at world level it's all about Monster Energy and extreme sports?'

Ask them about the future and whether, for example, there will ever be an independent body running British speedway, and Scott is in no doubt. 'In a word, no. I've never been more certain of anything in my life. There are some clubs who would maybe vote for it, but the majority wouldn't even entertain it because they see themselves as masters of their own destinies. What I hear after every single AGM in November is that the promoters have to look after their own business first. If there's an independent body, there's no way they could do that. Almost every single fan would say we need an independent body, like we have with Rob Painter and Vicky Blackwell at Team GB now, who can market the sport and go and get sponsorship.'

Graham agrees but feels that the BSP Ltd could spend their funds more productively without giving up control. 'The guys who run British speedway are successful businessmen in their own right, but they're not necessarily good at marketing. There's a big difference between running a successful garage and marketing a sport that you want to take to a national level. That would be the next step for me. If you're not going to give up overall control to an independent body, give up the things that you're not expert in, like marketing.'

I'm aware I'm drawing Scott and Graham into areas they avoid in their own podcasts. And I've taken up more of their time on a Friday night than I'd intended. But, listening to them talk so knowledgeably about a sport that so many often try to talk down has been a treat, almost like my own private edition of the *Talk Speedway* podcast.

* * *

Josh Auty loves riding his bike. But he hasn't been on one since the Ben Fund meeting back in the middle of March. He has managed a pre-season friendly for his Sunday league football team. But he's decided not to bother with the bike until meetings are guaranteed. He reckons there's no point wearing them out for no good reason.

'I miss competing, winning races, scoring points for the team and obviously the banter that you have with the lads when you're together as a group. It's just a real shame. This year for everybody has just been a complete write-off. But if speedway says, "Right, we're running next week," I'm ready to go. It's as simple as that. All the bikes are ready.'

With no prospect of riding, he's had to get a job. He's working five days a week, at an alloy wheel company in Oldham, packaging them up and sending them off. The company has worked through the whole pandemic and is really busy.

Josh says a lot of riders he knows have picked up jobs to see themselves through the summer. 'You've still got bills to pay, mortgages, taxes, we're no different from working-class people. If you've got nothing coming in, you're relying on your savings if you have any. And if you've got none of them, you're in trouble.'

Like Tom Bacon and Jitendra Duffill, Josh's sponsors have stood by him. They're also becoming one of the positive stories of the summer. And Josh says virtually all of the supporters for his cancelled testimonial date didn't want refunds either.. 'They said just hold the money, keep it to March 2021, which was superb.'

When we'd last spoken at the end of April, Josh had been staying at home, well out of the reach of the virus. But now, like many others, he's getting used to the new world. 'The lads I play football with, they're taking the same view as me. Yes, it is a virus and you can catch it, but generally the numbers for my age are very low.'

But, while social distancing for some has gone out of the window, Josh is sticking to the rules. He's turning 30 in September and would have had a big party with his friends, his family and his girlfriend Olivia's family. But there isn't room in the house for that to be done safely so he's staging his birthday party in two sittings; his family from noon until four and then Olivia's side of the family later on.

Josh isn't one for watching old videos of meetings online. He's been following football and, in particular, Manchester United, who had a mixed post-lockdown, securing third place in the Premier League but losing in both the semi-final of the FA Cup and the Europa League. Ask him about those defeats and it is telling how quickly he starts talking about speedway. 'Any defeat's disappointing, whether you're a supporter or a rider. You know, when Scunny's been defeated at home in a last-heat decider. One that stood out for me last season was when Glasgow beat us. Craig Cook got excluded in heat 15 in a collision with me, but Rasmus Jensen managed to beat me in the final and get the 3-3 that meant Glasgow won. You're deflated. Nobody likes getting beat at home.'

I sense this is one rider who really is missing his speedway.

* * *

It's Monday, 17 August, heat 12 of the rearranged Polish Ekstraliga meeting between Gorzów and Wrocław. Gorzów have a commanding

41-25 lead and can seal victory in this heat. They're up against Wrocław's three-time world champion, Tai Woffinden. One of the Gorzów riders is smartly out of the tapes though and, despite Tai's best efforts over the following four laps, manages to hold on to win. The rider? Nicolai Klindt who, just over two and a half months earlier, was delivering Tesco groceries around Telford.

For the majority of British-based riders, like Tom Bacon and Josh Auty, the 2020 season will be, through no fault of theirs, one to forget. But a small number of riders have been able to keep their careers moving on despite what's happened. Robert Lambert, with his win in the European Championships, is certainly one. Nicolai Klindt is turning out to be another.

While he'd enjoyed his Tesco job – 'it gave me a bit of income and got me out of the house' – he was keen to go to Poland and ride, as intended, for Ostrów in the First Division. When the season was given the go-ahead, he, like all riders in Poland, had to take a pay cut. Nicolai says it was a tough call and it took time to convince his girlfriend, Sarah, that it was the right thing to do, particularly as he'd likely be away from his family in Shropshire for the rest of the summer. Some of his friends said he was daft to ride for less money, but Nicolai worried that if he missed a whole season riding in Poland, he'd be at the back of the queue for contracts when it came to 2021. After all, he still has his dreams of making it to the Grand Prix. At the end of the day, he wanted to ride his bike.

He arrived in Ostrów in the middle of June and was given the use of a new flat in the town by the club. He was fortunate that, within two days, Polish quarantine restrictions were lifted, meaning he was free to go out to the supermarket or for a walk.

He's one of speedway's most prolific and professional contributors to social media and has provided frequent video updates on his Polish experience for his 11,000 Twitter followers. There's his first time back on a bike – 'awesome' – and his first competitive appearance in the northern Polish city of Gdańsk in a North v South representative meeting. He scores eight points, which he declares 'acceptable', although he's left cursing a puncture in his fourth ride. His first league meeting for Ostrów goes well – a solid 11 points – but he's a tough critic of his performance, concerned that he only made one out of his five starts. Watching his post-meeting video updates, you can sense that strong desire to keep improving that he'd talked about earlier in the year. His focus isn't on what's gone right but on what didn't work and what he needs to do better next time.

He's not surprised when news comes through that the British league speedway season has been cancelled. In an interview in *Speedway Star*, he says what many people back home are now thinking, that the British Government is just not doing a good enough job. 'They are always behind other countries, no matter what they do, which is both frustrating and disappointing. If you look at it, England is one of the countries with the highest infection rates in Europe, if not the highest.'

He'll be racing in Sweden in the top BAUHAUS league for Lejonen, but the lack of league racing in Britain is a blow. He estimates that he'll only make a third of his income from riding this year compared with 2019. But his expenses, apart from those he'd have incurred in Britain, are the same. 'It's going to be a hard year.'

Making a career in speedway is different this season in so many ways. There are intrusive – up the nostril and down the throat – COVID-19 tests every time he travels in and out of Poland. Polish authorities will also fine riders if they're found to have allowed selfies with fans and so contravened social-distancing regulations.

There's a dip in Nicolai's scoring at the start of August, but he bounces back well, scoring good points in both Poland and Sweden. He secures a five-ride maximum in the Danish national semi-final in Esbjerg to book his place in September's final.

His good form has clearly alerted teams in the Ekstraliga. That's why Stal Gorzów give him a late invite, to replace the erratic Polish rider, Krzysztof Kasprzak, for their meeting against Wrocław. It's a big opportunity and when Nicolai posts that 'it may only be one meeting, but I'm sure gonna do my best', you know he really means it.

He certainly manages that, finishing the meeting with 11 points. The ranks of socially distanced, yellow-clad Gorzów fans – Polish tracks are now allowed 50 per cent capacity crowds – obviously enjoy what they've seen and some call for him to be signed up permanently. While that won't happen this season, it's put Nicolai in the shop window for the following year's Ekstraliga team selections.

For now, with weekly racing commitments in both Poland and Sweden, it's very nearly business as usual for Nicolai, with long van journeys and hurried drives to catch overnight ferries. But even though he's doing what he loves – back racing, earning money and riding well – there's the knowledge that he's far apart from his family in Shropshire. At the very end of the month, he tweets two photos of his daughters, and says he's not seen them for two months and 20 days. Not that he's counting the days or anything.

* * *

Given what we've all just lived through, August is the closest thing to being back to 'normal' that the post-COVID world allows most Britons in 2020. In the middle of the month, the *Daily Mail* reports that coronavirus deaths have fallen to a new low and that six times as many people are dying from flu and pneumonia. As long as you're not living in one of the local lockdown areas – like Leicester, Blackburn with Darwen or Aberdeen – or having to scurry back from a hastily cut short holiday in somewhere like France or Croatia, there's a bearable routine to everyday life. Take a mask wherever you go, follow the arrows, use the hand sanitiser and keep your distance from strangers. There's talk of a Government campaign to get workers back into the office. It's not life as we knew it but we can go to pubs and restaurants and friends' houses.

Over bank holiday weekend, we leave London to visit Chester and struggle to get a table for an evening meal on the Saturday even though it's not even five o'clock. We're told the city is officially full, with no hotel rooms available. Liverpool on the Sunday and Birmingham on the Monday – the final day of the Government's 'Eat Out to Help Out' scheme – are similarly busy, their city centres full of people shopping and enjoying the unusually warm and dry weather. Predictions from earlier in the year, that we'd only be eating in restaurants at tables encased in plastic glass, prove unfounded.

Crowds are to be allowed back – at reduced capacity – to top-flight football matches from the start of October. They're already being allowed back in limited form at some non-league games and I get to my first match at Haringey Borough before August ends.

Speedway too is edging back to normal. The final August edition of *Speedway Star* has, for the first time since early March, a small box on page two advertising 'Where to go/Where to watch'. Admittedly it is small. There are only four meetings included – and two of those are the first Grand Prix in Poland – but it's a start.

Maybe, just maybe, the worst is over.

September 2020 – Best-laid plans

THE SPEEDWAY of Nations – it undoubtedly sounds more elegant in the FIM's native French language than its English translation – is the sport's world team championship. It was only contested for the first time in 2018, replacing the Speedway World Cup, which had been increasingly dominated by Poland, who won it eight times between 2005 and 2017. Some think the change – from the World Cup's four-rider teams to more of a pairs competition in the Speedway of Nations version – was made because Poland's strength in depth at international level meant they were almost certain to win every year. If a different format was needed to spice things up, then that happened, with Russia winning in both 2018 and 2019, their first-ever international honours.

This year, though, particularly with Belle Vue as a home venue, Great Britain are in with a real chance of winning their first international honours for more than 30 years. Since England last won at Bradford in 1989, five countries – the United States, Denmark, Sweden, Poland and Australia – have all won more than once. Going so long without a win at international level has certainly hampered speedway's profile in Britain. This year could change that.

There are good reasons for optimism. Tai Woffinden has made a good start to the first two rounds of the Grand Prix, which began in Poland at the end of August. His main partner will be European champion, Robert Lambert. The rules of the two-day Speedway of Nations require each nation to give at least one race each day to an under-21 rider. That will be Dan Bewley, who has been improving in Poland after returning from injury and, more importantly, counts Belle Vue as his home track – where, on his day, he can be very hard to beat. At this point, Britain have as good a chance – if not better – than anyone.

It's not just on-track efforts that matter. The GB Speedway team is completely dependent on commercial partnerships for its income. But getting sponsorship for a sport that doesn't get national headlines is hard enough at any time. Doing so when businesses – apart from those in the tech and healthcare sectors – are struggling in the teeth of likely the worst economic recession for nearly 100 years, is even more impressive. But that's what the Great Britain team has managed, with two national names being unveiled as media partners in the build-up to the Speedway of Nations.

Announced first are Smyths Toys, who'd first dipped a toe in the speedway world with fork-cover sponsorship of the Great Britain team at their international against Denmark back in October. That's followed by Marston's Brewery, who've sponsored Eastbourne but are now looking to promote the sport nationally throughout their large network of pubs.

GB Speedway managing director Rob Painter is in no doubt about how he wants the arrangements to work. 'What's important isn't just putting logos on a race suit. That just isn't good enough. You have to show value to a commercial partner because there has to be a reason why it makes sense for them to do it.' While Marston's are having a difficult time this year because of the pandemic, GB Speedway is looking at a number of giveaways to attract people back to their pubs in 2021.

The first display of the new sponsorship is on a promotional video released ahead of the Great Britain under-21 team's appearance at the world finals in Denmark early in September. It looks impressive. It tallies very much with Rob Painter's desire to build a real identity for the national speedway team, in addition to getting things right on the track.

'We spend a lot of time watching professional sport from all around the world: Big Bash Cricket in Australia and Super Rugby, for example. You just have to look at how they build their brands and how they build club identity. It's something that we don't have in British speedway and that makes it very difficult. You know, grandad goes along with his grandchild to watch football or rugby and they want to buy the scarf that's the same colours as the team they've gone to support. That's something that needs to be done in speedway. It's something we've done from the start with Great Britain. We've got a very clear brand. We've got a very clear identity. We're very strict on how it's portrayed.'

Those involved in speedway for some time have certainly been impressed. *Talk Speedway*'s Scott Frame, who works with one of the under-21 riders, Berwick's Leon Flint, says riders were sent a rundown before they travelled to Denmark, detailing what to wear, what sponsors they were allowed to advertise – essentially only those promoting Team GB – times for eating, training and when to be at the track, COVID regulations and what was expected of them when representing Team GB. It's clear that, at all levels of Great Britain squads, a new professionalism is being built with which big companies, national names too, are keen to associate.

Rob feels that the clubs could do their own bit to help build a British speedway brand that could become even more valuable, although he does admit that seems out of reach at the moment. 'It's difficult to be too critical of British speedway because all the clubs are in different situations. But in terms of the British speedway brand in particular, there's a huge amount of growth potential there.'

He says the GB Team have a good relationship with the BSP Ltd and that he personally has a great relationship with chairman Rob Godfrey. They have monthly meetings to discuss future plans. 'They all want speedway to grow and move forward. We want the same thing and we can focus all our attention on the Great Britain team, whereas that was never really possible before.'

He remains optimistic about the future of the sport in this country. 'It is just such a fantastic sport. I do think speedway has stood still in this country. If the ideas that we have as an organisation had all been tried and failed, then there would be no room for optimism. But there are so many things that could be done, and if they're put in place then speedway can grow, as we're seeing in Poland, as we see with the World Championship, as we see with the Speedway of Nations.'

Great Britain's under-21 team take the bronze medal in the World Team Cup Final behind Poland and hosts Denmark. Team manager, Neil Vatcher, says he's pleased with the progress of the youngsters. Next month, though, with home advantage and a strong trio to track, the senior team will be looking for gold.

* * *

One of those promoters trying to build a brand – and boost attendances – is Ian Jordan. In typical speedway style, he's not just doing it for one club; he's managing director of Eastbourne in the Championship and commercial director at Plymouth in the National League.

Ian is a relative 'newbie' to the business of speedway, if not the sport itself. Another aspiring speedway rider, he drifted away from the sport in the mid-1980s when he realised he was never going to make the grade. Three years ago, he was shopping in Sainsbury's and picked up a copy of *Speedway Star*. He read about one of Eastbourne's young riders, Tom Brennan, and decided to sponsor his race suit. From there, he started helping out on the commercial side. Then, at the end of the 2018 season, he was asked if he'd be interested in taking over Eastbourne speedway and he says it took him 'about a nanosecond' to agree.

Ian chooses his words carefully but it's clear his ideas for the sport are sometimes different to those who have been in speedway for longer. 'I've got massive respect for people who've been in speedway for 20 or 30 or 40 years, but what strikes me about it is that it's a bit like a goldfish bowl. They're just looking inside that goldfish bowl and they've almost become transfixed. One of the things I learned in business was that before you say or do anything, think of every question that's going to come and try and answer it before it's asked. You should also be prepared to say that you don't have the answer, if that's the case. At the end of the day, speedway to me is a business.'

As Ian freely admits, he's a glass-half-full kind of a guy who believes, despite the position British speedway finds itself in, that opportunities are there to be grabbed.

'I don't think there's a better product in sport than speedway. Four guys, four bikes, no brakes. To me it's the most exciting of sports. If you're a fan of it and you're passionate about what you're trying to sell, it makes it a lot easier.'

But he's clear about what needs to change. When he went back to Eastbourne (the first time he'd been there for 30 years) and walked around, he says he was meeting people who he'd known before. There were very few young people.

He's doing something about it, in a way that might be a blueprint for other speedway clubs up and down the country.

At the end of 2018, he contacted local junior football teams. Youngsters, along with their mums and dads, could come to Eastbourne speedway for free. After that, they'd be offered special discounted family deals. In 2019 a proper community project was launched that saw nearly 4,000 people – kids and parents who had never been before – come through Eastbourne's gates over the season.

Ian is 'big on data' and says 20 per cent of people who came for the first time on a free visit returned. He's proud they sold 20 adult season tickets over the winter to people who had never been to speedway before 2019.

They had planned for 2020 – now rolled over to 2021 – that children could come free to Eastbourne speedway. They have 65,000 '15 and under' free season tickets that will go out to schools, sports clubs and tourist attractions in and around the Eastbourne and Brighton area. Brighton and Hove Albion football club will have a separate batch of 40,000 to cover all their junior members.

'If you're going to let kids in for free, rather than just wait for them to come to you, you need to go to them. I want those season tickets on the mantelpiece so that on a nice warm Saturday or Sunday afternoon the kids will nag the parents: "Come on, can we go to speedway?" If the parents come once or twice then they're paying. If we had 5,000 or 6,000 people coming through at £15, £16 a pop, it just transforms your bottom line.'

Ian has sat down with Plymouth promoter Mark Phillips, who said they'll do exactly the same 'under 15s for free' initiative there. They've also identified sizeable Polish communities of around 9,000 in both Eastbourne and Plymouth, so they can encourage Poles to come to British speedway. Ian feels that community has been ignored for too long.

Plymouth were disappointed not to be allowed a Championship place over the winter. But it hasn't stopped them investing in the stadium, their new grandstand being a welcome addition during the summer. They've also separately launched a new business, which Ian calls his 'new baby', establishing the stadium as a venue for craft fairs, music events and car boot sales, which can generate significant income for speedway as well.

When we speak, it's a few days after Plymouth have become just the fourth British club to stage a meeting with spectators this summer in a three-team tournament.

Ian says it was quite a difficult and long process to arrange with both the local authority and the BSP Ltd. He says they were told they could have 25 per cent capacity and settled for 400 in the end, about 20 per cent, which felt comfortably within the guidelines; 400 is their average crowd for a National League meeting and they sold out within four days.

They also linked up with a streaming provider and sold about 300 units at £5. Ian says he was very pleasantly surprised by the quality of the streaming. 'We got very positive feedback. I'll be honest, I'm not a massive fan of streaming because my business head says that if you make it too easy for someone to sit in their armchair and watch speedway, ultimately they're not going to come. As an example, when the speedway Grand Prix is on, on a Saturday night, I lose 50–100 people at Eastbourne.'

He says they made money on the three-team meeting at Plymouth. 'At Eastbourne, with the higher pay scales of Championship riders, I probably need 800 to break even. But the capacity at Eastbourne is 4,000 so I can put meetings on with a crowd of around 800 to 1,000 and make a few quid. We're already working on how we optimise things for 2021. We have a very good, simple online ticketing system for both clubs that we can also use to create a whole new marketing base. Out of the darkness comes light.'

It's something that will be increasingly relevant next year. Ian doesn't expect the COVID-19 situation being much different by March. He believes they'll need to look at reduced capacities for possibly the whole of 2021, if not beyond.

* * *

If there's one event which sums up British speedway's luck – or lack of it – in 2020, it's the individual British Final.

Even if there isn't any league racing this summer, Rob Godfrey hasn't given up on running professional speedway before the end of the season and, in particular, staging a British Final. It's almost become his holy grail for the year. He and other BSP Ltd board members lobby MPs and various Government departments and finally manage to secure a Zoom call with DCMS officials at the end of July. It's put in the diary for just 30 minutes and no minister is present, but still, it's a step in the right direction.

Despite being told a decision is imminent, Rob is made to wait. 'We kept emailing them, "Come on, have you got this decision for us?" We even got an email back saying the Prime Minister has taken it to bed tonight to look at.'

Official confirmation finally comes in an official DCMS statement on 26 August. It details pilot events, where a limited number of spectators will be allowed, for football, rugby union, horse racing, cricket, basketball – and speedway. The British Final will be allowed to take place at Ipswich's Foxhall Stadium on Saturday, 26 September.

The choice of venue is a bit of a surprise. The British Final has been held at Manchester's National Speedway Stadium ever since it opened in 2016, but it's felt more spectators can be accommodated at Foxhall under COVID-19 restrictions. The stadium has already hosted stock car racing this summer, so some of the necessary measures are already in place.

You might think, then, that Rob Godfrey would be ecstatic to finally have a British Final to put in front of spectators, given all he's had to contend with this year, but, when I speak to him at the end of August, there's a new problem – selecting the 16 riders who'll take part. With no speedway this season, the obvious way is to choose based on their last available averages from 2019. But some riders don't want to take part. Many haven't raced for nearly a year and don't fancy getting their bikes out for just one meeting. The 2017 British champion Craig Cook is one of the first to say he won't be riding. He says there isn't enough time to get prepared and, with a title on the line and riders having done so little actual riding, he doesn't feel that's great for safety.

Former champion Scott Nicholls decides to give it a miss. The current British champion, Charles Wright, is also conspicuously quiet. With Tai Woffinden and Robert Lambert racing in Poland, they're already ruled out. But Rob, ever the optimist, promises that it will still be a very good line-up.

Tickets – limited to 2,200 for an elite sport pilot event – go on sale online on 8 September. The good news is that demand far exceeds expectations. Speedway supporters, starved of top-flight action, are keen to return. But there's bad news too. The promoters put their hands up and admit they'd not anticipated what they call 'stunning demand'. They didn't have enough staff to cope. Sales are suspended with a promise that work will go on through the night to have the remaining tickets back on sale the following morning.

Except external circumstances intervene. The number of COVID-19 infections in the UK has been steadily increasing, even if hospital admissions and deaths are still very low. The Government, clearly sensitive to accusations that they acted too slowly back in

March, are taking no chances. New restrictions accompanied by a now obligatory slogan – 'Hands Face Space' – are introduced. But there's also a rethink on pilot events for elite sports. As a result, Ipswich's 2,200 capacity is reduced to just 1,000. No more tickets will be made available. Those lucky enough to have been in the first 1,000 purchases will get in. Refunds will be given to the others.

But Rob and Chris Louis, the Ipswich promoter and former rider, want as many people as possible to see the meeting. They also need to cover their costs. The following week, they announce that the British Final will be streamed. It's something many have been asking for and good news for fans unable to attend or isolating at home. But, inevitably, there are those who find fault with it. Some comments on the Official British Speedway Twitter feed wonder why it's not being covered by Eurosport under the terms of its new five-year contract. It's pointed out that Eurosport's contract is being rolled over to start in 2021. Then there are those who claim that the £12.95 fee is the 'wrong price point' or a 'bloody rip-off'.

A more measured response comes from British rider Adam Ellis. He's not riding in the final – not because he doesn't want to but because he was injured in August's Grand Prix qualifier. He says, not unreasonably, that fans had been calling for the season to start behind closed doors with meetings streamed. Now that's happening and there are complaints about the cost. 'Looks like @speedwayGB can't win whatever they do.'

That's equally true when it comes to the riders selected for the final. Imagine putting a wedding list together, knowing very well you won't please everyone. But instead of just a few people sticking their oar in and wondering why you've invited so-and-so, your selection is open to scrutiny from thousands. As the finalists' names are steadily released, criticism inevitably follows.

There aren't that many surprises in the first nine names – 2016 champion Danny King, Dan Bewley and Lewis Kerr are all in there. I'm pleased too to see that Josh Auty will be getting his bike out for his first meeting since the Ben Fund in March. It's the tenth name that's announced, Australian Jason Crump, that causes an almighty rumpus. It's not that Crump won't be a welcome addition. After all, he was one of the marquee signings contributing to that pre-COVID feel-good factor back in February. It's the fact that this is supposed to be a British Final, and Crump, despite being born in Bristol, is Australian. He won his world titles as an Australian and rode, consistently, for the Australian team.

Some supporters are just glad that there's speedway and if Crump helps to make up a competitive field then so be it. Others feel that his inclusion means a young, up-and-coming British rider will miss out. Perhaps those complaining shouldn't be surprised. After all, Wolverhampton's Rory Schlein has already been included in this month's line-up. Australian too, he's been allowed to participate in British Finals since 2017. There are precedents for Crump's inclusion both in Britain and abroad.

For better or worse, the riders are chosen, the permitted 1,000 tickets all sold and live streaming made available. But fate is about to throw British speedway another curveball.

Infections are rising more quickly, alarmingly in the eyes of the Government's top medical advisers – Professor Chris Whitty and Sir Patrick Vallance. On the Monday before the final, 21 September, they warn that we could be heading to 50,000 infections a day by mid-October. While their forecasts are not accepted by everybody, reflecting a definite shift in the way some now view the threat from the pandemic compared with March, the Government acts. Further restrictions are announced across England, including a ten o'clock curfew on pubs and restaurants. Plans to allow a limited number of fans back into stadiums from the start of October are ditched – along with an immediate suspension of all pilot events for elite sports.

The following day, the BSP Ltd announce that the British Final will go ahead, but without any fans in attendance. Rob Godfrey describes it as a hammer blow for the sport and feels, in particular, for Ipswich promoter Chris Louis and his staff at Foxhall Stadium.

'He's been burning the midnight oil to plan everything, starting with 2,200 supporters, then down to 1,000, and now it's zero through something not of our doing.' That's not all. Anyone who's been faced with a long and complicated official form will wince when they hear what Chris Louis has had to do to make Foxhall Stadium compliant for the meeting. The documents include a ten-page event management plan, backed up by 18 documents making up another 160 pages.

Rob makes a plea for those receiving refunds to use £12.95 of it to buy the meeting's live stream. He says they're taking a financial gamble by going ahead and they need people to support it – and see what demand there is for live streaming in future.

While the official statement doesn't reveal the full depth of his frustration at the turn of events, an interview with a reporter from the Press Association the following day most certainly does.

Headlined 'We're down already and they keep kicking us – British Speedway fears for future', the interview is syndicated to regional newspapers up and down the country.

'If we don't start another season then it could end the sport. Yesterday's news really was a hammer blow, in the sense that it just cracked the skull. You've got to fear for our future – it's heartbreaking, real pit-of-the-stomach time.'

Then, no doubt thinking about all the hard work that's ultimately been wasted in trying to get spectators to attend a British Final, Rob's frustration really boils over. The 'they' of his anger aren't named specifically, but it's clear who he means.

'Speedway is the number-one sport in Poland and they are letting people into stadiums. There's no reason why it can't happen here. One thousand people can go to Tesco or go to the zoo, but they are not allowed to watch speedway.

'There's no strategy whatsoever in my opinion. You can't just keep kicking people in the b******s. We accept that we're a minority sport, we're down there already and they just keep kicking us. I can't emphasise just how ridiculous and demoralising it is. We put our hearts and souls into this sport and people should be allowed to go and watch it.'

The following day, he releases an official statement. The PA reporter had caught him at a bad time – 'My chin was on the floor.' He'd just had confirmation that all their hard work had been wasted. He'd been speaking from the heart, on a personal level and not at British Speedway Promoters Ltd level.

'I am a passionate man and I was personally feeling extremely low. I regret some of the things I said and, given more time, I would have put things differently.'

He goes on to congratulate those promoters – at Belle Vue, Leicester, King's Lynn, Plymouth, Edinburgh and Berwick – who have and will stage meetings this summer. He talks up the positives – the five-year TV deal with Eurosport, the ongoing attempts to find a league sponsor and the number of really talented youngsters coming through the British speedway system.

He ends with a plea: 'Please stay with us. Your support means everything. We cannot do this without you.'

If it's been hard for Rob Godfrey, organising the British Final has probably been even tougher for the Ipswich promoter, Chris Louis. But if Chris thinks there's nothing more that can be thrown at him, he's sadly wrong.

On the Friday afternoon, just over 24 hours before the meeting is due to take place, it's announced that it's being put back 48 hours to Monday evening – and that it will take place, not in Ipswich, but in Manchester.

The decision has been made because of heavy rain during the week in Ipswich – with more forecast for Saturday. Chris Louis is not wrong when he says that everything has been against them, with the bad weather being the final nail.

He'll later back up – in less emotional language – what Rob Godfrey said in his PA interview. The most important thing he's learnt from the whole pandemic is how important fans are for the future of the sport. Louis feels the Government has overlooked the concerns of smaller sports looking to survive by focusing on the top levels of football. 'Quite clearly, they won't want to see 70,000 people at Old Trafford, but that's not speedway or many other sports. In them being blinkered, we have all had to suffer greatly for it. We don't have the backing and finances. Many sports don't have the infrastructure. It has been tough.'

* * *

Belle Vue in Manchester has held a meeting in the city every year since 1928, no mean feat in the precarious world of British speedway. It's no surprise then that, having successfully kept going through the Second World War, the promoters aren't going to let the little matter of a global pandemic spoil that record. Even before being handed this year's British Final at short notice, Belle Vue have decided to stage their own top-flight meeting, the first to be live-streamed behind closed doors.

One of the prime movers of this is promoter Adrian Smith. Adrian is a relative newcomer to the sport – and one of those angling for a change in the organisational structure of British speedway.

While acknowledging the current situation is beyond anyone's control, he tells *Speedway Star* that he hopes the extended close season can be used constructively.

'What is important now is how speedway looks in the future. My mantra has always been the same, to see the sport independently managed so we can drive it into a new era, and I still want to see that at some stage. That's how we are all going to benefit in the long run, with a fresh approach. We have been working with the board [of British Speedway Promoters Limited] in that regard and on the whole they have tried to balance everyone's requirements.'

It's those three words 'on the whole' that stand out. It's been said that the crisis has brought promoters together in a way that hasn't been apparent before. While that might be true, it's inevitable there won't be complete harmony. Belle Vue, while accepting the original decision to move the final to Ipswich, say they were disappointed with how they were told about it.

But that hadn't stopped Adrian arranging a professional-level meeting, a team competition between the Belle Vue Aces and the ATPI

All Stars, proof of Ian Sinderson's determination to keep sponsoring speedway even in tough times.

In his programme notes for the meeting, Adrian says it hasn't been an easy decision to race behind closed doors without supporters. He admits there are risks but says it's vital to embrace all technologies and social media channels to attract new audiences and see the sport progress. 'The bottom line is that the sport simply has to keep evolving to remain relevant to a future audience. You are part of a groundbreaking night and one which we hope will be a great success and help drive the agenda for the sport.'

The online streaming – £10.00 for early birds and £12.95 otherwise – is provided by Sport Central TV, who've worked with British ice hockey for several seasons. They've promised a multi-camera production. That's indeed what we get, along with commentary from journalist and speedway fan Dave Rowe. Apart from one small glitch in the first race, it's a slick and enjoyable broadcast with live action, replays and lots of interviews with scrupulously bemasked riders, interspersed with adverts from the four main sponsors.

The Belle Vue team features four of the side they would have tracked in 2020 had COVID not intervened. There's also a place for Jason Crump, making his first appearance in a Belle Vue race jacket since 2008. You're reminded what a thoughtful individual Crump is. Interviewed before the meeting, he's asked how he's feeling and, instead of the usual platitudes about being really excited, he admits it's a little bit stressful given this will be the first time he's been in a competitive meeting in Britain for 12 years. What most people don't know – and which will only be revealed the following week – is that he'd actually broken his pelvis in four places, along with his wrist, in a motocross practice accident back in June. He's still not fully fit but it says a lot about his commitment that he's here tonight. He's interviewed again after his first two races – two third places – and admits it hasn't gone too well so far. 'It's like the start of my career again.'

Given quite a few of those riding haven't been in competitive action for six months, the meeting isn't bad either. Dan Bewley is the star, looking very fast indeed around the corners of his home track, but it's a good competitive match that is only decided, in Belle Vue's favour, in the penultimate heat.

It is hard – almost unbelievably – to find anyone on social media or bulletin boards with a bad word to say about the evening. Some are impressed by the racing and really pleased to see Jason Crump back on a bike. Others praise the quality of the streaming and say it's a step forward into what could be a bright future for the sport. If clubs can make money from pay per view, it has to be done. No official figures are made available for the sales of online streaming passes, but Belle Vue say the meeting paid for itself.

It's summed up by Richard John, a speedway fan and paint sprayer from Bristol, who tweets the following morning: 'A timeline full of happy speedway fans, blimey 2020 really is out of control.'

* * *

In some ways, speedway, although it probably wouldn't think so right now, has got off lightly in the latest round of restrictions compared to several other sports. After all, their 2021 season isn't due to start until the middle of March next year – unlike football, rugby union and rugby league. This winter's ice hockey season has been cancelled with clubs now unlikely to start league action until August 2021 at the earliest.

A meeting on 22 September between the Culture and Sport Secretary Oliver Dowden and representatives of leading sports has established that crowds will not be allowed back into stadiums before March next year. Dan Roan, the BBC's Sports Editor, says that British sport is facing a crisis the likes of which it hasn't faced before. While sports journalists are often given to hyperbole, this is an accurate summary of what's facing many long-established sports clubs. There's talk of a lost generation of sport and activity with the 'rule of six' now being applied to all team sports like netball and basketball. The Rugby Football Union – the richest rugby union in the world – says much of the game is heading for oblivion with clubs disappearing for ever.

The Premier League, whose clubs nevertheless continue to spend big sums in this summer's transfer window, says there will be a monthly £100 million loss.

Sports authorities point to countries in Europe where up to 50 per cent stadium capacity is permitted. With no likely income from fans for six months, there are calls for a financial rescue package, similar to the £1.57 billion announced for the arts sector at the start of July. While football's Premier League won't be given help, it is being asked to provide support to the EFL where clubs are already struggling. Macclesfield Town, in financial trouble before the pandemic, have been wound up and other clubs could follow.

Another sport in trouble, one with important links to speedway through their use of shared stadiums, is greyhound racing. Already in decline, the arrival of COVID-19 has accelerated that trend. News that greyhound racing is coming to an end at Wimborne Road in Poole has set alarm bells ringing for the future of the speedway Pirates. The Poole promoters offer, if needed, to take over the running of the stadium themselves but receive reassurances that it will continue to operate. They say they fully intend to run in 2021. British speedway without Poole Pirates, even in the second-tier Championship, would be a major blow to the sport.

At the other end of England, there are similar concerns for the Newcastle Diamonds. Their Brough Park venue is owned by greyhound operators Arena Racing Limited. While their immediate future for 2021 – assuming racing is allowed – seems secure, owner Rob Grant says there are no guarantees from the stadium owners beyond then. Grant, who took over last November, says he was always keen to find a new location to control the club's long-term future. He says this year has opened his eyes to the fact they're too reliant on a separate stadium owner – one of British speedway's Achilles heels for decades – and that he wants to find, or build, his own track. He believes a model, followed by the likes of Scunthorpe and Redcar, is the only way to operate. That way, they can generate new revenue streams through staging events and practice days at their own track.

While there's obviously a lot of work to be done before that can happen, Grant says he's been encouraged by the response of the four local councils in the Newcastle/Gateshead area to finding a site for a new venue.

It all must be wearily familiar to Dave Tattum who was, after all, brought in to work alongside Rob Grant last autumn after Stoke's closure. When I speak to him, it's a year to the day since the very last speedway meeting at Loomer Road. But, instead of dwelling on that, as I'd half expected, he's much more concerned about recent job losses at the local Stoke radio station, Signal Radio. 'They were very good to us but they've been bought out and closed down. All the DJs, all the news people, gone.' Signal is not alone, with dozens of towns and cities across the country losing their local radio station – often loyal supporters of speedway – after their owner, Bauer, decided to fold 50 regional stations into one national radio network.

Dave tells me that a few of the journalists have started up a small radio station and he's going along this Saturday with former rider Nigel Crabtree to talk Stoke speedway. 'To just keep it in people's memory and remember the good times, that sort of thing.'

You sense Dave's really enjoyed working with Rob Grant, that it has, in some ways, given him a new lease of life and zest for speedway. 'It's done me a huge favour. He will make it happen, Rob Grant will. He put a statement out that he was debt-free. Not many people in the speedway world can say that.'

While Newcastle won't be running any meetings in 2020, Dave's certain they'll be back next year. He says they've tried everything to get bikes back on the track in Newcastle, even training days, but the stadium owners didn't want crowds in during COVID. However, they have told Rob and Dave they're safe for 2021.

'I've just been talking to Rob Grant on the phone and he's been in meetings with the council this morning. There's a lot of positives going on. I think Rob Grant is the best thing that's happened to speedway in many years. He's got a helluva temper, and that used to be me in my younger days, so I quite like what he stands for. He will leave no stone unturned to get Newcastle speedway up and running, whether it be at Brough Park or on a new site.'

Given that Dave had been so realistically honest about the lack of prospects for Stoke speedway starting up again, I'm more than happy to believe his optimism for Newcastle's future.

* * *

Just four nights after their successful first meeting of the season, Belle Vue stage their second, the seemingly jinxed British Final. There have been a couple of late withdrawals, which means opportunities for 16-year-old twins, Dan and Joe Thompson, who've been busy riding in the British Youth Championships. There's no place for Tom Bacon, who would have been in last year's British Final if not for injury. While Tom's not one to make a fuss, he does wonder why the 2019 averages weren't used to select riders. He finds it very hard when things aren't done in a fair and transparent manner and believes the British Final should feature the best 16 available riders.

Inevitably – because it's the end of September and because it's Manchester – there's rain falling on the Monday evening. The reflected floodlights of the National Speedway Stadium glisten off the wet shale of the Belle Vue track.

Chris Louis is filling in as co-commentator on the live stream, something he did back in the days of Sky Sports' coverage. Whether it's the rain or it's because a few of the riders are taking part in their first meeting of the season, there are bike problems aplenty in the first eight heats – with just a classic Jason Crump manoeuvre in heat five to enjoy. Steve Worrall describes it as like peeing into the wind all night. He says he was ready to go home after his first two heats but his mechanic persuaded him to switch to another bike and get stuck in. Visibility is clearly a problem, particularly for those riders unlucky enough to be trailing after the first bend. They are, in speedway vernacular, 'filled in' with wet shale and mud; not an ideal welcome back to your job for the first time in months.

I'm hoping Josh Auty does well but, after a promising second in his first race, he's one of those with mechanical issues and doesn't finish in his second, which effectively ends his chances. He'll say later he hadn't protected the plug areas, which would be normal practice when it's so wet 'but because we hadn't been riding continuously, we weren't on the ball with things.'

Fortunately, the rain eases after heat six and the remaining races are better. The final is won by an Australian, Rory Schlein. He pumps his fist as he passes the line, indicating that winning the title certainly means a lot to him. Not everyone's impressed. Former British champion Craig Cook tweets that listening to how great the racing is while he watches what is actually happening is painful. For those speedway fans who lean to the negative side of life, the podium features two Australians – Schlein in first place and Jason Crump in third, with Britain's Richard Lawson second. For the rest of us, it's been another well-presented and welcome evening of speedway in a summer when there hasn't been much to watch.

Josh Auty says it was odd racing without spectators but that it's better to have sport behind closed doors than having no sport at all. For him, and for many riders, sport is not the same without supporters. 'It just doesn't have the vibe or feel to it.'

Chris Louis looks ahead to 2021 and, asked if we'll see speedway back in front of crowds, says there has to be an improvement in communications from the Government. He may be speaking on behalf of British speedway promoters but, in many ways, he's speaking for the whole country, given the confusing and complicated messages on what can and can't be done in our daily lives.

The following day, Rob Godfrey confirms that streaming numbers more than covered the cost of the event, 'which is a wonderful achievement.' But he reiterates his frustration with the logic that hundreds of fans can attend non-league football but none are allowed at speedway meetings.

As well as winning the title, Rory Schlein surely claims the award for the muddiest rider to feature on the cover of this year's

Speedway Star, his gold medal clenched between his teeth as if he's making sure it's not a chocolate imitation. Inside, the meeting report concludes that it was a night to appreciate everything that was done right with maximum effort, in tough conditions, and a worthy winner.

But there's also a plea by the magazine's Paul Burbidge that, while streaming has its place, fans need to be back in stadiums. He says supporters get more for their admission fee than 15 races. 'They get a night out, the chance to catch up with friends, the unique atmosphere on the terraces and the sound, smell and buzz of 500cc bikes up close and personal.'

That chimes very much with the findings of a Loughborough University survey highlighted in the *Financial Times* earlier in the year. When researchers asked supporters around Europe to document what football meant in their everyday lives, almost 90 per cent of the thousands of photographs sent in didn't show match action. Instead, there were bus interiors on the way to an away game, minute preparations before taking a child to the stadium and pre-match excitement in the stands. It may have been for football matches but it is unlikely speedway fans' feelings would be much different.

The beauty of fandom, especially for some men, is that conversation isn't even required. You can just be together. For speedway, that can mean standing in a customary spot on the first bend or along the back straight. But that's under threat. Burbidge's article concludes with some chastening words.

'Unless fans return to UK stadiums and soon, the oldest speedway leagues in the world will wither and die. We can only hope they [British speedway bosses] persuade the authorities that hosting supporters in sizeable sports stadiums in limited numbers poses a far lower risk than allowing revellers to pile into pubs and then pour on to the streets and continue the party at 10pm. And let's not get started on the lack of social distancing onboard an aircraft or on the south's beaches this summer. Common sense has gone out of the window in this country; we can only hope nearly a century of speedway heritage doesn't follow.'

October 2020 – The unluckiest break

IT'S THE first Saturday of the month and, across most of the country, it pours. It'll be the UK's wettest day since records began in 1891, the sort of weather that accompanies the climax of a British speedway season in a normal year.

October wasn't promising very much in the first place, given we're facing six months – the coldest and darkest ones too – with COVID restrictions very much back in place again.

The virus's political polarisation is now clear for all to see – if it wasn't already. Enormous amounts of data have been accumulated but, instead of providing clarity, they're used selectively to support anything from a complete lockdown to a Trumpian free-for-all. The Labour party produces figures to show that local lockdowns aren't working because all areas have seen rises in infections. But an Imperial College London study claims they have been successful because the 'R' number in Great Britain has actually fallen during September from 1.7 to 1.1.

In the middle of October, the Government unveils a new three-tier system, designed to simplify rules and regulations. It then puts many northern areas – whether they want to be included or not – into the highest-risk tier. There's opposition, short-lived from Middlesbrough's independent mayor, Andy Preston, high-profile from Manchester's Andy Burnham, and financially damaging for one Wirral gym, which defiantly remains open and is fined for doing so. By the end of the month, books, greeting cards and hairdryers are deemed non-essential items and banned from sale in Wales. In Europe, crowds take to the streets in Turin, Milan and Barcelona to protest against their national lockdowns. That wide acceptance of restrictions seen earlier in the year – when the virus was new and unknown – is no more.

At the end of the month, the Government – to no one's great surprise – announces what some of the papers deem a 'Hallowe'en Horror Show' for England – a lockdown until 2 December. Apart from keeping schools and universities open, it's broadly similar to what was put in place in March. Except this time it's set before a much more fractious, unhappy population. The *Daily Telegraph*, normally the stoutest of supporters of Tory governments, sums up Lockdown 2 thus:

'Here we go again. England is being locked down for a second time, as if we hadn't learnt anything or made any progress since this dreadful virus burst on to the scene at the start of the year. It is a depressing and debilitating development, one that will plunge Britain even deeper into a double-dip recession, a mental health crisis and a social, personal and cultural abyss.'

The new James Bond film – becoming an entertainment litmus test of how deeply we remain in the pandemic crisis – has its release pushed back again into 2021. Sport – including speedway – continues in its neutered, behind-closed-doors fashion, but deeper-seated worries remain. In football, EFL clubs say many will go bust without crowds; proposals and demands for Premier League clubs to bail them out come to nothing. The chairman of Surrey County Cricket Club says players will be playing for drink money next season if there are no spectators.

In some ways, speedway is lucky that it closes down at the end of this month. It can watch from the sidelines and prepare for next spring when things – with long-hoped-for vaccines available – may, just, be better.

* * *

The heavy rain from Storm Alex that lashes Britain bypasses Poland. That's fortunate because this first weekend of October is the final round of this season's individual speedway Grand Prix. The format for 2020 has been changed because of COVID, being staged over four weekends, with a Friday night meeting followed immediately by a second on the Saturday at the same venue. Three Polish tracks are selected along with Prague in the Czech Republic.

The first four rounds see some good, competitive racing and four different winners. While not one of them, Britain's representative, Tai Woffinden, scores consistently to remain in contention in fourth place.

The races between Woffinden and defending champion Bartosz Zmarzlik show speedway at its very best. Close, intense, unpredictable, always hard but fair, it's clear they both enjoy and respect the other, each race ending with a fist bump between the two on the way back to the pits, whichever of them has won. I find myself scanning the night's list of heats, looking for the one where they'll face each other, hoping they'll both make it into later stages so we can enjoy another race between them. It's a compelling speedway storyline of its own, with no one sure who'll come out on top at the very end.

The weekend in Prague – meetings five and six in this year's truncated programme – is pivotal. Woffinden does well, finishing second and scoring 18 points out of 20 each night. But Zmarzlik does even better, winning both. Going into this weekend's final meetings at Toruń, Zmarzlik is eight points clear of Woffinden.

Heat two on Saturday serves up one of those sublime speedway races that warm the heart. It helps that the world's top three riders – Zmarzlik, Woffinden and Sweden's Freddie Lindgren – are in it, each desperate for points.

Zmarzlik, off gate two, leads going into the first corner, pursued closely by Woffinden, with Lindgren seemingly out of it in third. Woffinden tries to sweep round the Pole, first on the outside and then the inside, without success. Going into the third bend of lap two, Zmarzlik leads. But that's when the fun and games really begin. Woffinden cuts inside Zmarzlik to take the lead on the fourth bend, but the Pole won't settle for second and, as they head into lap three, he cuts back inside Woffinden. Both go slightly wide, which allows

Lindgren, never a rider to shirk an opportunity, however tough it looks, to dive under the two of them. He somehow avoids colliding with Zmarzlik's front wheel as he does so. Into the back straight, the three of them are almost level, Lindgren on the outside, Zmarzlik in the middle, Woffinden on the inside. Woffinden turns first but drifts wider than he'd like, pushing Zmarzlik out with him, which allows Lindgren inside both of them as they emerge onto the fourth and final lap. It's breathtaking stuff – 'Fireworks have gone off here, mate!' says Kelvin Tatum. It's so good that words, any words, simply can't do justice to it: in the space of just six bends, one after the other, the lead has changed hands six times: Zmarzlik, Woffinden, Zmarzlik, Lindgren, Woffinden, Lindgren. In just 19 seconds. There is no other sport where this happens.

Zmarzlik only needs to reach the final to guarantee becoming world champion. Despite being off the outside gate in his semi-final, he rides bravely to take second place – enough to reach the final – which sets off wild celebrations amongst the Polish fans in the stadium. He'll go on to win the night's final too, meaning that no one can question his overall victory. Of the eight Grand Prix this season, he's won four. In his private battle with Woffinden, he's also come out on top – 11 wins to eight.

Interviewed on BT Sport afterwards, Woffinden says he's not been on form this season and feels he's been struggling. 'But the fire's burning for next year – massively.'

Natalie Quirk in the studio reminds him that this season isn't finished yet because he's still got the Speedway of Nations to look forward to. With Woffinden the world number two and the reigning European champion Robert Lambert forming their main pairing, Great Britain have a really good chance of winning, even though the meeting is no longer taking place in Manchester. Because of changing travel restrictions and quarantine requirements, it's been moved to Lublin in Poland. There are some who wonder whether Toruń, with its overhanging roof covering much of the track, wouldn't be a better choice at a time of year when the weather's not great.

Before then, on Sunday in fact, Woffinden has a league semi-final play-off for his Polish side, Wrocław, who only have a two-point lead from the first leg. They'll have a tough job to reach the final.

* * *

In many ways the history of speedway in Edinburgh mirrors the path the sport as a whole has taken in this country. It began in May 1928 in Portobello – Edinburgh's seaside holiday resort – at Marine Gardens, an existing pleasure complex which, at different times, boasted a zoo, circus and ballroom. When speedway started up again after the Second World War, and Marine Gardens was no longer available, it moved to Old Meadowbank Stadium. The home at the time of Leith Athletic football club, it was a city-centre location befitting a sport drawing weekly crowds in their thousands. But Old Meadowbank Stadium was demolished to build a new athletics arena for the 1970 Commonwealth Games and, with speedway falling out of favour, there was no place for it. It didn't return until 1977, this time at Powderhall greyhound stadium, closer to the port of Leith than the city centre. In 1995 a housing developer made an offer for the site and Edinburgh were evicted again. They raced at Shawfield in Glasgow in 1996 under the banner of the 'Scottish Monarchs', which was, in the words of co-promoter, Alex Harkess, a complete disaster: 'The fans didn't get on and they used to throw bread rolls at each other.' They managed to find a new home the following year at a greyhound stadium in the old mining community of Armadale in West Lothian just off the M8 motorway. The only people who'd make a claim for Armadale being part of Edinburgh would be budget airlines, given that it's a good 25 miles away. The Monarchs have remained there ever since.

That 90-year-long journey to out-of-town industrial area via leisure complex, city-centre stadium, greyhound stadium and a couple of evictions to boot is one with which many other speedway clubs can identify.

Even now, there's speculation about Edinburgh's future, with outline planning permission given for housing at Armadale. But Alex

Harkess is relaxed about it, saying the ground is unstable because of mine-workings and, with so many planning restrictions in place, no builder is interested. The Monarchs get on very well with the family who own the stadium and he says they'll be there as long as they want to be.

He admits that it's a tired old stadium but feels it offers some of the best speedway because of the shape of the track, which makes it tricky. Riders make mistakes, which makes the racing that much more interesting. That's not a view shared by all riders, however. Of those prepared to name their least favourite track in *Speedway Star*'s 'On & Off Track' weekly feature this year, Edinburgh gets the most mentions.

Riders making mistakes means injuries and Alex is justifiably proud of bringing in air fences to British speedway tracks when he was chairman of the BSPA. Previously they were made of wood or, in the case of Hull's Boulevard stadium, brick.

'Going back to our early days at Armadale, riders would hit that wooden fence and I'd hear the thud. I used to shut my eyes, thinking, "What the hell's happened to him?" The air fence has certainly made the sport an awful lot safer; they've got a chance of walking away. They are riding as fast as the bike will go now, right on the nail. Everything is faster and more powerful. The lower point of gravity on the laydown engines was supposed to make them a bit safer, but it means they're throwing it into the bend even harder. It only takes something, clipping the back mudguard of another bike, and you're going so fast you're catapulted to absolutely anywhere.'

Whatever the dangers, on the same Friday night as the Toruń Grand Prix weekend is getting underway, 11 riders, mainly National League level and below, have turned up at an autumnal Armadale for the annual Caledonian Riders' Championship. While some clubs have decided not to stage any meetings this year, Edinburgh were always keen, even if, like tonight's meeting, it's behind closed doors. It's their second meeting of the season, following their British Youth Championship round two weeks earlier.

Alex says it was important to get the meetings on because they wanted to test out streaming, which they've been working on for some time. They had made last September's home meeting against Somerset available to away supporters watching back at the Oaktree Arena clubhouse and wanted to develop that this season. 'We always felt that it was a way forward. I'm not saying it'll pay for everything, but if you get a steady income from people with no intention of coming because of where they are geographically, what's wrong with that? We're not trying to find a replacement for television. We're just trying to find an extra market.'

They would put a block on streaming in their own area to stop their own supporters staying at home. Alex says an extra £500 a match can, over the course of a season, help clubs keep their head above water.

Edinburgh plan to do the streaming themselves unlike, say, Belle Vue, where they'd contracted out to a production company. 'Other than a connection fee, which is probably less than £100, there are no other charges. We do it all ourselves. The cost of putting the Belle Vue one on was quite a few thousand pounds and that's a different ball game.' But Alex is keen to stress they wouldn't be happy to start a new season next March behind closed doors. They need spectators. 'You could probably do it in the top league if you have enough television money, providing you sit down and work it out sensibly. But that's not an option in our league because we don't have television money so we can't run a league campaign without spectators. That's just a fact.'

He remains upbeat for 2021. 'I'm an optimistic person and I think to survive in speedway for a long time, that has to be your frame of mind. The one big difference this time is that there's so much out of our hands. Normally it's what you do at your own club that matters, but this time you're depending on the Government. We're very good at Edinburgh in raising money and we'll continue to be. But I hate when it's out of our control. And that's what it is at the moment.'

* * *

Imagine, for a moment, a different version of 2020, one where COVID-19 doesn't wreak havoc, where social distancing is as unfamiliar a term as it was prior to March and that this year's Speedway of Nations is an undisputed triumph.

It's held, as planned, on the first bank holiday weekend of May at Belle Vue. Britain's record-breaking spring weather means Manchester is dry and sunny. With almost every speedway fixture going ahead throughout March and April, enthusiasm is high and there's a capacity crowd of 6,000 on both days. The Great Britain trio of Tai Woffinden, Robert Lambert and Dan Bewley look resplendent in their new kevlars, complete with their new national sponsors, proof of the hard work put in behind the scenes by Rob Painter and Vicky Blackwell.

On the track, the shale surface, as is nearly always the case at Belle Vue, has been prepared for entertaining racing. And it delivers, with passing in almost every heat. Equally importantly, building on all the hard work and good habits instilled in the Great Britain team over the winter by co-managers Simon Stead and Olly Allen, the home riders rise to the occasion.

Tai Woffinden goes through the weekend unbeaten by an opponent. #SuperTai trends on Twitter. Robert Lambert secures race wins against some of the world's best riders. And perhaps the highlight for true speedway fans is Dan Bewley sweeping around world champion Bartosz Zmarzlik on the final bend to take second place behind Woffinden on Friday. Bewley's spectacular effort goes viral on social media.

In Saturday's winner-take-all final, Woffinden and Lambert make up for the disappointment of 2018 by defeating the Russian pairing. It's Great Britain's first team victory since 1989. Woffinden and Lambert celebrate with a joint wheelie down the back straight, in front of a bank of Union flag-waving, cheering fans. Perhaps prompted by the fact that this weekend's bank holiday celebrates the 75th anniversary of VE Day, speedway – one of the post-war sporting successes – actually gets some unexpected mainstream media coverage. Their win is covered in national newspapers, on radio and TV. Tai, Robert and Dan are asked to appear live with their trophy on Monday evening's *The One Show* on BBC1. There's even talk of a visit to Downing Street.

But this is, sadly, an illusion; 2020, as we all know, is far from perfect. In reality, this month's Speedway of Nations pretty much mirrors the year as a whole.

* * *

Tai Woffinden's play-off semi-final at Gorzów proves as tough as expected. Wrocław's two-point lead from the first leg disappears by heat two. Woffinden does his best, taking eight points out of nine. Going into heat 10, Wrocław trail by six points overall, so it's not yet out of reach, but with world champion Zmarzlik in two of the final five heats, points here are vital.

Wrocław reserve Michał Curzytek surprisingly leads from the gate. Behind him, Woffinden is involved in a frantic battle for second place with home riders Anders Thomsen and Niels-Kristian Iversen. On lap two, he gets ahead of both of them only to be overtaken again a lap later. Going down the back straight of the final lap, Woffinden is still fourth, neck and neck with Iversen in third. But then, going into the penultimate bend of the race, disaster strikes.

Iversen seems to lose control and slides off. As he does, he twists around behind him to see Woffinden coming straight at him. Tai is literally feet away from his rival as Iversen hits the ground, leaving Tai no time at all to lay down his bike and avoid a collision. He drives right over Iversen, causing Iversen to tumble and bounce along the track. Woffinden is propelled off his bike, headfirst into the air fence amidst a jumble of metal and dust. There's an immediate hush from the crowd. Speedway fans know very well when they've just seen a very bad crash. And this is a bad one. The commentator's words, an excited flurry just seconds earlier, are now ponderous and slow in between ominous silences. Two ambulances are immediately sent onto the track.

Replays show that, miraculously, Woffinden had missed riding over Iversen's head but not his chest. Woffinden's first to his feet, holding his left hand. He refuses the medical staff's attempts to shepherd him into an ambulance, insisting that he go and check on Iversen who's now managing to sit up.

Both, not surprisingly, will take no further part in the meeting. On his way to hospital Woffinden tweets that he's really glad that Iversen had got up from that – 'I was going way too fast to miss him!' There's no squeamishness either as he helpfully provides a link to the crash on YouTube – 'If ya wanna watch it.'

Iversen turns out to have broken a rib, painful enough but, given the nature of the crash, not as bad as it might have been. Woffinden, in a year when British speedway really hasn't had any breaks, has perhaps now suffered the unluckiest one of all. A fifth metacarpal in his hand is broken in two places.

Olly Allen is one of those watching the meeting back on television. When he sees the accident, he phones his Great Britain co-manager Simon Stead straightaway to talk about what they should do now. Their talisman, the world number two, their best chance of salvaging something for the national team from this disrupted year, will miss the Speedway of Nations.

They resist calls to bring in one of the more experienced, older riders – fully supported by GB managing director Rob Painter. Instead, they look to youth, selecting Drew Kemp and Jordan Palin, who only turned 16 in February and hasn't raced above National League level. While it's unlikely Jordan will actually get to ride, it's still a huge honour for someone who's likely to be part of the national set-up for the next decade and beyond.

With Dan Bewley having his best weekend in the Polish league – paid 23 points in two meetings for Wrocław – perhaps there is still hope for Britain to secure a medal of some sort.

* * *

COVID-19, however, has a final kick in the stomach for the world of speedway in 2020. Faced with a record spike in the number of coronavirus cases, the Polish Prime Minister reimposes a partial lockdown on the country. Sports events will now be held without any fans at all. That includes the Speedway of Nations due to begin the following day, Friday, 16 October.

Except, it doesn't. With the original venue, Manchester, enjoying a dry weekend of weather, Lublin is cold, wet and miserable. Friday night's meeting is cancelled without even a practice taking place. Organisers say it'll now be run over one night instead of two. But the rain continues during Saturday and, as BT Sport's live transmission begins, there is still doubt as to whether the meeting will go ahead.

Each team sends out a rider for a practice lap. The track is bumpy and the riders seem to bounce around. It doesn't look great for racing. But the decision is made to go ahead.

Great Britain have been drawn against Poland in the very first heat. Robert Lambert, overly keen to make a good start, touches the tapes and is excluded. Dan Bewley takes a plucky second place behind Bartosz Zmarzlik, meaning Britain have three points after the first heat. The scoring system has been changed this year to encourage team riding, so instead of the usual three, two, one, zero points, it's now four, three, two, zero, meaning that teams can 'win' the heat by having their riders finish second and third. Conditions are difficult and it's hard to get excited about what we're watching. Britain's second heat, against the Grand Prix duo of Emil Sayfutdinov and Artem Laguta, is a processional seven-two for the Russians.

Word comes through that organisers are going to try and get to heat 14, at which point a winner can be declared, with every country having ridden four races. There's no time for track grading with heats quickly following on from the previous one.

'If this had been a league match it wouldn't have been on. We wouldn't have left home,' says Kelvin Tatum, bringing to mind the end of the domestic 2019 season.

Lambert and Bewley secure a seven-two of their own over the weakest pairing, the Czechs. But, in their fourth heat against Sweden, they somehow manage none at all, Bewley coming off on his own in the first race and Lambert suffering his second tape-touching exclusion in the rerun.

There's a wonderful move from Russia's Emil Sayfutdinov in heat 13, almost scraping up against the fence to get past Australia's Jason Doyle. It's one of the best moves of the season and almost justifies the meeting going ahead by itself, particularly when Sayfutdinov says that he couldn't really see where he was going because of rain getting into his goggles. We get to heat 14, which means there will definitely be a winner. But, in the next heat, Sweden's Freddie Lindgren is thrown off his bike on the last bend of the final lap, which causes the two riders behind him to come off too. Kelvin Tatum says you have to question why they're still racing because that wouldn't normally happen.

It turns out he's not the only one thinking that because, with rain continuing to fall, the meeting is called to a halt by FIM match referee Phil Morris. He's in one of those 'no-win' situations. The forecast for Sunday for Lublin doesn't look much better and he's got to juggle a whole host of conflicting demands – sponsors, TV companies, team managers and riders' safety. Russia are declared the winners because, despite finishing on the same number of points – 23 – as Poland, they had beaten the Poles in their head-to-head meeting.

Some wonder, given conditions weren't great from the start, whether they couldn't just have pushed through and run the remaining heats. Others contemplate the fairness of the decision. Russia hadn't yet tracked their weaker, under-21 rider, and Australia still had the two nations in sixth and seventh place – Britain and the Czechs – to face in their remaining races. Australia team manager Mark Lemon is seen – and heard – remonstrating with the referee about his decision. After the meeting he'll tweet a diplomatic 'no comment', but it's clear he's not happy about what's happened.

Back in Britain, BT Sport's normal host Natalie Quirk has contracted COVID-19 and is isolating at home. Her replacement, Charlie Webster, closes the programme by saying it's been a fantastic night. It hasn't. It's a night of racing which, Sayfutdinov's exploits aside, hasn't done the sport many favours at all.

When I catch up with Rob Painter, the managing director of GB Speedway, a couple of weeks later, he admits the Speedway of Nations had been a real challenge all round and not what they'd been hoping for.

Ask him for an assessment of 2020 overall and he'll talk about how the plan was always – even pre-COVID and Tai Woffinden's injury – to focus on developing the younger riders. He's pleased that their push to present GB Speedway as a professional, immaculately organised and turned-out squad has been noted by both the FIM and other national teams. At Lublin, all the riders had Great Britain carbon mudguards, heat shields, wheel discs, full bike covers and race suits, along with a strict dress code for everyone – including mechanics – who was part of the Great Britain travelling team. For his post-meeting interviews, Robert Lambert had appeared in a set of clean kevlars, his original ones covered in mud because of the conditions. Of course, there will be those who will say that the GB Team needs to show improvement on the track to really be successful, but looking after your sponsors – so you can end up attracting more – is a vital part too.

Rob's already looking towards 2021. 'We would have liked to have had a number of events in the UK this year which obviously couldn't take place, which is a shame. But we're talking about motorsport and there are bigger issues afoot that we need to be aware of. We're still driving forward, we're still making changes and we're still developing the structure of the Great Britain team. Regardless of how quickly we progress, it's probably never going to be quick enough for me, but that's just something I have to deal with.'

* * *

For riders, even in a truncated season like this, October is a month to take stock, to look back and forward.

Katie Gordon's been fortunate in that she's made real progress towards becoming the first female rider to appear in the Championship or Premiership. In the final round of the British Youth Championships at Belle Vue, she makes her first final in the 500cc Support Class and says it's one of her best-ever nights. The following week, at Redcar, she scores nine points in the 500cc Intermediate Amateur Championship, including two wins. She goes into the winter with much more confidence on the more powerful 500cc bikes, still hopeful of a team before too long and with huge support from the speedway fraternity.

Women are making strides in speedway elsewhere. Germany's Celina Liebmann becomes the first female rider to finish ahead of a male one in a Polish league meeting, a second-division fixture. The following day, in an individual meeting back in Germany, she continues her good form, winning two races before being hit by another rider, which leaves her with a broken arm and wrist.

Back in Britain, Josh Auty is experiencing a case of Groundhog Day. He's back, as he was at this time last year, contacting sponsors for his testimonial meeting. The difference is that he has no idea when it will actually go ahead. Nobody does. Everything is up in the air. 'It will go ahead. I simply don't know when. Everyone's been totally understanding.'

What is certain is that Josh will – once again – be lining up for Scunthorpe. He's looking forward to scoring points for the team again, 'racing with a good bunch of lads' and making up for what's been a complete write-off of a year.

He's moving to a new warehouse to work over the winter but, like so many, he's not enthusiastic about the next six months. 'I think people have been worn down by it all. I'm a bit of a conspiracy theorist so I don't watch the news. In the early days, it was deaths they were counting. Now, all of a sudden, it's cases and, of course, there are going to be more cases. Me, personally, I'm not too concerned about getting it. I get that we need to protect the elderly, but I think younger people are just saying let's get back to normal, as long as we're careful, washing your hands and not going in crowded places.'

Even though he wasn't selected for a place in the British Final, Tom Bacon's enthusiasm for the sport remains undimmed. He was out practising a couple of times in September and then at Scunthorpe towards the end of October.

'I'm even more determined than I probably was before. I still want to stay on the bike and try some new bits. You've got to look to next year as if we're going to go racing because that's the only way to prepare properly.' He admits it's been hard seeing all the youth meetings and knowing they've been riding and progressing when he's been missing out. 'But the reality is that a lot of guys haven't been riding at all and those that have, haven't actually got that much riding in this year.'

While he's worked through the year – for the company providing safeguarding for teachers – he admits he's fed up seeing the same four walls, particularly with the winter drawing in.

'If speedway wasn't to run again next year, I would go and do something different. I'm lucky to have worked all the time, but I probably wouldn't want to put it on hold for another year, to be honest. That's the dilemma really, all our lives are on hold.' He says it's particularly hard for his dad, Mike, who spends a lot of time working on Tom's bikes and is wondering what he should do and whether speedway will run as normal again next year.

I wonder, given the doubts over foreign riders being able to travel so freely post-COVID, whether there may be opportunities for riders like Tom in the Premiership. 'I've always thought we should be looking at one league anyway. If it's going to be more difficult for some riders to travel freely then it will be interesting to see what they do with the teams.' He then brings up another unanswered question. 'We've also got Brexit. I'm not sure how that affects all the foreign riders either, to be honest.'

In a parallel world, it's a much bigger issue. But not in the UK as it enters another lockdown at the tail end of October.

Nicolai Klindt, the Shropshire-based Danish rider, is unusual as he does know who he'll be riding for next summer. He's signed for Ostrów again in Poland and for Lejonen in Sweden. If it's a bit surprising that he's settled for another season in the Polish first division rather than moving up to the Ekstraliga, his logic is hard to fault. Ostrów had offered him a guaranteed place. Polish Ekstraliga teams are changing their rules to protect young Polish riders, which means fewer opportunities for foreign riders like Nicolai.

He's still ambitious and possibly being a squad member isn't for him. 'I was speaking to a few clubs and, while my priority was Ekstraliga, that wasn't going to happen because of the new rules. I will just have to wait another year now and work even harder to get myself a chance in 2022.'

Since we'd last spoken, he'd finished second in the Danish national championships, ahead of Nicki Pedersen and Grand Prix riders like Leon Madsen and Niels-Kristian Iversen. But he'd clearly had his sights set on winning. He hadn't done his regular post-meeting tweet for once, waiting until the following day to post a photo of himself on the podium with words suggesting that he'd been disappointed by that second-place finish. He's a rider who sets himself high standards.

'Overall, I had a really good season. I've learned a lot and I know some areas where I could have done better and handled different situations differently. But as long as you can learn from defeats or your mistakes then that's where you can improve. I'm still capable of being better.'

As he said at the start of the season, despite being 31, he's still firmly aiming to make the Grand Prix series. And the fact that next season's qualifiers include riders who he's beaten several times in both Polish and Swedish league action this summer both tantalises and frustrates.

Before then, though, there are more pressing issues. His mother is seriously ill and Nicolai's been caring for her back in Denmark. It's meant there's little time to see his partner Sarah and two young daughters who he'd been apart from for most of the summer, bar a couple of days back in England at the end of August. Financially, the season hasn't been great. He tells me he reckons his income is down by a considerable amount, about £100,000 less than he'd have expected had the season gone normally. He'd been riding under a capped salary in Poland and had no racing at all in Britain and Denmark.

That might mean returning to work for Tesco later in the year to make up the shortfall in his income. He wouldn't rule it out. 'If I was to do it, I would do it over December. In January I want to focus on my fitness and my diet. Even with a flexible full-time job, with the effort I want to put into next season, I don't want to do anything half-hearted.'

Based on this season, the 'new' Nicolai Klindt isn't capable of doing anything half-hearted.

* * *

I catch up with Paul Ackroyd the day before he flies off for a week's holiday in Cyprus. The chairman of the Speedway Riders Benevolent Fund had booked it back in January and, after having all the necessary tests, he's taking his grandchildren who he's not seen all year.

Paul says the Ben Fund – financially – is on an even keel at the end of the season. They've missed out on all their usual track collections so income is down about £30,000 on what they would ordinarily have achieved. But direct donations are up and the Fund's paid out less too. One of the few benefits – perhaps the only one – from having so little racing is that no riders have been injured. December is the Ben Fund's biggest month for expenditure because all their paraplegic and terminally ill riders get a big handout prior to Christmas. Once they've spent that, it'll change the Ben Fund's circumstances completely and they'll likely end the year £50,000 in deficit. Paul, though, says they can handle it.

They plan that if they don't have any income for a few years, there's still money there to keep things ticking over. 'We've got reserves that will keep us in good stead. We always have to plan for the worst contingencies and make sure there's something up our sleeve if a tragedy happens.'

There have been a few riders who've been retired for eight to ten years or so who, Paul says, have hit a few problems. They're mainly former riders who went into self-employment – electricians or joiners or tradesmen – and injuries have caught up with them. Because the NHS hasn't been able to operate on them this year, the Ben Fund has helped them out with private consultations. 'That's what we're here for. It's been weird, to say the least, the way things have panned out.'

In the 80s and 90s, when he was refereeing, Paul used to attend around 65 meetings a year. He only managed one this year – the Ben Fund Bonanza back in March. He reckons he must have been three or four years old the last time that happened.

* * *

That's one more than the venerable Peter Oakes, who started going regularly to speedway in 1959. This is the first time since then he's not been to speedway at all.

Has he missed it? 'I have to say, I don't think I have. And that's sad. I've missed the people, the camaraderie, the going along, but I couldn't actually say I've missed the speedway. That's the thing the sport's got to combat, isn't it? You do slip out of anything very quickly. And we are so far behind other sports in presentation at the meetings. There's no reason to go half the time.'

Those are worrying words coming from someone like Peter Oakes. Short of riding a bike, he's done pretty much everything else in speedway. Promoter and manager at various tracks over nearly 40 years from 1972 to 2011 – Barrow, Exeter, Swindon, Coventry and Peterborough – he was also personal manager to Ivan Mauger. He's written many books on speedway, the most recent being Tai Woffinden's *Raw Speed*. He's a columnist for *Speedway Star* while continuing to wave a lonely flag for speedway in the national press for the *Daily Star*. His knowledge of speedway is unparalleled.

I'd been struck by what Peter had written two years ago, in *Speedway Star*'s 'Speedway in crisis' edition. He'd outlined seven things that the sport needed to do to transform its fortunes – from attracting a younger audience, to appointing an independent chief executive as well as a social media guru, to reaching out to marketing or administrative experts in other sports. Ask him whether he feels there's been any progress in the last two years and his first reaction is to clarify which particular crisis article we're talking about. He says that over the last 20 years there's been a 'future of the sport' edition in *Speedway Star* every couple of years.

'There's probably been progress but I don't think it's been meaningful. Speedway isn't attracting new people. Social media certainly has improved but there's still enormous grounds for improvement.' He mentions how sponsors look on social media to check out companies and how that doesn't necessarily reflect that well on British speedway.

But if you think Peter Oakes is someone who just points out what's wrong, you'd be mistaken. One of the most honest things I've seen over the last year was when he was asked on Twitter about the demise of British speedway compared to the rise of Polish speedway.

His response? 'Probably the best I can do is cite complacency, self-interest, lack of inspirational leadership and failure to move with the times. I have been guilty of all those things during my days as promoter, so the wrong person to ask maybe.'

Ask him how he sees it now and he'll say it's worse 'because it is all run on self-interest. It's always going to be, as long as there isn't any independent control. All of us do what's best for ourselves, don't we, by and large? It's human nature. We want to look after our own. We all make decisions that suit us and our families. You've got to have someone, somewhere who will turn round and say, "Well look, no, we've got to do what is best for the sport."'

And yet, at heart, Peter Oakes is someone who still believes in the sport and is keen for it to prosper and recover its former glories. He has no interest in engines or the more mechanical aspects of speedway. It's the spectacle that attracts.

'It's probably better placed than any other outdoor sport, because you can see every inch of the race. I only went to one motorcycling Grand Prix and all you saw was flashes, you couldn't even tell they were bikes, going past – vroom, vroom, vroom – and you hadn't got the slightest idea what was happening round the next bend or on the opposite side of the track. Whereas speedway, you see it all. You see them come out, you see them go to the start, you see them on the first bend, the second bend, the third, the fourth, the second lap, you just keep seeing them. It's got so much over the other sports.

'You either fall in love with the sport or you think it's absolutely boring, not worth going to watch. On occasions, it's as bad as it's ever been. I'm not one of those who believes it was better in the old days. It wasn't. The racing today is as good as it's ever been. I don't think you can get a better sporting experience than a really good speedway meeting.'

I'm unashamedly in agreement.

* * *

The final action of the 2020 British speedway season – such as it has been – is at Belle Vue on Thursday, 21 October, with the Peter Craven Memorial meeting staged behind closed doors and streamed. Compared to the soggy mess of Lublin five nights earlier, it's a fine, dry autumn evening and a good meeting, with lots of passing and an innovative touch at the end, with five riders contesting the semi-final and six in the final, which is won by Jason Doyle.

It means there have been six matches open to the public since August – three at Scunthorpe, two at Plymouth and one at King's Lynn. A further eight have been held behind closed doors – four at Belle Vue, two at Edinburgh and one each at Leicester and Berwick – of which six have been streamed. Including the Ben Fund meeting back in March, British speedway's 2020 season has run to a total of 15 meetings.

Speedway goes into the winter, as it always does, facing questions about its future. But this time is different. For one, as Alex Harkess admitted, the decisions about its immediate future next season will be taken by people outside the speedway world. Whether it likes it or not, British speedway is being overseen by an independent body – an amorphous body of politicians and scientists and medical experts and councillors, brought together by the worst global pandemic to strike for a century.

Streaming meetings behind closed doors at a handful of clubs has made professional speedway possible. It's been well received. But there's no guarantee that league speedway behind closed doors will be widespread next year. Not all clubs can afford it. Not all clubs want to do it. And Eurosport will have an opinion too, given it will be starting its five-year broadcasting deal in 2021 covering Premiership speedway in the UK. Simon Downing, Head of Eurosport UK, says it's fantastic that streaming meant fans had an alternative means to watch high-quality action. While a lot of uncertainty still surrounds next season, he says Eurosport will be working closely with the BSP Ltd 'to deliver the best possible coverage to viewers'. The broadcaster has also unveiled a ten-year plan to promote speedway globally, which might attract new fans.

Continuing the positives, every British club that was due to operate in 2020 seems set – COVID notwithstanding – to run in 2021. Campaigners and enthusiasts are looking to reopen tracks at Oxford, Coventry, Bradford, Southampton, Workington and Exeter. But they all know that the work needed to do so is complex and lengthy with finances, approvals, infrastructure and planning processes all needed. Sadly, it's far easier and simpler to close a track than it is to open one. As we've seen, most people – many councils amongst them – don't particularly want what's seen as a noisy and dirty speedway track anywhere near their back garden.

Not everyone can be like Scunthorpe or King's Lynn, where the promoters own their stadiums and can pretty much decide their own meeting or practice schedules. Too many others are at the mercy of external operators or, ultimately, housing developers.

As it heads towards its centenary in 2028, one thing is clear about British speedway. It will survive. There are still enough riders keen to ride and people – promoters and sponsors – willing to put in the time and, more importantly, the money to keep it going. But the form in which it does survive is up for grabs. At one level there's the Great Britain speedway team. It's professionally run, keen to build a brand and benefiting from a new group of young and talented riders who promise a bright future for the next decade and beyond. It deserves its elite tag, requiring on-track success and wider media coverage for it to move to the next stage.

For bread-and-butter British league speedway, it's more difficult to be optimistic. It's easy to disparage its tatty stadiums, its ageing spectator base and the fact that, in many ways, its culture and attitudes have barely moved from its heyday in the mid to late 20th century. The top riders no longer see Britain as somewhere they have to ride, with the money on offer in Poland being so much better. That trend looks set to continue because Poland has, during 2020, strengthened its hold on the sport.

Whether that was providing the only full league season, the bulk of the venues for the Grand Prix series and the – admittedly damp – Speedway of Nations, Poland prevented the sport disappearing from international view.

It's clearly well aware of its new powers as well.

Eyebrows were raised the previous year when Poland scheduled league fixtures for live TV coverage on the Friday night before a Grand Prix. This clashed with the introduction of practice sessions for the riders by the FIM in an attempt to copy Formula 1. But, very often, they didn't have a full complement, with riders opting to miss the Grand Prix practice and turn out for their league clubs who, after all, pay their weekly wages. No action was taken against the riders or the Polish Ekstraliga.

Now, emboldened by this summer's developments and wanting to further protect their assets, the Polish speedway authorities announce another new ruling: to be able to take part in the Ekstraliga, riders may only compete in one other country. Those days of riders flying back and forth across Europe to ride in four leagues already looked, for a number of reasons, to be coming to an end. This ruling, however, seems likely to mean more of the top riders, not just those riding in the Grand Prix, will miss out on British speedway. Nicki Pedersen, already committed to ride in Poland and Denmark, has a huge question mark over his Sheffield place. Others who have a hard decision to make include Robert Lambert, Dan Bewley, Jason Doyle, Jack Holder, Niels-Kristian Iversen and Jaimon Lidsey.

But it's not just the top riders. Some of the younger riders from the GB Academy – realising that to reach the very top they need to compete abroad – are being signed by Polish first and second division clubs. They're happy to test themselves against the best to develop their careers, something many of their predecessors didn't want to do in previous years.

By accident rather than design, 2020 may be the year that paves the way for some supporters' long-held wishes for more British riders to be given team places in their home country. By the end of October, the laudable aim of British clubs keeping the same 2020 squads for 2021 is already on shaky ground. There's even talk of having just one league or reducing team numbers to six from seven. Doubling-up isn't going away anytime soon. The overall quality of rider in the British leagues looks set to decline further, although, as we've seen, that doesn't necessarily affect the quality of the racing.

There's one figure I've been reluctant to work out over the last year: the number of people who, in a normal week, pre-COVID, would head along to a speedway track in Britain. I finally do the maths and I check with a couple of people in the speedway world because it seems far too low and I want it to be right. But they agree that it's probably around 25,000 to 30,000. That's around a third of those attending one meeting back in the good old days at Wembley. Many of those are committed fans who will come back the following week, whatever they watch, or head to Wolverhampton on a Monday and Birmingham on a Wednesday. To survive and prosper, British speedway needs to attract those whose minds will be made up by the more uncontrollable variables of the weather or whether the track has been prepared well enough to produce competitive and entertaining racing.

For those who do venture along, the rewards are worth it, even for those who don't really know the sport. Read what broadcaster Stuart Maconie said about speedway in his 2016 book, *The Pie at Night: In Search of the North at Play*:

'When I was very young, somewhere at the blurry edge of memory, I recall that *Sportsnight with Coleman* would sometimes, on a thin football week I imagine, bring us speedway highlights from Wolverhampton, Scunthorpe or Workington. It seems to me, even as a child, that as a TV spectacular it was somehow lacking; gloomily monochrome and a tad predictable in that whoever was in the lead at the first corner stayed there all race. Overtaking was rare, if not unheard of.'

But then Maconie visits Belle Vue and has a sporting epiphany. For him, speedway 'is at the other end of the sporting spectrum from Test cricket. In place of the long contemplative stretches of ambient torpor, that delightfully textured boredom, is a compacted minute of crazed activity, a roaring whirlwind of helmets, shale and mud. The best view you can have is this one; close up, surrounded by noise and action, spinning around to catch the bikes as they circle you at speed. In this way, with the odd dash to the shed for lager, the next couple of hours pass in a hugely entertaining blur.'

Or listen to Sky Sports' production team. I'd been trying, for several months, to speak to them about their coverage of speedway which, after all, had lasted 20 years. When I finally did, I was heartened – and surprised – to find that their enthusiasm for the sport, one that's no longer part of their schedule, remains strong.

Producer Rory Hopkins worked on Sky's speedway coverage throughout. He talks, with genuine affection, about going away to foreign events with the GB Team and promoters like Poole's Matt Ford and says it's the friendliest sport he ever worked on. They had a fantastic relationship and, as broadcasters, they felt appreciated, that they were trying to do their best for the sport.

That's the same for Sky's Head of Multi Sport, Georgina Faulkner. She didn't know speedway very well before she started working on it, but found the riders and those involved in it to be good people to work with. She's happy to call herself a massive speedway fan and still has friends in the sport. Rory says they both want speedway to be a success whether it's on Eurosport or BT. 'It's a great sport and there's nothing more exciting than a great speedway race.'

Go back to that stunning Lindgren-Woffinden-Zmarzlik race from the final Grand Prix of the season. I was so thrilled by it that I showed it to the rest of my family, none of them speedway fans. 'Give me a minute of your time, just 60-odd seconds,' I say, 'and I'll show you something amazing.' I want them to be thrilled by it, to want to come along when life gets back to normal. I play them the clip on my phone. My wife seems reasonably impressed, saying that, yes, for her, it's more exciting than Formula 1. My son nods – 'that's decent' – although, as Everton are currently unbeaten and top of the Premier League, he might just be in a good mood and open to being positive about anything. My daughter is the one sceptic, saying it didn't do much for her because she's not 'invested' in the riders taking part. As she's got to know Formula 1 drivers this season, she finds that more interesting. I can understand where she's coming from but I'm a bit deflated. If this didn't do it for them, nothing will.

But then, maybe like Stuart Maconie, they need to get themselves to a track and breathe in the sights and sounds of speedway. Or, like Rory and Georgina at Sky, mix with some of the riders and the promoters. Maybe they won't see a race nearly as good as the one I've shown them. But if they do – one that mesmerises and catches the breath as riders throw their machines into the corner in a blur of shale – maybe they will get it and return. At its best, speedway is absolutely worth it.

* * *

We began the year with Dave Tattum closing the gates on speedway in Stoke. And, while I wasn't expecting it, that's where we end. Dave, remember, had been invited to join former rider Rob Grant at Newcastle, only for the season to be cancelled because of COVID-19. They'd then had to spend time looking for a new track on Tyneside because of doubts over the long-term future of Brough Park.

But, in the very final days of October, there's more bad news. It turns out that HMRC have been investigating Newcastle's former owners for 'historical liabilities' between 2013 and 2018. Rob and Dave have no option but to wind up the old company, Newspeed 2003, and put it into liquidation.

When I speak to Dave, he tells me it's been 'a rocky, rocky road'. He's been told not to say too much by the liquidators but mentions that Rob Grant had cleared off several debts that had been left behind from the previous promotion. They'd not known about the HMRC investigation.

Dave says most people would have walked away at that point, having ploughed thousands of pounds in already. But he says Rob Grant has jumped through hoops to keep it going. 'The people of Newcastle ought to carry him round on their shoulders.' Rob aims to begin again through a new company, Newcastle Diamonds Ltd, and Dave says they will still run speedway in 2021.

'It's been terrible. I wouldn't have thought what has happened, would have happened. But it has and we've dealt with it and come out the other side.'

In many ways, it's a metaphor for British speedway in general: troubled, often damaged by its own efforts, seemingly on the brink of collapse, but resilient and, in the end, emerging, blinking and still hopeful, into an uncertain light.

Postscript

ON 19 November, the Government announces its long-awaited coronavirus bailout for British sport. The statement from the Department of Culture, Media and Sport lists the sports that will benefit from the low-interest loans, which, it's claimed, will total £300 million. Nearly half goes to rugby union, with horse racing, women's football and National League football and rugby league next in line. Tennis, netball, basketball and ice hockey all receive £4–5 million. Badminton gets £2 million and greyhound racing £1 million.

There's £6 million for motorsports targeted, very specifically, at the owners of operators of the major circuits at Silverstone, Goodwood, the British Automobile Racing Club and MotorSport Vision.

No funds are allocated for speedway.

* * *

The annual meeting of the British Speedway Promoters Limited, when the big decisions for the coming year are taken, doesn't take place in November as normal. Because of the new national lockdown – even more dispiriting than the last one – it finally takes place, virtually, in the middle of January. Plans are made for the 2021 season to begin at the start of May but there are other issues for the promoters to discuss. Two clubs announce that they will not be taking part after all: the 2019 Premiership champions Swindon will sit out the year because of rebuilding work at their stadium and uncertainty around spectator sports in general as a result of COVID. Somerset will not run in the Championship. Their Oaktree Arena, which would normally host wedding receptions, conferences and dinners, has been badly hit by the pandemic which has led to 'concerns regarding the financial credibility of the club.'

Both say they hope to run again in 2022.

Select bibliography

Bamford, R & Jarvis, J., *Homes of British Speedway* (London: Tempus, 2001).

Dalling, P., *The Golden Age of Speedway,* (London: The History Press, 2011).

Henry, J. & Moultray, I., *The History of Edinburgh Speedway: The Marine Garden Years* (Friends of Edinburgh Speedway, 1997).

Jacobs, J., *Speedway in London* (London: Tempus, 2001).

Morrish, P., *British Speedway Leagues 1946-1964* (London: Midland Speedway).

Oakes, P., *The Complete History of the British League* (London: Front Page Books, 1991).

The Speedway Review 2019 (London: Curtis Sport, 2020).

Woffinden, Tai, *Raw Speed – My Autobiography* (London: John Blake, 2019).

Magazines

Backtrack (bi-monthly retro-speedway magazine)

Speedway Star (weekly magazine)

Podcasts and audio programmes

Humans of Speedway, Ian Brannan.

Speedway, Jenny Gow (Audible).

Speedway Chat Show, Gerry Sims and Wilbur Hancock.

Suzi's Breakfast Club, Suzi Perry.

Talk Speedway, Scott Frame and Graham Muncie.

Tatum & Pearson, Kelvin Tatum and Nigel Pearson.

The Speedway Podcast, Mike Bacon.

UK Speedway Tavern.